Islam after Communism

Islam after Communism

Religion and Politics in Central Asia

Adeeb Khalid

UNIVERSITY OF CALIFORNIA PRESS
Berkeley · Los Angeles · London

University of California Press, one of the most
distinguished university presses in the United States,
enriches lives around the world by advancing scholarship in the humanities, social sciences, and natural
sciences. Its activities are supported by the UC Press
Foundation and by philanthropic contributions from
individuals and institutions. For more information,
visit www.ucpress.edu.

University of California Press
Berkeley and Los Angeles, California

University of California Press, Ltd.
London, England

© 2007 by The Regents of the University of California

Library of Congress Cataloging-in-Publication Data

Khalid, Adeeb, 1964–.
    Islam after communism : religion and politics in
Central Asia / Adeeb Khalid.
        p.   cm.
    Includes bibliographical references and index.
    ISBN-13: 978-0-520-24927-1 (pbk. : alk. paper)
    1. Islam — Asia, Central.   2. Islamic renewal —
Asia, Central.   3. Islam and politics — Asia, Central.
4. Religion and politics — Asia, Central.   5. Asia,
Central — Politics and government.   I. Title.

BP63.A34K535   2007
297.2'720958 — dc22   2006021901

Manufactured in the United States of America

15   14   13   12   11   10   09   08
10   9   8   7   6   5   4

This book is printed on New Leaf EcoBook 50, a 100%
recycled fiber of which 50% is de-inked postconsumer
waste, processed chlorine-free. EcoBook 50 is acid-free
and meets the minimum requirements of ANSI/ASTM
D5634–01 (Permanence of Paper).

For Cheryl

Contents

Maps and Tables

Acknowledgments

This book marks a departure from my usual research interests, which my historian's instinct have kept focused on the early twentieth century. My turn to the current topic was dictated by world events. After September 11, Central Asia, perhaps one of the least-known regions of the world, found itself in the global limelight. I saw a need for a broad, accessible treatment of Islam in cotemporary Central Asia and put aside my other projects to write this book. This book was therefore written without the usual preliminaries of grant proposals and leaves from teaching, and thus owes more than usual to the help, advice, encouragement, support, and good humor of friends and colleagues.

Many individuals and groups heard excerpts from this book, but I owe a particular debt to Sergei Abashin, Laura Adams, Stéphane Dudoignon, Adrienne Edgar, Marianne Kamp, Shoshana Keller, and Russell Zanca, who shared their insights and their own research with me. Grants from the National Council on Eurasian and Eastern European Research and Carleton College allowed a trip to the region in summer 2004. Many thanks for hospitality and guidance to Franz Wennberg and Muzaffar Olimov in Dushanbe and to Nurbulat Masanov in Almaty. I owe a great deal to many friends and acquaintances in Uzbekistan, who over the years have taught me a lot about Central Asia, but I think it prudent to leave them unnamed here.

I marvel at the luck that brought Shahzad Bashir to the small college where I teach and made him a colleague and a friend. In addition to providing support and encouragement, he read the whole manuscript as it progressed. Fran Hirsch read an almost complete version of the manuscript. Muriel Atkin, Daniel Brower, and one other referee who chose to remain anonymous evaluated the manuscript for the University of California Press. Their advice and criticisms made this a better book. I have not been able to use all the advice I received, but I hope that the finished book does not disappoint those who gave of their time and energy.

Working with the University of California Press has been a pleasure. Lynne Withey's enthusiasm for the project from the outset was crucial. Without Monica McCormick and Reed Malcolm, the process of completing the book would have been longer and unhappier.

Haroun and Leila have lived with this manuscript for large chunks of their lives; they will be even happier than I am to have it out of the way. Cheryl Duncan first suggested that I write this book. She has read every word of it, many times over, and given criticism and encouragement in equal measure as it has progressed—all this on top of her abundant supply of love and care. It is to her that I dedicate this book.

St. Paul, Minnesota
October 31, 2005

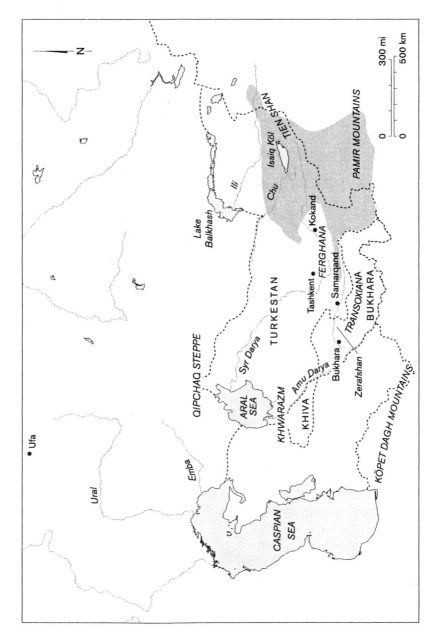

Map 1. Central Asia: political boundaries in the tsarist period.

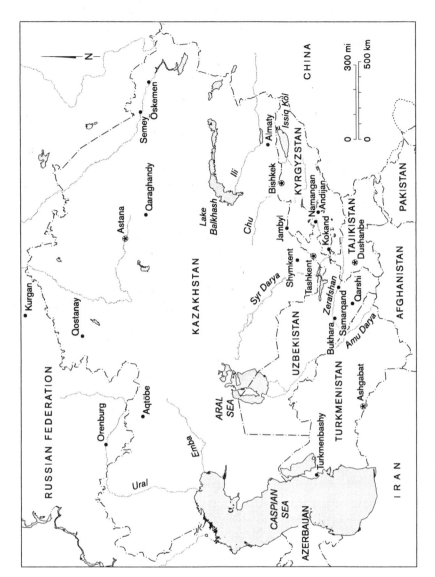

Map 2. Central Asia: current political boundaries.

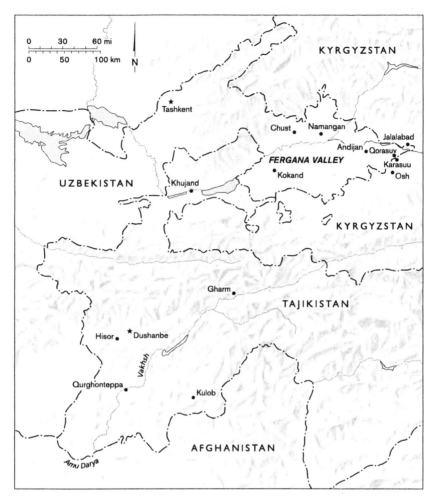

Map 3. Tajikistan and the Ferghana Valley.

Introduction

Waiting in line at a cafeteria in Tashkent one day in 1991, in the last months of the Soviet era, I fell into conversation with two men behind me. They were pleased to meet someone from the outside world, to which access had been so difficult until then, but they were especially delighted by the fact that their interlocutor was Muslim. My turn in line eventually came, and I sat down in a corner to eat. A few minutes later, my new acquaintances joined me unbidden at my table, armed with a bottle of vodka, and proceeded to propose a toast to meeting a fellow Muslim from abroad. Their delight at meeting me was sincere, and they were completely unself-conscious about the oddity of lubricating the celebration of our acquaintance with copious quantities of alcohol.

This episode, unthinkable in the Muslim countries just a few hundred kilometers to the south, provides a powerful insight into the place of Islam in Central Asian societies at the end of the Soviet period. Clearly, being Muslim meant something very specific to my friends. Seven decades of Soviet rule had given Central Asians a unique understanding of Islam and of being Muslim. Islam after Communism had its peculiarities.

A few months after my encounter, the Soviet Union ceased to exist, and the republics of Central Asia became independent states. As old barriers—political, ideological, personal—came down, the region experienced a considerable Islamic revival. Mosques were reopened, new ones built, links with Muslims outside the Soviet Union revived. Islam has indeed experienced a rebirth in the region.[1]

For many, especially in the West, this return of Islam boded ill. According to this view, Central Asia would become another hotbed of Islamic fundamentalism, a breeding ground of terrorism—essentially a natural extension of Afghanistan and other anti-Western regimes in the Middle East. Westerners had reasons enough to fear this outcome. In November 1991, demonstrators in the Uzbek city of Namangan besieged the country's president and demanded that he declare Uzbekistan an "Islamic republic." In neighboring Tajikistan, independence degenerated into a bloody civil war that was widely seen as pitting resurgent "Islamists" against the incumbent "Communists." By the late 1990s, militant organizations had emerged in Uzbekistan that sought the overthrow of the regime there and its replacement by an Islamic state. The Islamic Movement of Uzbekistan (IMU), the most prominent of these organizations, developed links with militant groups in war-torn Afghanistan, and its members fought alongside the Taliban during the American invasion in the autumn of 2001. For many observers, the IMU represents the future of Islam in the region—a "natural" culmination of the rebirth of Islam. This view is based on certain assumptions, often unstated by its proponents, about Islam itself. According to this view, Islam is inherently political and naturally leads to anti-Western militancy. For this reason, the seventy years of Soviet rule were of no consequence, for once Islam reemerged, the paths to its politicization and militarization were foretold.

This book argues that history *does* matter. The way in which Central Asians relate to Islam, what Islam means to them, can only be understood by taking into consideration the experience of seventy years of Soviet rule. Although those years may seem like the blink of an eye in the long history of Islam in Central Asia, the Soviet period was one of enormous transformation in society and culture—transformation, moreover, in a mold that set Central Asia apart from much of the rest of the Muslim world. All forms of Islamic expression came under sustained assault in the Soviet period: patterns of the transmission of Islamic knowledge were damaged, if not destroyed; Islam was driven from the public realm; the physical markings of Islam, such as mosques and seminaries, disappeared. The Soviet period also saw the emergence of strong secular, ethnonational identities among Central Asians, as well as the creation of new political and cultural elites firmly committed to such identities. Independence has not meant the evaporation of these identities, nor of the elites that shaped them. For much of the 1990s, a certain naïve optimism made Westerners believe that the countries of Central Asia, along with the rest of the former socialist states, were in the midst of a transition from Soviet authoritarianism to something "more normal," perhaps a free-market democracy in which people would think just like them. It is now amply clear that the trajectories of these countries cannot be understood in such simplistic terms. Instead of a neat transition, in which the people and their rulers jettison their past, we have "postsocialist" forms of society and politics that are new in that they combine aspects of Soviet authoritarianism with those of the neoliberal order into which they have emerged. Older understandings of the world have not simply disappeared; they are being shaped and reshaped in interesting ways. Soviet understandings of culture and identity remain dominant in Central Asia. Thus, we can understand little about the region's contemporary politics or about the role that Islam plays in it unless we take serious account of the Soviet period.

. . .

It is probably fair to say that Central Asia remains one of the least-known and least-understood parts of the world. Soviet xenophobia cut off the region from the rest of the world; its languages are little known, and its history is practically a blank slate. A decade and a half after the collapse of the Soviet Union and the opening up of the region and its archives, no single decent source is available to nonspecialists who want to look up the broad outlines of even the political history of the region. The contours of cultural and religious change are even harder to discern. In the absence of information, many writers simply opt to dismiss the Soviet period out of hand. Mixing arrogance and ignorance in equal measure, Ahmed Rashid writes, "When independence finally came, in 1991, the Central Asians, ideologically speaking, were still back in the 1920s. The crisis in Central Asia today is directly related to this stunted political and ideological growth, which the Communists ensured by their actions in 1923 and afterwards."[2] The dismissal of the Soviet period is connected to broader, ahistorical conceptions of Central Asia as an eternal land, whose peoples and cultures stand outside of time and (can) never change. If Islam or traditional culture or patriarchy or authoritarianism is strong today, it is strong because such is the region's tradition. One is left to wonder, how strong can a tradition be to survive even the murderous assault of the Stalinist regime unscathed?

Admittedly, contending with the Soviet period is not easy. The triumphalist mood following the collapse of the Soviet Union has produced

an easy tendency outside the academy to dismiss the entire Soviet era out
of hand. In such circles, the Soviets appear at best as ham-fisted buf-
foons, incapable of creating anything and bent on destroying everything
they touched; at worst, they are portrayed as pure evil, and the seven
decades of Soviet rule presented as an extended nightmare. In countries
of the former Soviet Union, the disavowal of the Soviet past stems from
different impulses, such as the need to legitimize the new post-Soviet
order, stake a claim in the new world order as "normal" states, or simply
put the past behind. In either case, the dismissal of the Soviet past is
entirely unhelpful in understanding the extremely complex developments
of that era and the many peoples and nationalities it touched. This book,
therefore, aims to explore the consequences, intended and unintended, of
the Soviet attempt to remake Central Asia. The Soviets did not achieve all
their goals, but Central Asia was utterly transformed by them.[3]

.   .   .

The biggest problem, however, is with talking about Islam. No discussion
of Islam can take place today without reference to the vigorous public
debate over Islam that has raged since September 11, 2001. The market-
place is full of books about Islam, and the periodical press and the electronic media have contributed their share to this debate. All shades of
opinion are represented in this new literature, from somber academic
tomes to sensationalist bestsellers and everything in between. For many,
the answer is straightforward: the religion of Islam is innately political,
intolerant, oppressive of women, and inimical to "the West" and its values. Moreover, the religion determines all aspects of its believers' lives in
a way that Christianity and Judaism do not. In this view, the political and
social behavior of Muslims can be discerned from a reading of the scriptures of Islam, which are beyond the realm of human intervention or
interpretation. The most extreme forms of militancy that take place in
the name of Islam—acts by al-Qaeda or Hamas—are thus the true and
logical manifestations of Islam. Such judgments come from all points of
the political and cultural spectrum: the left, the secular right, the religious
right, Muslims critical of their tradition, Hindu fundamentalists, friends
of Israel, and Serbian nationalists all find this vision of a homogeneous,
hostile Islam compelling.

More sympathetic or apologetic authors, Muslims and non-Muslims,
argue instead that Islam is "really" a religion of peace that has been
hijacked, corrupted, or perverted by militants' "incorrect" interpreta-

tions of Islamic teachings. They posit the "real" Islam, which is the opposite of the commonly held stereotype—a religion that is tolerant, spiritual, and moderate. We can see a possible step forward in the distinction, often made in public discourse since September 11, 2001, between "good" or "moderate" Islam, on the one hand, and its "bad" or "extremist" counterparts, on the other: Islam has two faces, one tolerant and spiritual, the other intolerant and violent. Not all Muslims are alike—there are "good" Muslims and "bad." The problem with this binary vision is that too often, the yardstick for measuring moderation is agreement with U.S. geopolitical goals. Muslims who agree with U.S. foreign-policy goals are "good" and "tolerant"; those who do not, are not. Thus, for years, Saudi Arabia was routinely touted as a "moderate" Islamic state, whereas other, more secular states in the Muslim world have been relegated to the "extremist" camp simply because they disagreed with the foreign-policy goals of the United States. Because this distinction has been invoked repeatedly to wage war on Muslim populations, its utility for understanding the world is gravely limited.

The apologetic and "two faces" arguments share a fundamental problem with the views of Islam espoused by its most hostile critics: these views all take for granted that a "real" Islam exists about which one can make such generalizations. The apologetic and "two faces" arguments also locate the sources of Islam in the same places—its scriptures—and assume that the political behavior of Muslims emerges directly from them.

These arguments are essentialist in that they derive their explanation from the purported existence of a certain essence of Islam that is immune to historical change and that exists beyond the realm of society and human intervention. (Essences can be found in anything—race, culture, religion—and, as we shall see, they need not be negative.) No matter where Muslims live or what they do, the most important thing about them is that they are Muslims and that they act as such. Essentialist arguments are attractive for their simplicity, for they allow the public to make sense of a world it does not know very well. Although critics have argued that many Western authors have long held essentialist views of Islam and Muslims, essentialist arguments are enjoying a boom these days. With the end of the Cold War, questions of ideology or of economic conflict have receded from the public arena, and "culture," in all its manifestations, has come to provide explanation for all conflict, struggle, and inequality. Over the past decade, this form of cultural essentialism has been given academic cachet by two thinkers with immense influence among policy makers and the media.

The Harvard political scientist Samuel Huntington claims that future conflict on the planet will take place on the lines not of ideology or national interest but between "civilizations." He discerns a number of discrete civilizations that he defines broadly by essentialized cultural features. "Islam" is one of the civilizations, and it is the one that, according to Huntington, is most likely to get into conflict with "the West." The proof of the existence of civilizations is in history, but the history in his book is remarkably thin.[4] His book *The Clash of Civilizations and the Remaking of the World Order* and its thesis have been routinely invoked since September 11, and indeed the current U.S. paperback edition features a rather crude depiction of this conflict in the form the green banner of Islam battling with the U.S. flag (which presumably signifies all of "the West"). All Muslims, apparently the "good" and the "bad" both, are fated by virtue of belonging to their civilization to act in a particular way, which is hostile to the West.

Much of Huntington's argument about Islam comes from the work of the British-born Orientalist Bernard Lewis, who taught for many years at Princeton University, and who since September 11, has become a one-man industry producing essentialist analysis of Islam and the Middle East. In 1990, the year after the Cold War ended, Lewis argued in a cover story for the *Atlantic Monthly* that conflict in the Middle East is part of a much broader phenomenon: "It should now be clear that we are facing a model and a movement far transcending the level of issues and policies and the governments that pursue them. This is no less than a clash of civilizations—the perhaps irrational but surely historic reaction of an ancient rival against our Judeo-Christian heritage, our secular present, and the worldwide importance of both."[5] At issue are not policies but a reaction to—a rage about—civilizational difference. Muslim rage has roots in Islam itself, according to Lewis. "In the classical Islamic view, to which many Muslims are beginning to return, the world and mankind are divided into two: the House of Islam, where the Muslim law and faith prevail, and the rest, known as the House of Unbelief or the House of War, which it is the duty of Muslims ultimately to bring to Islam."[6] To Lewis, the "classical Islamic view," not interests and aspirations, determines how Muslims act in the world. He also blurs the distinction between "Islamic radicals" and Muslims at large, implying that all Muslims, regardless of where or who they are, face the same compulsions: "What is truly evil and unacceptable is the domination of infidels over true believers. For true believers to rule over misbelievers is proper and natural. . . . But for misbelievers to rule over true believers is blasphemous and unnatural, since it leads to the corruption of religion and morality in society, and to the flouting or even abrogation of God's law. This may help us to understand the current troubles in such diverse places as Ethiopian Eritrea, Indian Kashmir, Chinese Sinkiang, and Yugoslav Kosovo, in all of which Muslim populations are ruled by non-Muslim governments."[7] The fact that the conflicts in Eritrea, Xinjiang, and Kosovo were all purely nationalist struggles in which "Islamic radicals" played no part matters little to Lewis's argument. Islam, for Lewis, is immutable and impervious to change brought about by history or society. He contrasts the Muslim compulsion to act according to Islam to "our secular present," as if religious motivations were entirely absent in the conduct of affairs in the West. Such essentialist arguments are much loved by today's Islamic extremists, who proceed from the assertion of total incompatibility of Islam and the West. Osama bin Laden and Bernard Lewis completely agree on this point.

Essentialist arguments efface history. In them, civilizations are like billiard balls, bouncing off each other on a table, acting and reacting but remaining indivisible wholes all the while. Moreover, all the behavior of a civilization is internally generated, a product of each civilization's unique (and again, unchanging) characteristics. Essentialist arguments thus hide the political or international contexts of the phenomena they seek to explain. All explanation (and responsibility) for the political behavior of Muslims has to be sought in Islam itself with the broader context of Muslims' involvement with Europe and the United States studiously avoided. The denial of interconnections between civilizations is also necessary to create a positive image of the West, as the storehouse of the best achievements of humanity. The West is identified only with lofty ideas such as freedom, democracy, human rights, and free markets; other achievements, such as colonialism, slavery, the near extermination of the indigenous populations of three continents, the industrialization of warfare, and the Holocaust, are never invoked. The "West" is just as clearly essentialized an idea as "Islam"—it too is self-contained and internally homogeneous, but here the essence is entirely positive. When Americans think more narrowly about the United States rather than the West in general, they have access to other mechanisms that enable them to avoid drawing connections between the United States and the rest of the world. Acceptance of the myth of the Innocent Nation precludes doubts about American goodness.[8] This view is buttressed by the fact that few Americans pay attention to foreign affairs, even though the reach of U.S. foreign policy is truly global. The only possible remaining question, then, is "Why do they hate us?" (a question in which both the "they" and the "us" are problematic, as is the verb), and in the absence of a dispassionate discussion of interconnections, no answer is forthcoming. George W. Bush could only express amazement in answer to this question: "How do I respond when I see that in some Islamic countries there is vitriolic hatred for America? I'll tell you how I respond: I'm amazed. I'm amazed that there is such misunderstanding of what our country is about, that people would hate us. I am, I am—like most Americans, I just can't believe it. Because I know how good we are, and we've go to do a better job of making our case."[9]

·   ·   ·

Like all religions, Islam is internally diverse. Individuals and groups can take vastly different, even opposing positions within the framework of a religious tradition. Over the centuries, Christians have used the Bible to argue for waging war against non-Christians and for persecuting Jews living amid Christians; many Americans justified slavery, apartheid, and Jim Crow by invoking scriptural injunctions. Yet Christians have also used the Bible to fight against slavery, to preach tolerance, and to fight for social justice and civil rights. The same scriptures that yield the doctrine of the poverty of Christ can be made to produce the gospel of wealth. These mutually opposed positions are explicitly and self-consciously Christian. Muslims, too, can and do debate among themselves and derive opposed positions from their sources of religious authority.

To speak of "Islam" as a homogeneous phenomenon is analogous to speaking of Christianity as a single whole that includes Catholics and Orthodox, Protestants and Copts, and members of countless other sects, including such marginal ones as the Mormons, the Scientologists, and Jehovah's Witnesses. Of course, we never speak of Christianity in this way because we intuitively recognize that the label loses all meaning when applied to such a diverse group. We seldom have such qualms, however, in defining Islam, even though the label *Islam* covers just as wide a spectrum of geographic, cultural, and sectarian diversity as the label *Christianity* does. If anything, Islam is more internally diverse than Christianity, which crystallized around an institutionalized church from the beginning. In Islam, such an institution never developed. There is no religious hierarchy and no single individual qualified to pass final judgment on questions of belief or practice. Within thirty years of the death of the Prophet, the Muslim community had split on matters of doctrine.

Since then, Muslims have relied on multiple and simultaneous sources of authority. Authority resides not in church councils and such but in individuals who derive their legitimacy from their learning, piety, lineage, and reputation among peers. This feature gives Islam a slightly anarchic quality: authoritative opinions (*fatwas*) by one expert or one group can be countered with equally authoritative opinions, derived from the same sources, by another group; or one set of devotional practices held dear by one group can be denounced as impermissible by another. In more extreme cases, such conflicts of opinion can turn into "wars of fatwas," fought out, in the modern age, in the press or in cyberspace. (If Islam were held in a more positive light in the West today, this diversity would be described as a free market of ideas!) To speak of Islam as a homogeneous entity ignores this fundamental dynamic of its tradition.

This pluralism extends to the most basic level of belief. The major sectarian divide in Islam, between Sunnis and Shi'is, goes back to the origins of Islam. The two doctrines evolved in parallel; therefore, to see in them an orthodox/heterodox divide is incorrect. All Muslims share certain key reference points (the oneness of God, loyalty to the Prophet and his progeny, the need to prepare for the Hereafter, to take a few examples), but different sects and movements have played upon these points in different ways. Moreover, each of the two sects has many branches and supports a variety of theological and legal schools, and many modern ideological groups straddle the divide between the two sects.

For better or worse, Islam today is identified most closely with law. One of the central ideas in the Islamic tradition as it emerged was that of the *shari'a* (or, in the Turko-Persian form used in Central Asia, *shariat*). The usual rendering of the shariat as "Islamic law" is not wholly accurate. Shariat means "the path," the way of proper demeanor in this world, dictated by God, that paves the way for salvation on the day of judgment. As such, it encompasses only the broadest ethical norms of the Islamic tradition. Law in the narrower sense of passing judgment on concrete cases in real life evolved into the discipline of *fiqh*, jurisprudence. Fiqh grew rapidly in the second and third Islamic centuries, when concern with proper governance and the limiting of possible alternatives led to its codification. Fiqh, too, was, from its inception, plural. Sunnis came to hold four schools (*mazhab*) of fiqh as equally legitimate, if not always interchangeable. Fiqh was, almost by definition, an exercise in interpreting the basic commandments of the shariat in concrete cases. Contrary to common misconception, the Qur'an is not the sole source of Islamic law. The example of the Prophet, preserved both in the practice of the community and in written traditions (*hadith*), the compilation and sifting of which became a major preoccupation of scholars, is also authoritative, as are reasoning by analogy and the consensus of scholars. Whereas the point of fiqh was to discern and implement what God had ordained, the discernment and the implementation of it were recognized to be distinctly human endeavors. The elaboration of legal doctrine was the work of jurists, who were seldom agents of the state. On the most mundane level, then, Islamic law retained an element of anarchy. Courts executed law, but they did so on the basis of opinions (fatwas) issued by legal scholars (in this case, *mufti*) at the request of petitioners. The fatwa was a legal opinion whose authority derived directly from the authority of the mufti who issued it. One fatwa could be countered by another from a different mufti, leaving the job of adjudication to the judge (*qazi*). A major goal of Islamic jurisprudence was to maintain social order. Islamic law was thus fully integrated into Muslim societies.

But law was always just one source of authority. The ethical tradition in Muslim societies also looked to classical antiquity for inspiration, and Aristotelian and neo-Platonic thought exercised immense influence in Muslim lands.[10] A third ethical tradition was Sufism, which coexisted with sectarian divides and the legal and philosophical traditions. Usually glossed as Islamic mysticism, Sufism represents a complex of diverse religious trends that include mystical philosophy, a cult of saintly figures with miraculous powers, and distinctive liturgical practices. It originated as a movement of personal piety in the first century of Islam. Its adepts, or Sufis, emphasized an esoteric path to the knowledge of God, which they were to achieve through prayer, asceticism, and withdrawal from society, all of which they traced back to the example of the Prophet himself. True knowledge of God could not be achieved through the rational and philosophical traditions beloved of the *ulama*. A tradition of the Prophet that is popular with the Sufis holds that legal knowledge encompasses only one-third of all knowledge; the rest has to come through the direct experience of God. Over time, expressions of Sufism have covered the entire spectrum, from radical antinomian rejection of a rational and legal approach to salvation, to accommodation of the world, and the assimilation of many aspects of the legal tradition of Islam. Influential thinkers such as al-Ghazzali (d. 1111) worked out a synthesis of the esoteric and exoteric currents of Islam. By the thirteenth century, Sufism had become an integral, not to say a dominant, part of the cultural life of much of the Muslim world. It was organized in Sufi brotherhoods (*tariqat*) centered around the followers of individual Sufi masters and housed in networks of hospices (*khanqah*) supported by followers and pious benefactors of the Sufis. The synthesis proved to be enduring: it produced an aesthetic that underlies the bulk of the literary production in Muslim societies of the past millennium.

.   .   .

If Islam is not homogeneous, it is also not self-contained or discrete. Muslims have always interacted with their neighbors. Islamic civilization was never coextensive with Islam as a religion; it was a hybrid, multicultural venture in which Christians, Jews, and Hindus participated as central actors. If we can now call the Western tradition "Judeo-Christian" (which both underestimates the extent to which the civilization of the West has historically been identified with Christianity alone and dispenses entirely with non-European Jews), then surely Islamic civilization was at least Judeo-Islamic, if not worthy of an even more complicated label.[11] As the great American historian Marshall Hodgson pointed out more than three decades ago, the lands of Islam were the global *oekumene,* in contact with all other civilizations of the old world, for several centuries.[12] Hodgson also coined the adjective *Islamicate* to describe the civilizational, as opposed to the religious, aspects of Islam. It is a great pity that the term has not taken hold, for it describes accurately such varied phenomena as poetry by Hindu poets in praise of the Prophet, Hebrew poetry indistinguishable in its aesthetics or its structure from its Arabic counterpart, or Christian theological debates in the lands where Christianity was born.

This interaction has been particularly sustained in the past 200 years, during which time it has taken many forms. The notions of progress, the nation, and the will of the people; new means of organizing society and state power; and new means of communication all have transformed how Muslims think about Islam and the world of which they are a part. Similarly, Islamic political and religious movements today take place in an international geopolitical context in which Western powers are active agents. Whether Islamic movements react to Western military or political involvement in the Muslim world or are, at times, even actively encouraged by the West, they are never entirely innocent of the West. "What went wrong?" asks Bernard Lewis about the Middle East, and he proceeds to give an answer that explains everything through Islam and makes no reference to the intense intertwining of the history of the Muslim world with that of the West. It is a very flimsy understanding of current realities that invokes obscure texts a millennium old but ignores the political context of today.

The classical tradition of Islam, in fact, is of singularly little help in understanding the actions of Muslims today, which have been shaped in a profound way by the ideas, technologies, and modes of organization of the modern age. Muslims' relationship to Islam is shaped by modern ways of relating to religious authority, which distance Muslims from the classical tradition. The crucial concept in understanding Islam is modernity, which refers to the emergence of new understandings of the world (a hankering for certainty and classification, disenchantment with the supernatural, and the rise of the authority of science) and new forms of organization (the modern state and its many attributes), communication (the advent of print and, more recently, of electronic media), and socialization that have transformed the world, beginning with Europe in the early modern period. Modernity wreaks havoc with the established order of things, but it does not have a fixed trajectory. It is thus different from the concept of modernization, which assumes an end-driven scheme of historical change in which certain economic changes ("development") lead to similar social and cultural transformations (secularization, the rise of democracy, the equalization of gender roles, and so forth).

The Muslim world has not been immune to modernity. Over the past century or so, new forms of power and new epistemologies have redefined how many Muslims relate to Islam. The introduction of print and mass public education have given ever-larger numbers of Muslims access to the sources of Islam, which has in turn undermined older patterns of learning and put to question the authority of the traditional guardians of Islam. Increasingly, Islamic debates have turned back to the Qur'an and hadith. Scholars have called this process the "objectification" of Islam, which extracts Islam from custom, tradition, and interpretation and reinvents it as a stand-alone object composed of certain original sources.[13] To a certain extent, Islam has undergone "protestantization," with classical understandings of Islam often giving way to new formulations.[14]

This objectification of Islam has produced varied results. In the late nineteenth and early twentieth centuries, an influential current of opinion called Muslim modernism argued for the complete compatibility of Islam and modernity. In this view, progress was inevitable and desirable and fully consonant with Islam. Indeed, for the modernists, Islam *demanded* progress of its followers. Muslim modernists argued for the reform of education and of family life, changes in the position of women, new notions of public health and hygiene, and much besides: in effect, they wanted Islam and Muslims to modernize. Islam itself, they thought, was in a poor way: Muslims had allowed it to become encrusted with alien influences. The modernists placed much of the blame for the situation on traditional elites, such as the ulama and Sufi sheikhs, who had caused the corruption of the faith. A generation later, different groups in society, faced with rather different problems but informed by the same understanding of an objectified Islam, came up with a very different argument. The modernists, they argued, had succeeded only in imitating the West and taking Islam on the path to corruption. The solution was not to make Islam accord with the dictates of the modern age, but rather to make the modern world fit the demands of Islam. In other words, modernity had to be Islamized. Muslims could succeed in this world or the next only by reinventing modernity on truly Islamic principles. We will call this movement *Islamism*.

Islamism is modern in that it presupposes the objectification of Islam, for only when Islam is separated from custom, tradition, and indeed history can it become a stand-alone object that can in turn be applied to the practice of politics. In effect, Islam becomes a political ideology, in which all political goals and actions derive from certain abstract notions embodied in the "true" scriptural sources of Islam. In 1929, Hasan al-Banna (1906–49), an Egyptian schoolteacher, founded the Society of Muslim Brothers in Egypt (the organization soon spread to several other Arab countries). The Muslim Brothers were self-consciously a modern political party that took political action for the conquest of power in order to Islamize law and the state. Another major thinker of political Islam was Sayyid Abu'l Ala Maududi (1903–79), who established the Jama'at-e Islami (Islamic Party) in north India in 1941. Although he opposed the creation of a separate state for the Muslims of India (on the principle that such a state would be a secular state and thus no better than an independent India), he nevertheless moved to Pakistan when that country was established in 1947, and from his base in Lahore, presided over a political party that acquired a vocal presence all over South Asia and, later, in the South Asian diaspora. For both al-Banna and Maududi, the goals of politics were not simply the prosperity and strength of Muslims (as most modernists and nationalists had articulated them) but the utter transformation of the individual and of society along principles extracted from the authentic sources of Islam.

Three seemingly disparate currents of modernity came together in the movements of al-Banna (and his more illustrious successor, Sayyid Qutb) and Maududi. First, the three leaders experienced a radical transformation in their understanding of religious authority, an experience similar to that of evangelical fundamentalists in the United States. For Islamists, religious authority resides in texts, which they see as transparent vessels of meaning available to readers without the help of interpretation. They thus disavow the authority of the interpretive tradition through which Islam has evolved in the world. Second, Islamist politics is part of a much broader search for cultural authenticity that has appealed to many different groups (religious, cultural, ethnic, racial) for its promise to restore purity and dignity in a world built on colonialism and the oppression of others. Islamists seek to reject all sorts of "encrustations" on an authentic tradition they seek to "resurrect." Finally, the political goals of Islamist movements owe a great deal, in their formulation, to modern revolutionary ideologies, and to Marxism-Leninism in particular. During the Cold War, Islamists tended to be rabidly anti-Communist in their stance because Communism was a rival ideology, one that rested on universal principles and was hostile to all religions besides. That stance should not blind us, however, to the fascination that Marxism-Leninism had for Islamists and the model it provided for successful political action. The Russian revolution was, after all, the most successful revolt against the bourgeois world order in the early twentieth century, and the resulting Soviet regime trumpeted its anticolonial credentials loudly. For al-Banna and Maududi, the organizational structure of the Communist Party held the key to its success, and both patterned their parties closely on the Communist model. Maududi's Jama'at-e Islami saw itself, in Leninist fashion, as a vanguard party of committed revolutionaries, membership in whose ranks was to be carefully controlled. The ranks of member, candidate member, and supporter—and the establishment of a youth wing for work among students—were patterned directly on the ranks within the Communist Party. The revolution for which the Islamists worked was, of course, to be an Islamic one.

For both leaders the goal was not just to overthrow established "un-Islamic" regimes but to bring about the inner transformation of individuals. This objective, too, was a modern conceit, and is shared by many ideologies of the modern world. In other ways, too, the Islamist way of posing the question bears all the marks of the contemporary world. The struggle to remake the world through anticolonial struggle, concerns with social justice, a fascination with revolution, and an insistence on seeing politics as the primary space of action are all concerns of modern radical politics worldwide, and their appropriation by Islamists gives us a clue to the appeal of their message in the Muslim world. That appeal was not always huge. The middle decades of the twentieth century were dominated by secular nationalism in much of the Muslim world, and Islamist parties appealed only to tiny minorities. The political space for Islamism opened up because of several interrelated factors. The nationalist regimes failed to deliver on their promises (partly because of corruption but largely because of global structural problems beyond their control), and the 1967 defeat at the hands of Israel put the claims of secular nationalism under renewed scrutiny, especially in Arab lands. Ever-larger numbers of citizens felt the need for a more "authentic," more moral response to the crisis posed by Israel. Indeed, the conflict with Israel (whose establishment came at the expense of Arab aspirations and against the wishes of the majority of the population on the ground) has driven politics in much of the Muslim world for the past several decades. Since 1967, as the conflict has taken on religious overtones on all sides, it has provided a major boost to the fortunes of Islamist parties.[15] Finally, we might note that the global defeat of the left and the collapse of the Soviet Union removed other alternatives for formulating an opposition to the discredited status quo.

If Islamism is modern, so are the Islamists.[16] Both al-Banna and Maududi were men of the twentieth century with little formal training in the tradition of Islamic learning. Both al-Banna and his successor, Qutb, were schoolteachers; Maududi came from a learned family, but he did not attend a madrasa. He entered public life through journalism instead and managed to live off his writing for much of his life. Engineers and doctors figure prominently in Islamist parties everywhere. Print and the public sphere have allowed Islamists to circumvent the entire tradition of Islamic learning. However, as parvenus, they have little feel for the flexibility of the tradition and take more absolutist positions than do traditional ulama. Because they see the original texts as the transparent vessels of meaning for all time, Islamists tend to denounce interpretation as evil in itself.

The Muslim Brothers and the Jama'at-e Islami do not exhaust the spectrum of modern Islamic movements. The Islamic revolution in Iran belongs to yet a different trajectory. Ayatollah Khomeini, the leader of the revolution, was not a lay intellectual but a high-ranking member of the Shi'i establishment with impeccable scholarly credentials, which he used to articulate his theory of the "rule of the jurist" (*vilayat-i faqih*). Yet this theory is strikingly modern, without precedent in the Shi'i tradition. Indeed, it owes a considerable debt to the work of lay Islamist intellectuals such as Jalal Al-e Ahmad (1923–69) and Ali Shariati (1933–77), who combined Islamic arguments with Western critiques of modernity. Equally at home with Marx, Sartre, and Fanon, Al-e Ahmad and Shariati articulated an "Islamic" critique of modernity that was a product of Iran's century-long encounter with the West and modernity—and as such, it was modern to the core. It is no surprise then that the Islamic revolution resulted in an Islamic *republic*, complete with a constitution, separation of institutional powers, and the principle of electoral representation.[17] Islamic movements in Turkey or Malaysia present yet other varieties of contemporary Muslim politics.

· · ·

The militant groups that make the headlines today—al-Qaeda, Hamas, the many outfits in Pakistan, and the IMU—represent a strand of radicalism that we will call *jihadist*. These groups differ from Islamists, because they have little or no political program beyond the conquest of power and the subsequent imposition of the shariat as the law of the land. They interpret *jihad* in a purely military sense, and unlike the Islamists, have no interest in the transformation of society beyond policing norms of behavior.

The genealogy of jihadist Islam is shorter still, going back no further than the 1980s, to the final drama of the Cold War, the extremely bloody proxy war in Afghanistan. Far from being the "natural" product of a coherent, self-contained civilization, jihadist Islam emerged in the hurly-burly of the contemporary world, its birth made possible by various regimes, Muslim and non-Muslim, each of which, for reasons of its own, fostered the development of a peculiar blend of militancy, religious radicalism, and social conservatism that was new in the history of the Muslim world. Because jihadist Islam is the main declared enemy in the "war on terrorism," and because its specter haunts the incumbent regimes in Central Asia today, its origins are well worth closer attention.

The Soviet invasion of Afghanistan, which was ostensibly to help an indigenous revolutionary regime fight counterrevolution, provoked a "civil" war that transformed much in the world beyond Afghanistan. The Soviet move threatened many actors, both global and regional. For the United States, the Soviet invasion, coming on the heels of the revolution in Iran, threatened to destabilize the American position in the Middle East and its access to the region's oil. The conservative monarchies of the Arab world, led by Saudi Arabia, felt directly threatened by both the Iranian revolution and the Soviet advance, as did the military regime in Pakistan, which had long had uneasy relations with Afghanistan, common faith notwithstanding. The three sides came together to back the Afghan resistance. The resistance was conceptualized as a jihad against Soviet atheists and did a great deal to heighten the profile of Islamic militancy in the region. The resistance fighters, the *mujahidin* ("those who undertake jihad") were lionized in the West as "freedom fighters." (Ronald Reagan, welcoming several mujahidin leaders to the White House, compared them to the founding fathers of the United States). The mujahidin were not a homogeneous group, but all of them had a strong dislike for the socialists and their largely progressive social agenda, which emphasized women's rights to education and employment, redistribution of wealth, and free and mandatory public education.

The United States supported an Islamic opposition to the Soviet invasion out of doctrinal principles long held sacred. Throughout the Cold War, conventional wisdom in the West saw Islam as an antidote to Communism and thus as a strategic asset to be cultivated. The Soviets' hostility to religion would, it was hoped, make them unpopular in Muslim countries and also keep local socialists at bay. U.S. government agencies spent considerable effort drawing attention to Soviet hostility to religion.[18] The problem was that many Muslims did not see socialism and Islam to be so starkly opposed. Indeed, throughout the twentieth century, a substantial current of opinion in Muslim societies held that Islam's message was one of social justice and that socialism was inherent in Islam. Therefore, only the more extremist and inflexible versions of Islam could effectively counter Communism. The need to counter Communism with Islam thus drew the United States close to the most conservative regimes in the Muslim world, whose wariness of the Soviets coincided with implacable hostility to social or political change at home and which used an appeal to Islam to crush secular leftist opposition at home. (This pattern was, broadly speaking, evident in friends of the United States in the Muslim world, especially Egypt, Saudi Arabia, and Pakistan, and, to a certain extent, even Turkey in the 1980s.) American goals for the proxy war were modest in the beginning; they amounted largely to "killing as many Communists as possible" and making sure the Soviets paid for their misadventure. Quickly, however, the war moved to the center of the Reagan administration's resolve to "use all means necessary" to win the Cold War.[19] For the Saudis, who provided matching funds to the effort, the Afghan war was an opportunity to channel Islamic activism away from themselves and their patrons, the Americans. For Pakistan's military, which had taken power in 1977, the war was a godsend, for it brought in massive military aid from the United States and financial aid from Arab monarchies.[20] The last act of the Cold War was an American-sponsored jihad against Soviet atheism.

Political violence motivated by Islam was new then, and mostly confined to militant offshoots of the Iranian revolution. But the war in Afghanistan made political violence against "unbelievers" a full-blown form of action. Saudi money not only armed the mujahidin, but it also opened a network of schools for the sons of the refugees who poured into Pakistan. These schools purveyed a message of unbending and often bloodthirsty struggle against enemies of Islam. The war also attracted enthusiasts from all over the Muslim world, who congregated in Peshawar to fight the good fight for Islam. Al-Qaeda was to emerge from the ranks of these warriors, which included one Osama bin Laden. The Afghan war also militarized Islamic movements across the Muslim world and did much to produce the Islamist militancy that exists today. With the Soviet withdrawal from Afghanistan in 1989 and the Soviet collapse two and a half years later, the United States lost all interest in Afghanistan, but the jihadist militancy that it had created (as well as the narcotics-based economy that supported the jihadists) continued to thrive. The jihadist groups did not have to wait long before the first U.S. war in Iraq in 1991 provided another target for their rage. Mahmood Mamdani quite correctly calls al-Qaeda and the events of September 11 the "unfinished business of the Cold War."[21]

Clearly, the Afghan jihad cannot be explained without mentioning non-Islamic actors and geopolitical motivations that have nothing to do with Islam. History, we find, is not irrelevant to explaining the political behavior of Muslims. Indeed, it is the very explanation. And if history matters, then we need to pay attention to the concrete historical experiences of real Muslim societies. The Muslim societies of Central Asia experienced the twentieth century in a radically different way than Afghanistan or Saudi Arabia or Pakistan did, and any attempt to understand Islam has to take into account their experience.

CHAPTER I

Islam in Central Asia

In 1805, Eltüzer Khan, the reigning khan of Khwarazm, the oasis principality at the mouth of the Amu Darya, commissioned a history of his dynasty that would "place our august genealogy on a throne in the divan [chancery] of words and to set the names of our glorious ancestors into the seal of history." The resulting work was undertaken by a court historian by the name of Sher Muhammad Mirab Munis, and continued after his death by his nephew Muhammad Riza Agahi, who carried its account down to 1828. The work bore the appropriately grandiose title of *Firdavs ul-iqbâl* (The Paradise of Felicity) and gave an appropriately grandiose account of the achievements of the dynasty. The hefty text contains an enormous amount of information about the history of Central Asia, but perhaps more important is what it tells us about the mental universe of its author and intended audience and about the literary tradition from which it emerged. Like all traditional Muslim histories, it begins with an account of the origin of the community whose history it recounts. In this case, an account of Creation is followed by a short first chapter recounting the Muslim version of the descent of Adam to earth, his reconciliation with Eve, and the Flood. After the Flood, Noah had three sons, who later propagated the human race. The eldest was Japheth, from whose eight sons sprang all the peoples who inhabited Inner Asia (Turânzamin). The eldest of the eight was Turk, the eponymous ancestor of the Turks. The Turks lived peacefully under the sons of Turk, a series of model rulers, until corruption set in during the reign of

Alanja Khan. "The children of Japheth had been Muslims from the time of Noah until this time," but now they fell off the true path and ceased to be Muslims. Events came to such a pass that if a father heard of Islam, his son murdered him, and if a son understood anything of the faith, his father killed him. Then was born Oghuz Khan, who could speak at the age of one and whose first word was "Allah." He rebelled against his father, eventually slaying him, before embarking on a series of conquests that brought Islam to all of "Transoxiana and Turkestan." He ruled for 116 years, before passing away to the afterworld, whereupon his descendants split up. Eventually, one descendent called Jurliq Markan produced Qonghirat, who was the forebear of the Qonghirat tribe that ruled Khiva in the nineteenth century. Jurliq Markan's younger brother Tusbuday sired Qorlas, whose line ultimately produced Genghis Khan. Qorlas's descendants conquered the children of Qonghirat well before Genghis Khan appeared, and the children of Qonghirat were active participants in the rulership of Genghis Khan and his descendants. But during this time, the sons of Qorlas had fallen off the path of Islam again, until they were reconverted. Then the mystic Sayyid Ata, accompanied by Naghday, a Qonghirat notable, went to the court of Özbek Khan, the ruler of the Golden Horde, and brought him into the fold of Islam.[1]

Muslim belief holds that Adam and Noah were the first among a vast number of messengers that God sent to humanity as bearers of divine guidance. They were thus Muslims, part of a chain of divine intervention in human life that culminated with Muhammad, the "seal of the prophets." In Munis's account, then, the Turkic peoples of Central Asia appear as having always been Muslim. They might have fallen off the correct path, but local heroes always brought them back to it. Remarkably, the history makes no mention of the Prophet, the rise of Islam in Arabia, or the Arab conquest of Central Asia. In the text, Islam becomes completely indigenized, an innate part of the genealogical heritage of the Turkic peoples of Central Asia. It is also intertwined with rulership: the Qonghirat dynasty that Munis and Agahi served bears an august lineage that goes back, through Oghuz Khan and Japheth, to Adam himself.

The story is obviously "legendary," and it is very easy to dismiss it as nonsense. But it tells us a great deal about how Central Asians related to Islam. For Munis, the origins of the community, and of the dynasty that ruled over it, were not a matter of explication through profane history. Rather, the origins were sacred, and only sacred history could explicate them. Other myths of origins connected cities and towns in Central Asia directly to the origins of Islam. The celebrated thirteenth-century Arab geographer Yaqut quoted a hadith in which the Prophet reportedly said, "There shall be conquered a city in Khorasan beyond a river which is called the Oxus; which city is named Bokhara. It is encompassed with God's mercy and surrounded by His angels; its people are Heaven-aided; and whoso shall sleep upon a bed therein shall be like him that draweth his sword in the way of God. And beyond it lieth a city which is called Samarqand, wherein is a fountain of the fountains of Paradise, and a tomb of the tombs of the prophets, and a garden of the gardens of Paradise; its dead, upon the Resurrection Day, shall be assembled with the martyrs."[2] Numerous other hadiths connected lesser cities and towns to the Prophet and the very origins of revelation.[3] Such hadiths might be considered unsound by Muslim scholars of hadith and by modern historians, but they were a true measure of the Islamization of Central Asia, for they allowed local identities to be imagined in Islamic terms. Such accounts of divine or Prophetic intervention in local histories dissolved time and space and connected Central Asia to the core of the Islamic tradition. The local and the global were thus intertwined.[4]

·   ·   ·

Before the Russian conquest, for the bulk of the population, being Muslim meant being part of a community that saw itself as Muslim. It had little to do with the mastery, by every individual, of the basic textual sources of Islam. The Qur'an is central to Islamic ritual: its recitation is a pious deed, its verses can serve as protection from misfortune, and the use of selected phrases from it in appropriate social contexts is the true measure of "comprehension." However, it was not central to the everyday conduct of Muslims. Not even the learned were expected to be able to explicate given passages of the Qur'an. Rather, communities asserted their Muslim identities through elaborate myths of origin that assimilated elements of the Islamic ethical tradition with local norms and vice versa. The account of sacred origins of local Muslim communities provided by *Firdavs ul-iqbâl* was replicated in other, more "popular" accounts. One of the most commonly disseminated myths was that of Baba Tükles, who converted Özbek Khan, the Genghisid ruler of the Golden Horde, to Islam by beating the khan's court shaman in a religious contest.

The legend goes as follows: Four Muslim holy men arrived as Özbek Khan participated in a drinking ceremony at a sacred burial ground. In the holy men's presence, the presiding shamans lost their miraculous powers. Impressed, the khan ordered the shamans and the Muslims to "debate with one another . . . ; whoever among you has the religion that is true, I will follow him." The two parties agreed to a trial by fire: one member from each party would enter an oven fired with ten cartloads of tamarisk, and "Whoever emerges without being burned, his religion will be true." When the time came, Baba Tükles, one of the Muslim saints, volunteered for the ordeal. He walked into the oven, reciting the Sufi *zikr* (remembrance) and survived; his counterpart, however, had to be forced into the oven and was instantly consumed by the fire. Seeing this miracle, the khan and all those present became Muslims.[5]

Baba Tükles was a "friend of God." Islam does not have officially canonized saints, but early on, Muslims came to accept that certain individuals have an intimate relationship to God and may intercede with him on behalf of ordinary Muslims. This cult of sacred persons replicated patronage networks that existed in society. Friends of God could be recognized as such in their lifetimes, and after their deaths, their mausoleums became shrines, places of pilgrimage, and foci of communal identity; their disciples, connected to them through chains of initiation, provided a living link to sacred origins. Many of these bringers of Islam were of foreign origin (usually they were ascribed Arab origins), but they were also fully indigenized as ancestors. Their successors were the living links to the community's sacred origins, whereas their shrines made the landscape itself sacred. It was these locally esteemed figures and their shrines that provided local communities with their links to Islam and to the rest of the Muslim world.

And the identity was communal. It was played out through the communal celebration of august ancestors, annual holidays, and life-cycle events. In turn, the community acquired a sacral aura, and its customs and traditions became "Islamic" in their own right. The veneration of shrines, codes of social intercourse rooted in local societies (showing respect for elders, the position of women, which could vary greatly across time and space, and obedience to those of higher social rank), or political authority could all be understood as Islamic. This dual process of localizing Islam and Islamizing local traditions led communities to see themselves as innately Muslim. Local customs were sacralized, and Islam was made indigenous. For most people, there simply could not be a distinction, let alone a contradiction, between Islam and local customs.

Such local ways of knowing Islam or being Muslim are hardly unique to Central Asia or to the past. Over the past few decades, anthropologists have created a substantial literature documenting cases of "local Islam" in many places, from Bosnia to the Comoro Islands, from Morocco to the Philippines. The diverse ways in which Muslims relate to Islam tests our assumptions about the unitary or homogenous nature of Islam. Conventionally, there are two ways in which such diversity is explained. One explanation posits the existence (in this case) of a "Central Asian Islam" that is allegedly moderate or liberal. This Islam stands in contrast to a harsher and less tolerant (but perhaps "more real") "Arab Islam." This view thus connects the diversity of Islam to national or ethnic categories and makes it subordinate to them. However, these national categories are themselves of modern vintage, and in no case is each "national" version of Islam internally homogeneous. Instead, such categorization of Islam transposes ethnic for religious essentialization (thus, not all Muslims think or act alike, but all Central Asians or all Uzbeks do). As we shall see in chapter 7, current repressive regimes in Central Asia are quite fond of such arguments and put them to brutal use.

Another way of making sense of Islam's diversity is to argue that Islam "sits lightly" on communities where Islam is thus localized, and indeed, that Muslims who identify with Islam in this manner are not "real Muslims." Implicit in this argument is the notion that "true Islam" exists and that it may be seen in practice in certain Middle Eastern societies. This position is canonized by many Western experts. Bernard Lewis thus writes, "Great numbers of Muslims live outside the Middle Eastern Islamic heartlands—indeed, by now the Muslims of South and Southeast Asia vastly outnumber the Arabic-, Persian-, and Turkish-speaking Muslims of the Middle East. But they have developed their own political and other cultures, much influenced by those of the regions in which they live."[6] The assumption that certain societies lack any culture other than "Islam," whereas others have only local culture with a coloration of Islam is highly dubious. Ethnographies of Middle Eastern societies, for instance, show the same kind of melding of the local and the global that I describe for Central Asia above. Asserting that Middle Eastern societies exhibit "real" Islam in its purity renders Islam synonymous with a narrow part of the spectrum of its diversity and mischaracterizes this global phenomenon. The Middle East represents only a small proportion (between a fifth and a quarter, depending on one's definitions) of the total Muslim population of the world, most of which resides in Pakistan and points east. Finally, Lewis's argument echoes that of the more exclusivist groups of modern Muslims, for whom "real Islam" is a prescriptive, rather than merely a descriptive, tool.

Neither of these arguments helps us understand Islam as a phenomenon of this world. Islam takes many local forms, but none of them is stable or internally homogeneous. Perpetual tension exists within Islam, and all forms of Islam are open to challenge on "Islamic" grounds, from within the Islamic tradition. "Customary" or "local" understandings of Islam are countered by more "normative" versions of Islam that draw their authority from greater adherence to injunctions or strictures elaborated by scholars who specialize in fiqh or other aspects of Islam's normative tradition. This tension between different ways of understanding Islam creates the most characteristic inner dynamic in Muslim societies.

We should not assume, however, that "normative" Islam is any more stable or homogenous than "customary" Islam. Muslims can use the resources of the Islamic tradition to take any number of positions, including diametrically opposed ones, on questions that confront them. The absence of a churchlike hierarchy in Islam, which might have a monopoly over the determination of what is normative, complicates the situation further. The answer to the question of who speaks for Islam is that *any* Muslim may speak on behalf of Islam. Indeed, at any time in any society, there are competing claims to authority based on Islam. Ultimately, it is this contention over competing interpretations that defines Muslim politics. Totalizing statements about Islam, therefore, grossly misrepresent this reality. Characterizations that present Islam simply as wicked or tolerant are equally incorrect. Muslims can draw any number of lessons from Islam. The tradition is much too rich and diverse to be reduced to a single evaluative adjective.

The analytical task, then, is not to ask what Islam is or whether *it* is good or bad but to ask why certain interpretations of it are more compelling to some groups in society than to others and how views change over time? And we can answer these questions only by asking how religious authority is constituted around Islam in a given society, how it interacts with other kinds of authority (that of the state, or of science or progress, and so on), how religious knowledge is produced and transmitted, and by whom. What "Islam" or "real Islam" are and what they ought to be are thus questions not primarily of theology, but of cultural and social politics. The political implications of these debates depend on what historically contingent forces play a role (which groups in society have what vested interests) and by the historical baggage these groups bring with them. The burden of the past is absolutely crucial in defining the parameters of debate.

. . .

Islam arrived in Central Asia with Arab armies at the dawn of the eighth century. Arab expansion had brought the armies of the caliphate to the banks of the Oxus (or Amu Darya) by the middle of the seventh century. "The land beyond the river"—*Mâ warâ al-nahr* in Arabic, Transoxiana in English—boasted an old sedentary civilization, Iranian in speech and predominantly Zoroastrian in religion, that sat at the crossroads of trade between India, China, and the societies of the Mediterranean. Although Arab armies had been raiding the region since the 670s, it was only in 709 that they captured Bukhara and incorporated it into the Umayyad caliphate. The conquest led to the conversion of many local inhabitants, although we have few concrete facts at our disposal about the pace of conversion. The Arab conquerors considered new converts to be their clients, *mawâlî,* whose conversion freed them from taxation but did not lead to equality with the Arab conquerors. The ethnic nature of the Umayyad polity changed with the coming to power of the Abbasid dynasty as Islam transformed into a universal religion, and the rate of conversion of the sedentary population probably picked up. By the ninth century, Muslim geographers considered Transoxiana to be an integral part of the Muslim world. Over the next two centuries, its cities became connected to networks of Muslim culture and of Islamic learning. Indeed, some of the most important figures in Islamic civilization came from Transoxiana. Sunni Muslims hold six compilations of hadith to be authoritative. Two of the six compilers, Abu Isma'il al-Bukhari (810–70) and Abu 'Isa Muhammad al-Tirmidhi (825–92) were from Transoxiana. The influential jurists Abu Mansur Muhammad al-Maturidi (d. ca. 944) and Burhan al-Din Abu'l Hasan al-Marghinani (d. 1197); the great scientist Abu Nasr al-Muhammad al-Farabi (d. ca. 950), known as "the second teacher" (after Aristotle); and the rationalist philosopher Abu 'Ali Ibn Sina (980–1037, known in the West as Avicenna)—figures of absolutely central importance in the history of Islamic civilization in its so-called classical age—were all born in the region. They were part of broader networks of travel and learning, which served to make the cities of Transoxiana part of the heartland of the Muslim world. This position was cemented by the emergence, at the end of the tenth century, of Bukhara as the seat of the independent Samanid dynasty, which patronized the development of "new Persian" (i.e., Persian as a fully Islamized language) as a literary language.

The surrounding steppe, with its largely Turkic-speaking nomadic population, remained a borderland. Many nomads entered the orbit of Muslim civilization and began migrating to the Middle East from the tenth century on, but conversion to Islam was a gradual process that lasted into the eighteenth century. Meanwhile, in the early thirteenth century, non-Muslim steppe nomads burst upon Central Asia in the form of the armies of Genghis Khan, and dealt a massive blow to the region. For their sheer ferocity, the Mongol conquests quickly became proverbial. For the contemporary Arab historian Ibn al-Athir, they were a "tremendous disaster such as had never happened before, and which struck all the world, though the Muslims above all. If anyone were to say that at no time since the creation of man by the great God had the world experienced anything like it, he would only be telling the truth."[7] The wholesale slaughter and eviction of populations from cities laid waste to whole provinces. Although the Mongols did not bear any particular animus toward Islam, their actions had a destructive impact on the religious and cultural traditions of Transoxiana. Islam was displaced from its position as the recipient of political protection or patronage, and its moral and ethical imperatives were subordinated to Mongol practices. For example, when Genghis Khan rode into Bukhara, he entered the main mosque, mounted the pulpit, and exclaimed to the assembled multitudes, "'The countryside is empty of fodder; fill our horses' bellies.' Whereupon," we are told by Ata Malik Juvaini, the Muslim historian in Mongol employ who is our best source on the events, the Mongols

> opened all the magazines in the town and began carrying off the grain. And they brought the cases in which Korans were kept out into the courtyard of the mosque, where they cast the Korans right and left and turned the cases into mangers for their horses. After which they circulated cups of wine and sent for the singing-girls of the town to sing and dance for them; while the Mongols raised their voices to the tunes of their own songs. Meanwhile, the *imams, shaikhs, sayyids,* doctors and scholars of the age kept watch over their horses in the stable under the supervision of the equerries, and executed their commands. After an hour or two Chingiz-Khan arose to return to his camp, and as the multitude that had been gathered there moved away the leaves of the Koran were trampled in the dirt beneath their own feet and their horses' hoofs.[8]

Though Transoxiana escaped more lightly than some other regions conquered by the Mongols, the damage to both its economy and its cultural traditions was great. The Mongols had their own code of law and ethics, the *yasa,* which they set against the shariat. Mongol rule thus undid the

Mongols

hegemony of Islam in the political realm. The devastation also unleashed
a lengthy period of religious change, in Central Asia and beyond. The
thirteenth, fourteenth, and fifteenth centuries witnessed numerous mes-
sianic movements in the Islamic East (Central Asia, South Asia, Iran, and
Anatolia), one of which, the Safavids, ended up taking political power in
Iran and imposing Shi'ism on the country. This period also saw the emergence of Sufi movements and their institutionalization in tariqats. The
Sufis' attitudes varied enormously. Some were openly antinomian, seeing
salvation only in the renunciation of the world. For such Sufis, norms of
society had to be trampled; outrageous forms of social deviance (going
around naked, consuming narcotics and hallucinogens, renouncing work
and reproductive sexuality) became the ultimate measure of true devo-
tion to God.[9] Other Sufi orders adhered more closely to the norms of
society and of juridical Islam, and were intertwined with political power
to different degrees. Many of the most prominent Sufi orders (such as the
Naqshbandiya and the Kubraviya) originated in Central Asia in these
centuries and then spread far beyond its boundaries.

.   .   .

One of the enduring stereotypes of Islam is that religion and politics are
intertwined in it. Unsympathetic observers in the West (who contrast the
Muslim world unfavorably with the Christian West with its supposedly
clear demarcations between the realms of God and Caesar) are not the
only purveyors of this view; many contemporary Muslims, too, insist
that "Islam is not just a religion, but a way of life." Historically, however,
this is simply not the case. For the bulk of Islamic history, religious and
political authority have lain in different hands, a division of labor that
was often explicitly formulated by theorists. The earliest caliphs claimed
both political and religious authority, but already by the beginning of the
third Islamic century, the ulama had supplanted the caliphs as guardians
of the faith. The political might of the caliphate, in contrast, disappeared
with the rise of numerous independent dynasties, whose legitimacy came
primarily from military conquest. The majority of the ulama came to accept the new political order, and they appreciated the security and order
that the rulers provided. Indeed, the fear of anarchy, *fitna*, when the supposedly natural order of the social world would be rent asunder, was a
fundamental stabilizing force and helped reconcile the ulama to the new
order. As the fourteenth-century jurist Ibn Taymiya put it succinctly, forty
years of despotism are better than a day of anarchy. But religion and

state—*din va davlat*—were distinct entities: "The state was not a direct expression of Islam, but a secular institution whose duty it was to uphold Islam; the real community of Muslims was the community of scholars and holy men who carried on the legacy of the Prophet in daily life."[10] The Hanafi school of jurisprudence, which predominated in Central Asia, in particular, came to articulate an explicitly quietist attitude toward political power, which in the colonial period led many ulama to reconcile themselves to European rule.

Rulers, for their part, professed to uphold Islamic ethical norms and to serve Islam through the patronage of Islamic learning and the construction of mosques, madrasas, Sufi lodges, and shrines to significant personages. But otherwise, the daily conduct of politics was dictated by *raison d'état.* The practice of Muslim rulers—which included plenty of war with other Muslim rulers—can seldom be explained by injunctions laid out in the scriptural sources of Islam. Far more useful for understanding the political conduct of Muslim rulers are the numerous "mirrors for princes" and advice manuals written by literati over the centuries. These writers took the model for the ideal ruler not so much from the Qur'an as from pre-Islamic imperial traditions—Mesopotamian, Iranian, Byzantine—important elements of which were fully assimilated into the new Islamicate political order.

This process was particularly evident in post-Mongol Central Asia. Over the course of the fourteenth century, the Mongol empire crumbled, and its successors in Central Asia converted to Islam, which thus regained its status as the religion of the ruling elite and the object of royal patronage. But the descendents of the Mongols never renounced their heritage. The principle that only true-blooded descendents of Genghis Khan had the right to rule retained wide currency, and later rulers laid their claims to legitimacy through a combination of Genghisid and Islamic factors. In the late fourteenth century, a Turkic notable named Timur established a major empire out of the chaos of feuding Mongol principalities. Timurid culture was thoroughly Islamized. For all the violence of Timur's ceaseless military conquests, he and his descendents presided over a period of remarkable cultural efflorescence. Samarqand, Timur's capital, was adorned with numerous architectural gems, and the Timurid court provided generous patronage for scholarship and the arts. Timur sought to legitimate himself through both Islam and the *yasa.* The Timurid empire lasted for several generations, but eventually Timur's descendents were ousted from Transoxiana by the nomadic followers of Shaibani Khan, a Muslim Genghisid prince who arrived from the north to reestablish Genghisid rule in the region. Known as Uzbeks, these nomads sedentarized quite rapidly and established what became the khanate of Bukhara. Shaibani Khan's successor, Ubaydullah Khan (d. 1540), made a vow at the shrine of the Sufi master Ahmed Yesevi in the town of Turkistan (in the south of present-day Kazakhstan) that he would rule fully in accordance with the shariat if he were successful in battle against Babur, then allied with the extremist Shi'i Safavid dynasty in Iran. Upon gaining victory, Ubaydullah Khan commissioned Fazlullah Ruzbihan, a scholar from Shiraz in Iran who had found refuge in Samarqand from the Safavids, to compose a manual of governance for him. Fazlullah's *Sulûk ul-mulûk* (The Conduct of Kings) was one of the most comprehensive Islamicate manuals of governance written in Persian. It is largely a synthetic work that describes the consensus of Sunni ulama of the time. It also provides valuable insights into the assumptions that lay behind statecraft in Central Asia in the post-Mongol period.

Fazlullah starts with the assumption that political authority is an absolute necessity and therefore a religious obligation. "Man is social by nature, and bound to cooperate with human society in providing for himself. Because the capacities for lust and anger invite tyranny and conflict, it is necessary for a just ruler to remove [such] tyranny and create proportion and equality among things that are not proportionate."[11] The community of Muslims needs a leader, an imam, to act as a vicegerent of the Prophet "for the sake of establishing the faith and protecting the community's domains." Although Fazlullah cites several ways of choosing an imam, he also recognizes "domination and sheer exercise of power" as legitimate. A leader who becomes a ruler over Muslims through power and military force is legitimate, and it is incumbent upon Muslims to obey all his orders and prohibitions "as long as he does not oppose the shariat." More positively, the ruler has to undertake to "protect the shariat" which here means "the solicitude of the ruler that the laws of the shariat should be guarded and protected among the community, and no manner of rupture may occur in its fundamentals or its branches. It is possible to consider a ruler just only to the extent that he protects the divine decrees and the observance of its commandments." The ruler should fulfill this responsibility by appointing learned men to offices such as *shaykh al-islâm,* "the leader of Islam," and *a'lam al-'ulamâ,* "the most learned of the learned," and by patronizing the cultivation of religious knowledge and showing respect to the learned.[12]

In return, Fazlullah was willing to grant Islamic legitimacy to all the royal pretensions of the rulers. A ruler who upheld the shariat could draw on the treasury for "anything needed to uphold the majesty of his rule." This practice was different from the precedent of the early years of Islam but necessitated by the new era. "Monetary allowances in our times differ from the days of the Prophet or the caliphs," Fazlullah wrote, "because the Prophet was victorious through the respect he inspired, and in the caliphal period, Islam was vigorous and young and people feared the rulers because of prophecy's lingering effects. Today, things have changed and hearts are no longer in their original place. Now if the imam does not undertake the ceremonies of houses, property, horses, and slaves for the sake of appearances, [and] chooses instead to follow the caliphs in his way of living, people would not obey him and all affairs of the Muslim community would come to a standstill."[13] Without social order, of course, there could be no hope for the maintenance of the shariat.

Fazlullah was not particularly original or unusual in presenting matters thus. His views represent a consensus that Sunni ulama of the region had arrived at by this time. The reconciliation of fiqh to the state ruled by military elites that acquired their legitimacy from conquest alone was of long standing. The events of the three centuries preceding Fazlullah, rife with political violence and religious experimentation, had only strengthened the ulama's faith in the necessity of order and of a harmonious relationship between themselves and the state. Indeed, the early sixteenth century saw the consolidation of stable empires throughout the Muslim world—the Ottomans, the Safavids, the Mughals, and the Uzbeks—that did much to curb the religious experimentation of the previous three centuries and establish a certain orthodoxy of state-ulama relations. In that sense, the Central Asian case is part of a much broader phenomenon.

The ensuing three centuries did see the emergence of an alliance between the state and the ulama along the lines indicated by Fazlullah. The sixteenth century saw the construction of several madrasas—places where knowledge could be transmitted to future generations and the ranks of the ulama replenished. Sufi hospices proliferated as well. Madrasas were funded through the institution of the *waqf*, property endowed in perpetuity for a given purpose. Waqf was a major institution in Muslim societies, anchored in fiqh and serving a host of purposes. The establishment of a waqf was a pious deed by the benefactor. If the latter were a ruler, then the act was part of his claim to being a just and legitimate ruler. The property thus endowed could take any form—agricultural land, shops, other forms of rental property—and was usually free from taxation. The waqfs were under the supervision of trustees, who normally came from the ranks of the ulama. To a certain extent, then, waqfs gave the ulama considerable financial autonomy from the state.

Although it is hazardous to generalize about a period spanning three centuries, we can say that the post-Timurid period saw a resurgence of Islamic learning in the cities of Transoxiana. Samarqand, Tashkent, and the cities of the Ferghana Valley boasted numerous madrasas, but the pride of place went to Bukhara. Juvaini had described the city on the eve of its sacking by the Mongols as the "cupola of Islam" in the Islamic East, comparable to the very seat of the caliphate, Baghdad. "Its environs are adorned with the brightness of the light of doctors and jurists and its surroundings embellished with the rarest of high attainments."[14] That status returned to Bukhara in the post-Timurid period, when its madrasas attracted students from throughout Central Asia and beyond, from India in the south and Kazan to the north. The city became *Bukhârâ-yi sharîf*, Bukhara the Noble, the center of Sunni orthodoxy in the region.

This orthodoxy rested on a synthesis of juridical Islam with Sufism. Shariat and tariqat came to be seen as complementary sources of authority. All ulama had Sufi affiliations, and Sufism realigned itself to the norms of juridical Islam. Networks of scholarly and Sufi activity were indistinguishable from one another, and the same individuals offered instruction in both exoteric and esoteric sciences.[15] Therefore, we can speak of the ulama and the Sufis as a single group. The synthesis was also self-consciously a tradition of interpretation and as such, was quite conservative. As in the rest of the Muslim world, Central Asian madrasas were not formal institutions that admitted students or granted degrees. Rather they were places where students learned from masters, whose authority derived from their learning, piety, and reputation. The master-disciple relationship was an individual one, and it revolved around the study of a standard body of texts. Most of these texts were commentaries and supercommentaries on older works of law. The Qur'an and the hadith were not studied as such. The ulama of Central Asia had little recourse to the texts that we think of as the original sources of Islam. This fact strikes modern sensibilities as incomprehensible (and, as we shall see, the modernist Muslim critique of madrasa education focused on this point), but it made perfect sense within the logic of the tradition as it had evolved. *Tafsir*, the science of the explication of the Qur'an, was a high-stakes endeavor left to a few specialists. The task of the tradition of learning embodied in the madrasa was to conserve certain truths revealed by God and the sciences elaborated by the masters. Furthermore, law was the central discipline in Bukharan madrasas of the post-Timurid epoch, and it could be mastered without direct recourse to the Qur'an and the hadith. Besides teaching the shariat as thus understood, madrasas taught "Arabic sciences," such as grammar, prosody, and history, and "rational" sciences, such as logic, philosophy, and metaphysics. Curious students could seek out professors with whom to read books in other disciplines as well.

The possession of Islamic knowledge gave the ulama immense prestige and status and turned them into a self-conscious elite. Nevertheless, the relationship between the rulers and the ulama was dynamic. In times when the state was weak, the ulama or the Sufis could exercise power in their own right. In fifteenth-century Samarqand, the Sufi sheikh Khoja Ahrar had played a significant role in the social and political life of the city, whereas in Tashkent, the ulama had ruled in their own right for much of the eighteenth century, when the city was a state unto itself. At other times, rulers honored the ulama and placed them in places of high influence, granting them tax exemptions as well as control of substantial waqf property and patronizing madrasas and khanqahs. This practice was especially common among rulers of the Manghit dynasty, which took over Bukhara in the late eighteenth century. The Manghits could not claim Genghisid descent and therefore had no choice but to assert their legitimacy through Islam. (For this reason, they could not use the title of khan and instead called themselves *amir,* which had strong Islamic connotations.) The first two rulers of the dynasty formed especially strong alliances with the ulama, even intermarrying with the more august families in their ranks. Such connections were mutually beneficial: they provided the amirs with legitimacy and access to august lineages while placing considerable authority in the hands of the ulama.[16]

Did this arrangement make Bukhara a theocracy? Contemporary Russian and other European observers and later Soviet-era critics thought so. The rulers conceived of rulership and politics in a conceptual framework that derived from Islam. The requirements for compliance with shariat were quite minimal. The ulama recognized the permissibility of *raison d'état,* and of the proclamation of non-shariat laws. The rulers of Bukhara, like all other rulers in the Muslim world, decreed all sorts of laws about extracting obedience and revenue on their own authority with the full approval of the ulama. The "Islamic" aspect of the governance of Bukhara was rulers' willingness to honor and hold in high esteem the carriers of Islamic learning, the ulama. The sources indicate

that the ulama themselves were believed that the affirmation of their
elite status was the factor that made rulers just. (The notion of an Islamic
state belongs to the twentieth century.) During the reign of Shah Murad,
we are told, the son of an *âkhund* killed a shopkeeper who was rude to
him. The victim's father petitioned the amir for justice, but the amir was
so outraged by the temerity of the victim that he imposed a fine on the
father instead, exclaiming that if the victim were not already dead, the
amir would have had him thrown from the Minar-i Kalan, the tall
minaret that overlooked the city and was used for executing criminals in
this manner. "It is clear from the aforesaid," our source informs us, "how
knowledge and its servants were in ascendance at that time, and how
strong were the opinions of the ulama and the rulers."[17] The shariat was
honored when its carriers were honored.

In the nomadic societies beyond Transoxiana, where the tradition of
book learning in madrasas was practically nonexistent, access to Islam
lay primarily through sacred lineages. Communities paid allegiance to
individuals, usually Sufi shaykhs, who belonged to lineages that had
"brought Islam" to the community. The Turkmens had been in the
Islamic orbit since the tenth century, but the Islamization of the Kazakhs
was a longer process, completed only in the late nineteenth century. In
both societies, members of sacred lineages—the Qojas among the
Kazakhs, the *övlad* among the Turkmens—had immense social prestige
and often wealth, but political power remained in the hands of tribal
chiefs. Power in nomadic societies was imagined in genealogical terms,
and to the extent that state structures existed, they derived their moral
authority from *âdat*, tribal custom and the traditions of the elders (who
were Muslims by definition), rather than through the juridical tradition
of the shariat as it was developed in urban societies by generations of
ulama. Later, during the colonial period, the Russian state formalized the
distinction between âdat and shariat by establishing sharply different
administrative practices in areas governed by two variants of colonial
law.

CHAPTER 2

Empire and the Challenge of Modernity

On June 15, 1865, Russian troops under the command of General M. G. Cherniaev broke through the city walls of Tashkent. After two days of resistance, notables of the town sued for peace and accepted Russian overlordship. The conquest of Tashkent, a major entrepôt for cross-regional trade and the third largest city in Transoxiana, was a significant landmark in the history of Central Asia. The Russians had been encroaching southward for more than a century and a half, and had, slowly but surely, extended their control over what is now Kazakhstan over the course of the nineteenth century. Tashkent, however, was the first major city in the sedentary zone of Central Asia that they had annexed. The subjugation of the rest of Transoxiana proceeded with great speed. The military forces of the three major states in the region— Bukhara, Khiva, and Kokand—proved woefully inadequate in the confrontation, and they were overwhelmed. The Russians annexed large chunks of territory from each of them but left the three rulers on their thrones to rule their rump states as Russian protectorates. (Kokand was later annexed *in toto*.) By 1889, when the Turkmen tribes of the Qizil Qum desert had been finally subjugated, Russia had emerged as the paramount colonial power in the region. The lands annexed from the local states or tribes were consolidated in the province of Turkestan, ruled by a governor-general answerable directly to the tsar. The two protectorates of Bukhara and Khiva were enclosed within Russian customs boundaries and denied the ability to conduct foreign relations on their own.

Internally, however, the rulers of the two protectorates were left to their own devices. As the administrators of many other European colonial empires had discovered, protectorates were much cheaper than direct rule.

Central Asia had seen many empires in its long history, but the Russian conquest brought new forms of political control and new forms of knowledge to justify it. It brought Central Asia into the modern world via colonialism. This fate was shared by much of the world outside Europe and North America in the nineteenth century. Russian administrators of Central Asia saw their position there as directly equivalent to that of the British in India or the French in Algeria or Vietnam.

Everywhere in the colonized world, conquest and subjugation produced new challenges for the conquered: How have we come to this pass? Why have we been conquered? What can we do? Different groups in society came up with different answers. But they all formulated their answers within a framework that was the product of colonialism. Many of the answers came from new groups of modern intellectuals that appropriated to their own ends the new kinds of education and new ways of looking at the world that empire made possible. They demanded political rights from the imperial power, but they also asserted the need for change in their own societies. The new order unleashed by empire transformed the dynamics of intellectual life in colonized societies, although change was seldom unidirectional. Central Asia was no exception to this pattern. Let us examine these changes in more concrete detail.

•   •   •

Islam and Muslims have had a constant presence in Russian history. Genghis Khan's grandson Batu had conquered the principalities of Rus', and the conversion of his descendant Özbek Khan to Islam in 1327 meant that political overlordship of the lands of Rus' was in the hands of Muslims for over a century. That relationship was soon reversed, as Muscovy, the principality that grew to be the Russian empire, gained strength while the Golden Horde, the Mongol successor state, disintegrated into numerous smaller entities. Muscovy acquired its first Muslim subjects as early as 1392, when the so-called Mishar Tatars, who inhabited what is now Nizhny Novgorod province, entered the service of Muscovite princes. Nevertheless, it was in 1552 with the conquest of Kazan, one of the remnants of the Golden Horde, that Muscovy first acquired a sizable Muslim population. Over the next two centuries,

Muscovy acquired numerous Muslim subjects as it asserted suzerainty over the Bashkir and Kazakh steppes. In 1783, Catherine the Great annexed Crimea, the last of the successors of the Golden Horde, and late eighteenth-century expansion brought Russia to the Caucasus. Although the annexation of the Transcaucasian principalities (including present-day Azerbaijan) was accomplished with relative ease, the conquest of the Caucasus consumed Russian energies for the first half of the nineteenth century. The final subjugation of Caucasian tribes was complete only with the capture of the tribes' military and spiritual leader Shamil in 1859. By the time the Russians conquered Transoxiana, they had long experience with Muslims. The conquest of Transoxiana doubled the size of the empire's Muslim population, inducting the inhabitants of the region into the wider community of "the Muslims of Russia."

Nevertheless, it is difficult to discern a single Muslim policy in the Russian empire. The Russian empire was conceptualized as a vast array of differences in which groups paid allegiance to the tsar-emperor in their own ways. The Russian state's interaction with Islam and Muslims therefore varied greatly over time and place. In the immediate aftermath of the conquest of Kazan, the state followed a policy of harsh repression. Repression returned in the early eighteenth century, when Peter the Great and his successors began to see religious uniformity as a desirable goal. In 1730, a new campaign of conversion led to the destruction of many mosques. For much of the rest of the imperial period, however, the state's attitude was essentially, in the words of Andreas Kappeler, one of "pragmatic flexibility."[1] Service to the state was the ultimate measure of loyalty and the source of privilege. Tatar landlords who survived the dispossession of the sixteenth century were allowed to keep their land and were even able to own Orthodox serfs.

The reign of Catherine II (1762–96) marked a turning point in the state's relationship with its Muslim subjects. She made religious tolerance an official policy and set about creating a basis for loyalty to the Russian state in the Tatar lands. She affirmed the rights of Muslim nobles and even sought to induct the Muslim clerisy in this endeavor. In 1788, she established a "spiritual assembly" at Orenburg. The Orenburg Muslim Spiritual Assembly was an attempt, unique in the Muslim world at that time, by the state to impose an organizational structure on Islam. Islam was for Catherine a higher form of religion than shamanism, and she looked favorably upon the Islamization of the Kazakhs by Tatar ulama. This stance, was of course intertwined with the goals of bringing the Kazakh steppe under closer Russian control and outflanking Ottoman diplomacy there. Headed by a state-appointed mufti, the assembly was responsible for appointing and licensing imams throughout the territory under its purview and for overseeing the operation of mosques.

Although Catherine's policies survived until 1917 in their broad outline, her enthusiasm for Islam did not. The Enlightenment had also brought to Russia the concept of fanaticism, and fear of fanaticism tended to dominate Russian thinking about Islam in the nineteenth century. Islam was now deemed to be inherently fanatical, and the question now was how to curb or contain this "fanaticism." If Catherine had hoped for the Islamization of the Kazakhs as a mode of progress, nineteenth-century administrators sought to protect the "natural" religion of the Kazakhs from the "fanatical" Islam of the Tatars or the Central Asians. These concerns defined Russian policies toward Islam in Central Asia in the nineteenth century.

Russian policies in Turkestan bore a deep imprint of the first governor-general, K. P. Kaufman, who served in office from 1867 until his death in 1881. For Kaufman, the ultimate goal was to assimilate the region into the Russian empire, but full assimilation could happen only in the long term. The Russian presence was too tenuous, the local population too dense and too "fanatical" for full assimilation to take place. The fanaticism inhered in Islam, and the solution was to undermine the influence of Islam. Such "fanaticism" could be lessened by ignoring Islam and depriving it of all state support, which Kaufman was confident would lead to the decay of Islam, while working on a long-term goal of encouraging trade and enlightenment as a way of assimilating the region to the empire. Ignoring Islam meant denying government recognition to religious dignitaries and distancing them from the new institutions of power. Thus, Kaufman forbade the Orenburg Muslim Assembly to extend its jurisdiction into Turkestan. Islam was to be ignored, not destroyed: colonial empires were seldom interested in this type of massive intervention in society. The Russian policy of ignoring Islam did not mean that local social and cultural practices remained untouched by the new circumstances. The mere presence of the Russians, the incorporation of the region into the world economy as never before, and the advent of new forms of communication and organization all produced far-reaching changes. But the changes were complex and cannot be understood simply as either "Russification" or "resistance."

The local population remained subject to indigenous law in civil and personal matters, although the colonial regime brought about many changes here too. From the beginning, the Russians made a sharp distinction between the nomadic and sedentary populations. The former were allegedly close to a "natural" way of life, in which Islam provided merely a thin veneer over ancient customs. They were to be governed by customary law (âdat). The sedentary populations, in contrast, were associated with "real Islam" and thus were under the domain of the shariat. Both forms of indigenous law were to be administered by judges elected by local notables. Although in theory election was open to any male over twenty-five years of age, in practice, offices for both qazis (judges in shariat courts) and *biy*s (those in âdat courts) remained predominantly in the hands of those with traditional qualifications. This assumption of innate differences between âdat and shariat crystallized a situation that had been much more fluid, leading nomadic and sedentary societies along separate paths. The state's official recognition of the two modes of law began a process of bureaucratizing and codifying them. Here, Russian policies had much in common with those of other European powers in their colonies. For our purposes, the shariat courts are important because they provided a space for the continued influence of the ulama in the sedentary regions of Transoxiana.

The ulama reacted to the Russian conquest in a number of ways. In some cases, they mobilized armed resistance to Russian armies. In 1866, for example, Muzaffar Khan, the amir of Bukhara, showed little enthusiasm for taking on the Russians when they approached the town of Jizzakh on the way to his capital. The ulama from the madrasas of the city led a throng to the gates of his palace, demanding that he take on the invaders. A similar protest erupted in Samarqand, where the populace had already been complaining about the exactions of the local governor. The protest turned into a riot, which was brutally suppressed by the amir's troops, with large numbers of students and many leading ulama of the city being massacred. Later, in 1898, a Sufi sheikh by the name of Dukchi Eshon led two thousand followers in attacking Russian barracks in Andijan in the Ferghana Valley, killing twenty-two soldiers as they slept. Some ulama are known to have emigrated from lands annexed by the Russians, either to Bukhara, where the amir retained internal autonomy, or to Afghanistan. But such cases were exceptional. The Andijan uprising, quickly suppressed with great brutality, was the most serious armed revolt against Russian rule in Central Asia until 1916. The ulama fell back on a long tradition of quietism well articulated in the local Hanafi tradition. As we saw in chapter 1, Fazlullah Ruzbihan had argued that as long as a Muslim ruler upheld the shariat, his rule was legitimate. In the late nineteenth century, Fazlullah's successors extended this recognition to the Russians. As long as the new rulers did not harm the shariat, and as long as Muslims as a community retained a space in which Islam could be practiced and the bearers of the shariat could adjudicate in matters of civil and personal law, colonial rule was legitimate. Far from decaying as a result of government disinterest, Muslim institutions flourished. The half-century of Russian rule before the revolution of 1917 saw marked growth in the size of cities, as new economic links to empire (most importantly, the introduction of cash-crop agriculture centered on cotton) led to substantial economic growth. Many new madrasas were built, and attendance in them increased. The policy of nonintervention in local life allowed recognition of Muslim society as different. The ulama came to see themselves as the gatekeepers of this difference.

Things turned out somewhat differently in the protectorates. Bukhara acquired a reputation as a bastion of conservative orthodoxy in which the ulama ruled the roost. This generalization had an element of truth, but the reality was complex. The ulama certainly emerged as the gatekeepers of tradition there, too, but Bukhara was no theocracy. The Russians had stopped short of total conquest of Bukhara, in part out of fear of provoking the "fanaticism" of the population to a degree that they could not control. Left to the rule of a Muslim monarch, the Russians calculated, the Muslims were much more likely to be quiescent. The amir of Bukhara thus became a guarantor of the stability of Russian rule in Central Asia. Muzaffar, the defeated amir of Bukhara, brilliantly turned this situation to his own purposes. To his own population, he portrayed himself as the last remaining Muslim ruler in Central Asia, who was thus a defender of the last bastion of Islam in the region. With the Russians at the gates, traditional practices came to be valorized as the measure of true Islam, and Muzaffar fashioned himself as the upholder of local ("Islamic") traditions. To the Russians, he presented himself as the best means of keeping the "fanaticism" of the local population in check, provided the Russians did not interfere in everyday life in the emirate. At the same time, by giving the Russians a stake in keeping him and his descendants on the throne, Muzaffar was able greatly to strengthen his position internally. He had not forgotten the uprisings of the ulama in 1866. Once peace was restored, he acted quickly to assert his authority over them. Over the next few years, he turned the ulama into a subservient estate. He created numerous sinecures for readers of prayers at his palace. He also revived the old Bukharan tradition of the *dehyak*, a stipend that the amir gave to madrasa students, as a way of buying the loyalties of the ulama. The amirs also used appointments to offices and

ranks as levers to enhance their position vis-à-vis the ulama.[2] Although
the amirs could not completely disregard scholarly credentials in making
appointments, they nevertheless could choose between similarly qualified
candidates.

The amirs' control of the ulama was never complete, but the constraints placed on the latter were real. Many ulama accommodated themselves well to the new situation, but tensions remained. Bukharan ulama
could, by withholding their assent, stymie any of the amirs' initiatives
that they did not like, and if the need arose, they could even assert their
power against the amirs through open agitation. But open agitation also
brought to the fore divisions *among* the ulama. Bukhara's status as the
most important major center of Islamic learning in Central Asia was not
affected by the Russian conquest. Students continued to arrive in
Bukhara from all over Central Asia. This scholarly population was of
central importance both to the economy and to the politics of the city,
which gave the impression of being one citywide campus. Among the
ulama were a number of factions, each of which found a constituency
among the students, who were tied to their teachers with bonds of loyalty and patronage. The resulting factional struggles over access to influence and wealth defined the parameters of politics in Bukhara under the
protectorate.[3]

•   •   •

In the generation following the Russian conquest, then, the ulama gradually accommodated themselves to the new order in Central Asia. The
new regime left enough space for the practice of Islam and the fulfillment
of basic legal codes that the ulama could focus on maintaining that space.
In this arrangement, they were happy enough to cooperate with the
Russian administration and to accept state honors and decorations. They
could respect many of the developments introduced by the Russians—
modern medicine, the telegraph, railways—but felt no need for Muslim
society to change. That feeling began to change by the turn of the century, when voices for reform began to emerge from other groups in society. Here is a typical example of this new discourse:

> O coreligionists, o compatriots! Let's be just and compare our situation with
> that of other, advanced nations. Let's secure the future of our coming gener-
> ations and save them from becoming slaves and servants of others. The
> Europeans, taking advantage of our negligence and ignorance, took our
> government from our hands, and are gradually taking over our crafts and

trades. If we do not quickly make an effort to reform our affairs in order to safeguard ourselves, our nation, and our children, our future will be extremely difficult. Reform begins with a rapid start in cultivating sciences conforming to our times. Becoming acquainted with the sciences of the present age depends upon the reform of our schools and our methods of teaching. Our present schools take four or five years only to teach reading and writing, and our colleges take fifteen to twenty years merely to study introductions [to canonical texts]. . . . To hope for them to impart a knowledge of the sciences of the present age is as futile as to expect one to reach out to a bird flying in the sky while standing in a well. . . . If we ignore this [now], it will be too late.[4]

Munavvar Qori, the author of this passage, which appeared as a front-page editorial in *Xurshid* (The Sun), a newspaper launched in 1906 in Tashkent, was a teacher who had studied in the madrasas of Tashkent and Bukhara. Well versed in the knowledge possessed by the ulama, he nevertheless argued from different premises. Munavvar Qori and others like him believed that the Muslim society of Central Asia was in a serious crisis, in which its survival was at stake. Everything was in need of change, with traditional education at center stage. The course of action was clear: enlightenment and modern education would solve all the problems of the community, but the community and its members would have to reorganize themselves in order to achieve this goal.

Munavvar Qori was one of the leading figures of a new reformist movement called Jadidism then gaining a foothold in Central Asia.[5] The movement derived its name from its advocacy of the *usul-i jadid*, the new method of teaching the Arabic alphabet to children in the *maktab*, the ubiquitous elementary school of sedentary Muslim societies of the region. Implicit in the concept was a new way of looking at the world. The most important item in the lexicon of Central Asian Jadidism was *taraqqiy*, a term that covered the notions of progress, development, rise, and growth. The Jadids' assimilation of the idea of progress, the notion of history as open-ended change, altered the way in which they saw the world and their place within it. If progress were a fact of nature, then it was incumbent upon Muslims as a community to strive for it too. Progress begat civilization, which for the Jadids was a singular entity. They would have utterly rejected the notion of a clash of civilizations. Rather, progress and civilization were accessible to all; the only precondition was the cultivation of knowledge. Hence came the centrality of the new-method school in the Jadid project; hence also came the emphasis on self-improvement.

Knowledge also explained for the Jadids the superiority of the "more advanced" societies of Russia (and Europe in general) over Muslim society. These societies were living examples of the links between knowledge, wealth, and military might that the Jadids constantly asserted. Such positive images were not simply the result of the Jadids' Europhilia. They had a didactic purpose: to exhort the Jadids' own society to acquire all the aspects of Europe that they admired: knowledge, order, discipline, power. This fascination with Europe coexisted with a fear that if Muslim societies did not "catch up," their situation would become even more difficult. The practically unchallenged encroachment of European powers over the rest of the planet sustained these fears. But fear alone did not drive the Jadid agenda. The Jadids genuinely admired the new forms of order and discipline in industrial society and appreciated its technological achievements. The task was to join this civilization, an imperative that the Jadids believed was commanded by Islam itself. The Jadids hoped that Muslims ultimately would join the modern world as respected and equal partners. They wanted the modernity of Europe for themselves.

The call to reform was made from a self-consciously Islamic position. The acquisition of modern knowledge, the Jadids argued, was mandated by Islam itself. In common with other modernists of the period, the Jadids ascribed the "decline" and "degeneration" of their community to its departure from the true path of Islam. When Muslims followed true Islam, the Jadids argued, they were leaders of the world in knowledge, and Muslim empires were mighty. Corruption of the faith led them to ignorance and political and military weakness. The solution was a return to "true Islam."

True understanding of Islam for the Jadids meant recourse to the scriptural sources of Islam without the commentaries and glosses painstakingly developed by centuries of scholars. The textual sources of Islam—the Qur'an and hadith—were now deemed to be self-sufficient and accessible to all educated Muslims. If commentaries and glosses were a hindrance to true knowledge of Islam, other customary practices, such as seeking intercession from "friends of God" or visiting shrines, were blatant signs of polytheism, the biggest sin in the Islamic tradition. For the Jadids, Islam existed in certain texts, not in the customs and traditions of Muslim communities. Jadidism represented, in essence, a new way of knowing Islam.

Jadidism may have started as simply the advocacy of a new method of teaching the alphabet, but in emphasizing the importance of literacy as a functional skill, rather than as a sacred activity, it was profoundly subversive of established patterns of cultural authority. Much of the ulama's authority rested in their command of the tradition of the interpretation of the sacred texts of Islam. The Jadids denounced the long tradition of interpretation that was reproduced in the madrasas; they criticized this tradition and argued that the basic texts were accessible to all those who possessed the literacy provided by the new-method schools they championed. Debates about religion could now take place in print, rather than in the rarefied precincts of scholastic circles. Received understandings could be questioned by new groups acting in a new arena; the transformations that had affected religion in Europe in the early modern period were now happening in the Muslim world. Madrasas faced criticism for not meeting the needs of the age, for producing corrupted versions of Islam, and even for being hotbeds of laziness and docility. The texts that the ulama mastered were now deemed to be full of *safsatalar va xurofot* ("sophistry and superstition") that obfuscated the true message of Islam and kept the Muslim community in the darkness of ignorance. The Jadids mounted a sustained critique of the ulama for their alleged venality, greed, and, most of all, abdication of their responsibility to the Muslim community. The ulama had corrupted the real teachings of Islam and led the nation into ignorance, and hence into colonial subjugation.

The life of Abdurauf Fitrat (1886–1938) is illustrative of the fate of Jadidism in Central Asia. Fitrat was born in Bukhara when the protectorate was almost two decades old. The son of a merchant who had wide literary and scholarly interests and who had traveled abroad for trade, Fitrat received a traditional Muslim education in Bukhara, studying with the eminent scholars in the city's madrasas. In 1909, however, he received a scholarship from the newly established Education of Children Society (a benevolent society funded by the city's merchants who were frustrated by the inability of their children to acquire a modern education in Bukhara) to go to Istanbul for higher studies. The four years Fitrat spent in the Ottoman capital were tumultuous. He arrived there the year after the Young Turk revolution had rekindled debate about the future of the Ottoman Empire. Fitrat's Istanbul experiences were to be central to the development of his view of the world.

The contours of Fitrat's notion of reform—and of Jadidism in general—are most clearly visible in two reformist tracts that he published in Istanbul. The first tract, *A Debate between a Bukharan Professor and a European in India on the Subject of New Schools* (1910) harks back to a long tradition in Islamicate letters of *munâzara*, "disputation," but it addressed a topic of current importance. Even more surprising is Fitrat's choice of a mouthpiece. The European in the title is an Englishman fully conversant with Islam and sympathetic to the needs of modern Muslim society. As a paragon of modern learning, he easily bests his Bukharan interlocutor. The Bukharan professor, clearly representative of all Bukharan ulama and the entire tradition as it existed in Fitrat's time, was ignorant of the world, narrow-minded, quick to temper, and not even proficient at his job. The Englishman speaks better Arabic than does the Bukharan, who has studied the language for years using the traditional methods. Fitrat turns the defense of new-method schools into a condemnation of traditional Bukharan ulama, whose conduct the Englishman criticizes for going against the injunctions of Islam and countering the best interests of Muslims: "What is this conduct that the ulama of Bukhara have!" exclaims the European interlocutor upon hearing that the ulama receive large sums of money from their students. "Are they not afraid of God or ashamed before the Prophet? . . . Are they not embarrassed to consider legal the imposition of this futile sin [of greed] on their helpless students—which God and the Prophet have declared illegal?"[6] In his second tract, *Tales of an Indian Traveler,* Fitrat dispenses with the European and uses a fictional Indian Muslim in the role of a sympathetic but stern outside critic to list the desiderata of Bukharan reformers: public order through policing, long-term economic planning, the creation of a system of public health and hygiene, and above all, a system of modern education at all levels. In this project, the state has the central role as the initiator and executor of reform.[7]

•   •   •

The tension between customary and normative understandings of Islam is a defining feature of the tradition. In criticizing customary practices in the light of textual sources, the Jadids put themselves in a long tradition within Islam of seeking renewal of faith and community. The Jadids were part of a broader current of modernist thought in the Muslim world of the period, which sought renewal of faith and community in a more rigorous approach to Islam. Figures such as the itinerant activist Jamal ad-Din Afghani (d. 1897); his disciple, the Egyptian mufti Muhammad 'Abduh (d. 1905); and a host of other luminaries sought to break from the accepted wisdom of the time by arguing for a return to the example of the "virtuous ancestors" (*al-aslâf al-sâlihûn*) of Islam—that is, the Prophet and his companions, whose lives were to be exemplary for all Muslims.[8] But they wedded this call, and the critique of traditional learning that it encompassed, to notions of progress and civilization and arrived at a radically innovative position.

The idea of a return to the sources is a fundamentally modern one, and not surprisingly, it underlies all reformist movements in the modern Muslim world. But returning to the sources can yield all sorts of political and religious stances. Other groups have used the same premises to argue for more rigorous adherence to Islamic norms without putting that rigor in the service of "progress." In Central Asia on the eve of World War I, a circle of ulama published the journal *al-Isloh* in Tashkent, which criticized customary practices associated with Sufism and called for more rigorous attention to requirements of fiqh. This call was a vision of piety rooted in hadith and fiqh, with no concern for yoking Islam to progress and modernity. Such concerns were taken to their extreme by a movement called "Wahhabism." Because Wahhabism figures large in later chapters of this book, a few words about the movement are in order here.

This radically puritanical sect arose in the Najd province of Arabia in the eighteenth century. Najd, a largely barren tract of land beyond the beaten path, had largely been forgotten by history. In the eighteenth century, it was formally claimed by the Ottoman Empire, but local tribes lived an autonomous existence. Here, Muhammad ibn 'Abd al-Wahhab began to preach a strictly puritanical doctrine that broke with the general consensus of Muslims. He took an expansive view of *shirk*, the sin of compromising God's unity, and of *bid'a*, "innovation." For 'Abd al-Wahhab, any concept not derivable from the Qur'an or a very restricted corpus of hadith was un-Islamic. In taking this position, 'Abd al-Wahhab dismissed the long tradition of Muslim jurisprudence (fiqh), which had accepted a much larger range of sources as authoritative. Mainstream Muslim opinion, both Sunni and Shi'i, had also long agreed on the permissibility of seeking the intercession of the Prophet or other "friends of God" in one's dealings with the deity in the form of petitionary prayer, supplication, or the visitation of shrines. 'Abd al-Wahhab denounced all of these acts as *shirk*. Even poetry in praise of the Prophet or other exalted figures, a genre that had produced some of the noblest verse in the Muslim world, was for 'Abd al-Wahhab merely a form of idolatry. The sins of *shirk* and idolatry turned Muslims into infidels. Denouncing all other Muslims for having strayed from the true path, 'Abd al-Wahhab saved the worst for Sufism and Shi'ism, which he denounced root and branch. Nor was denunciation enough: 'Abd al-Wahhab outlined a theory of armed struggle against infidels, but especially those Muslims who had fallen off the true path.[9]

The movement might have disappeared without a trace, had not 'Abd al-Wahhab made an alliance with Muhammad ibn Sa'ud, the petty ruler of a town in Najd. In 1746, the two together declared war (jihad) on all Muslims who did not share their views on Islamic purity. This alliance gave rise to a sectarian state built of conquest that in time conquered much of the Arabian Peninsula, except the province of Hijaz with its holy cities of Mecca and Medina. These cities too fell in 1806. The conquest aimed to bring lapsed Muslims back into the fold of Islam and was accompanied by a distinctly Wahhabi form of iconoclasm. Wahhabis were fond of destroying tombs and shrines, demolishing domes over houses and palaces, burning books other than the Qur'an, forcing people to pray communally, and policing moral conduct and personal behavior. This fate was visited upon the holy cities of Mecca and Medina, where the Wahhabis desecrated the tombs of the wives and the companions of the Prophet and a host of other luminaries of Islamic history, destroyed the dome over the house where the Prophet was supposed to have been born, and forced the ulama of the two cities to accede to their doctrine. Eventually, the Ottomans ousted the Wahhabis from Hijaz, and the Saudi-Wahhabi state retreated to its core in Najd. Eventually, the Saudi-Wahhabi state reemerged at the turn of the twentieth century in the context of the weakening of Ottoman power, when Muhammad Ibn Sa'ud conquered much of the Arabian Peninsula, including the cities of Mecca and Medina, and established the kingdom of Saudi Arabia in 1932.

The current prominence of Wahhabism in the Muslim world can easily lead us to believe that the movement's influence has always been great. In fact, much of its present success is a product of the late twentieth century, during which its fortunes have been tied intimately to those of the Saudi state and its geopolitical requirements. We need to remember that in the era in which the Jadids lived and argued, Wahhabism was a minor current of opinion, its influence limited to the more lawless expanses of the Arabian Peninsula. In the world beyond, Wahhabism served largely as a polemical foil in sectarian arguments among Muslims, enabling opponents of reform to denounce their opponents as "Wahhabis," whether or not an actual connection existed between the reform and the teachings of 'Abd al-Wahhab. This practice was especially common in India, where "Wahhabism" was tossed around as an accusatory label for many reform movements. The British rulers of India joined in as well, and established an imperial tradition of labeling all troublesome Muslim opponents as Wahhabi. In the lands of the former Soviet Union, the term has come into indiscriminate use to denote any and all expressions of nontraditional Islam. Thus, we need to remember that Wahhabism serves the purpose of accusation as much as that of description and to use the term with circumspection.

•   •   •

The emergence of Jadidism was not uniformly welcomed in Central Asia. Quite the opposite, in fact. Implicit in the advocacy of reform were large political issues. Who should exercise leadership in society? Who should set the terms of debate? What was really at stake? These questions represented a debate about society and politics as much as one about religion. The Jadid message provoked the opposition of many groups whose position in society was challenged by the message of reform.

Among those who opposed the Jadids were men of traditional Islamic learning. Not all ulama were against the Jadids: many Jadids came from learned families, and they could count on the support of many reformist ulama as well. Nevertheless, the Jadids' harsh criticism of traditional modes of understanding Islam arrayed the majority of ulama against them. These men mustered enormous prestige in society, which had scarcely been dented by the criticisms of the Jadids. In opposing the Jadids, the conservative ulama had the support of other established groups in society whose preeminence was threatened by the Jadids: merchants who might find literacy in Russian useful for their children but who saw little need for the thoroughgoing reform of society that the Jadids advocated, urban notables who felt that the Jadids threatened their positions as intermediaries between the indigenous population and the Russian state, and many others who felt little sympathy or need for the challenges the Jadids posed to their way of life. The fact that most Jadids were very young—Russian observers instinctively compared them to the Young Turks—made their task more difficult in a society in which age garnered enormous respect.

Yet the Jadids had made their mark on Central Asian society by the time World War I summoned the end of the old regime in Russia. Their use of the printed word and theater and their support of new-method schools and benevolent societies had, for all the group's limitations, destabilized the traditional order and challenged the authority of traditional learning. On the eve of the great upheaval of the Russian revolution, Central Asian society was beset with a fundamental conflict about where it was to go and who was to lead it there.

The debate between the Jadids and their conservative opponents was not, it must be understood, a debate between "secularists" and "Islamists." Both sides used Islamic arguments. Rather, the debate was about different interpretations of Islam—what being Muslim meant, who had religious authority, and how this authority was to be used. Nevertheless, the two sides arrived at radically different answers, providing an apt example of the internal diversity of Islam. Islam does not produce uniform or homogeneous kinds of political action. Rather, the sense Muslims make of their tradition, and the political action they undertake, depends on their sense of their place in the world, the problems they face, and the resources they have. Political actions of Muslims are a product of concrete historical circumstances and of conflicts and debates among human actors.

·   ·   ·

The conflicts that beset Central Asian Muslims under Russian rule extended beyond those between the established elites and their Jadid challengers. Conflict between nomads and peasants over land use often took on an ethnic coloration and pitted the Kyrgyzes against the Uzbeks in the Ferghana Valley and Turkmens against Uzbeks in Khiva. In addition, Russian rule brought new ethnic complexity. The conquest prompted substantial immigration from the European parts of the Russian empire, as Russians and members of the empire's numerous nationalities (Ukrainians, Jews, Poles, Germans, Tatars, and Armenians) appeared in the region. The growth of the economy also attracted labor immigrants from Iran and Chinese Turkestan (Xinjiang). Most of these immigrants came to the cities, which grew in size (or, in the case of the steppe zone, appeared for the first time), but an organized settlement of Russian and Ukrainian peasants also existed in the area. This ethnic patchwork tended at most times to be subordinated to a European/Muslim divide, but it could never be completely reduced to this division.

Indeed, the stiffest challenge to Russian rule in the tsarist period was a massive revolt by Kyrgyz and Kazakh nomads in 1916. Faced with labor shortages during World War I, the imperial government abolished the exemption from conscription that native inhabitants of Turkestan had enjoyed since the conquest and announced plans to recruit large numbers of them for work in the rear. The announcement immediately triggered a rebellion, first in the oasis towns of Turkestan, then among the nomadic populations of present-day Kyrgyzstan and southern Kazakhstan. In the towns, crowds gathered in front of administrative buildings to protest, destroying conscription lists and killing many government functionaries, both Russian and local, in the process. The oasis revolt was quashed by late summer. In the steppe, however, protest turned into a full-blown rebellion against Russian rule. Tens of thousands of nomads—armed with lances, swords, and the odd rifle—attacked government offices and Russian peasant settlements (the expropriation of land by officially sponsored settlers had long been a point of complaint), destroying them and killing their inhabitants. The government hastily armed the settlers and diverted soldiers from the front to quell the rebellion. Ultimately, in true colonial fashion, the suppression far surpassed the revolt in its brutality: as soldiers and settlers attacked nomads indiscriminately, the latter fled across the mountain passes to Chinese-ruled territory, only to face epidemics, hunger, and a freezing winter. Those who returned the following spring found their livestock dead and their land expropriated. Russian casualties in the uprising numbered 2,246, but no figure could be attached to "native" casualties (in some districts, they constituted as much as a fifth of the population).[10] The revolt was a protest against colonial oppression, land expropriation, and military conscription; Islam was never an issue.

CHAPTER 3

The Soviet Assault on Islam

On February 23, 1917, in the middle of the third winter of a brutal war, riots broke out in Russia's capital, Petrograd. It was international women's day, a major holiday celebrated by socialist parties all over Europe, and women workers poured into the streets to protest the shortage of bread. They were joined by many men who were already on strike. Banners demanding bread were quickly joined by red flags and inscriptions that read, "Down with Autocracy." The empress Alexandra thought it all of little consequence: "Its a *hooligan* movement," she wrote to her husband then away at field headquarters, "young boys & girls running about & screaming that they have no bread— . . . if it were very cold they wld. probably stay in doors. But this will all pass & quieten down. . . ."[1] But the crowds did not quieten down. Almost three years of war had rotted the ties that bound Russian society together and had undermined the legitimacy of the monarchy. The crowds continued to make ever more radical demands for political change. On the fifth day of rioting, officers from elite regiments refused to obey orders to shoot at the demonstrators; on the seventh, Nicholas, tsar of all the Russias and heir to a political tradition that dated back several centuries, abdicated. The Russian monarchy had ceased to exist.

The collapse of the monarchy unleashed a massive upheaval that was to convulse the length and breadth of the Russian empire for several years, shaking the many societies within it to their core. The numerous strains that had lain latent between and within various societies of the empire came into the open, were often transformed to higher levels of complexity, and were resolved through violent means. Among other outcomes, the Russian revolution utterly redefined the context in which Islam existed in Central Asia. The end result of the revolution, largely unforeseen at the beginning, was the conquest of power by the Bolsheviks, a party with a radical vision of remaking the world. The Bolsheviks put the Russian state back together, but on radically different terms than before. Theirs was a universalist vision that had little place for the toleration of local particularities that had marked the tsarist regime. The new regime was highly intrusive and sought to create a new and better world. The appalling cruelties of the Soviet period were underwritten by utopian ideals born of the Enlightenment tradition. The tsarist regime could not contemplate the massive projects of social and cultural engineering that the Bolsheviks happily embarked upon. The Bolsheviks did not always succeed, and the unintended consequences of their actions were often more important than those they intended. Nevertheless, the seven decades of Soviet rule left Central Asian society utterly transformed. The Soviet impact was deep, and we can understand little about Islam in post-Soviet Central Asia if we fail to take it into account. Thus, this and the following chapter explore the Soviet impact on Islam in Central Asia.

·   ·   ·

The abdication of the tsar was universally acclaimed as "the dawn of liberty," the beginning of a new era for the various peoples inhabiting the empire. In a series of sweeping reforms, the Provisional Government, formed from among the members of the State Duma, the quasi parliament the tsar had unwillingly granted in 1905, abolished all legal distinctions between citizens on the basis of rank, religion, sex, or ethnicity and granted every citizen over the age of twenty the right to vote. It also guaranteed the absolute freedom of press and of assembly. Russia was the freest country in the world in 1917.

The effect of the revolution on Central Asia was electric. The enthusiasm was captured by the Tashkent poet Ahmad Makhdum Sidqiy, who rhapsodized: "Praise be that the epoch of freedom has arrived. The sun of justice has lit the world. . . . The time of love and truth has come. . . . Now, we have to set aside our false thoughts; . . . the most important aim must be to give thought to how we will live happily in the arena of freedom."[2] The ensuing weeks saw public meetings that brought together

thousands of people in the cities of Central Asia; all manner of cultural
and political organizations appeared, and elections to councils of various
kinds took place. The First Turkestan Muslim Congress met in Tashkent
from April 16 to 22 to discuss matters of import to the Muslim community of Turkestan and to elect delegates to a similar congress of Muslims
from all over the Russian empire in Moscow in May.

What the goals of the community should be and who should define
them came to be the crucial questions. For the Jadids, the revolution was
a summons to action. Failure to seize the opportunity to act, wrote a
Jadid teacher, "will be an enormous crime, a betrayal of not just ourselves, but of all Muslims."[3] The Jadids also believed that they, with
their new knowledge and their awareness of the world, were the natural
group to lead their community into the new world. This claim was, however, contested by many other groups in society, who had little patience
for "half-educated, inexperienced youth" such as the Jadids. By May, the
conflict had come into the open, and two sets of parallel organizations
appeared among the Muslims of Turkestan. The Jadids created a network of "Islamic Councils" (Shuroi islomiya), whereas their conservative
opponents grouped around the Society of Ulama (Ulamo Jamiyati).
Although many Jadids had impeccable credentials as ulama, the majority
of the ulama mobilized against them. The conflict escalated throughout
the year, as accusations of insincerity, gullibility, perfidy, and treason flew
back and forth. On numerous occasions, the conflict descended to violence. In municipal elections in several cities in the summer and autumn,
the Jadids were defeated handily by their conservative opponents.

This conflict was not only about authority in society but also about
Islam: questions about the nature of Islam and the meaning of being a
Muslim were clearly at stake. Both sides argued from self-consciously
Islamic positions, even though they meant vastly different things. For the
ulama, the crucial goal was to safeguard the boundaries of their community from erosion in the new universalist order unleashed by the revolution. This objective called for establishing their control over their community, while forming alliances with conservative Russians who were
amenable to recognizing the cultural peculiarities of the local population.
Given the circumstances of 1917, many such Russians were to be found
in Turkestan. A congress of ulama in September resolved "the affairs of
religion and of this world should not be separated, i.e., everything from
schools to questions of land and justice should be solved according to the
shariat." Of course, because the only people capable of interpreting the
shariat were the ulama themselves, this resolution guaranteed the

entrenchment of their authority in the new regime. The Jadids, for their part, drew up in the same month a proposal for the future of Turkestan that called for complete autonomy in the economic realm and for the equality of all citizens of Russia, regardless of religion, nationality, or class. They also called for the establishment of a shariat administration (*mahkama-yi shar'iyya*) in each oblast. The crucial point was the proviso that the electoral principle be maintained in the establishment of this administration and that its members be "educated and aware of contemporary needs"—that is, people like the Jadids themselves. Education was to be free and compulsory, and under Muslim control, but all traditional Muslim schools—the bastion of the ulama—were to be reformed and regulated.[4] Significantly, although both the Jadids and the conservatives favored wide-ranging autonomy for Turkestan in a future democratic Russia, neither side demanded independence or secession from Russia.

The conflict was even sharper in Bukhara. Bukharan Jadids, who came to be known as Young Bukharans, had long hoped that the amir would do his duty (as they saw it) as a Muslim sovereign and institute reform from above. In 1917, however, they sought to pressure him into reform. In March, they telegraphed the Provisional Government in Petrograd, asking it to push the amir in the direction of reform, to institute some of the liberties that had been proclaimed in Russia after the collapse of the monarchy. The amir complied and issued a manifesto in April, only to turn his back on the Jadids when they organized a public demonstration to "thank" him for the reforms. As order disintegrated in Russia, the amir of Bukhara focused on maximizing his maneuvering room and gaining as much independence as he could. In the process, he relied on the most conservative elements in society for support and unleashed a wave of vicious persecution against the Jadids, many of whom fled to Turkestan. There, in the maelstrom of revolution, the Jadids embraced the idea of revolutionizing the East, a process that was to begin with the overthrow of the amir. From "the kind father of the Bukharans, the king who protects his people," the amir became a bloodthirsty tyrant who lived off the toil of the peasants and whose concerns did not extend beyond his own body. The Young Bukharans' relations with the Bolsheviks were always uneasy, but each side had some use for the other. In 1920, the Red Army invaded Bukhara, toppled the amir, and installed the Young Bukharans at the head of a "people's soviet republic."

Events turned out differently in the nomadic areas inhabited by Turkmens and Kazakhs. With Islamic book learning a much weaker tradition than in the sedentary regions, the nomads lacked the main actors

that defined conflict in Turkestan and Bukhara. The ulama were over-
shadowed by tribal aristocracies and small Russian-educated elites who
struggled to establish a national order on the steppe. The main demands
of the Kazakh intelligentsia were national autonomy and a halt to
Russian settlement. The question of Islam scarcely appeared on the political horizon.

There was more to this chaotic age, however, than simply conflict
between the Jadids and the conservatives. By the end of 1917, the eupho-
ria of March was a distant memory, and the deepening crisis of the
empire made more radical approaches attractive to ever-larger numbers
of people. The Bolsheviks took power in St. Petersburg in October and
inaugurated an armed conflict that was to rage until 1921. In Central
Asia, the situation became more pressing when a famine broke in full
force in the autumn of 1917. Cotton had come to occupy an ever-greater
percentage of cultivated land in Turkestan during the war years and had
made the region dependent on grain shipped in from other parts of the
empire. The revolution seriously disrupted transport networks in 1917.
At the same time, the rain failed that summer, plunging the region into a
devastating famine. Between 1915 and 1920, the amount of cultivated
land in the region declined by half, and livestock decreased by 75 percent. Cotton production practically ceased. The losses were not uniform
across social groups, of course. Russian peasants saw a decline of 28 percent in their cultivated land and lost 6.5 percent of their livestock; the figures were 39 percent and 48percent, respectively, for the sedentary
indigenous population, and 46 percent and 63.4 percent for the nomads.
The civilian population of Turkestan fell by a quarter over the same five
years, from 7,148,800 in 1915 to 5,336,500 in 1920. The indigenous
rural population declined by 30.5 percent.[5]

Against this backdrop, Russian settlers attempted to secure their privileges from the depredations of democracy. From the beginning, they had
argued for separate representation in the proposed parliament as well as
for separate local budgets. As the famine pushed questions of survival to
the fore, Russian settlers found such practices as the forced requisitioning
of food from "hoarders" and "speculators" in the old cities and the
forced "socialization" of land in the countryside to be convenient ways
to give revolutionary legitimacy to their search for food. As the countryside descended into chaos, local peasant society organized around armed
insurgents to protect itself and its food supply. This peasant movement
has had a curious career in historiography. The Soviets dubbed the bands
Basmachi, "bandits," and vilified them as forces of religious fanaticism

and dark reaction. In the West, evaluation of these groups has shifted over time. Some scholars have seen them as embodying valiant national resistance to Soviet rule, a view that has been embraced by the post-Soviet regimes in Central Asia itself.[6] In the 1980s, during the Soviet war in Afghanistan, the Basmachi were often seen as precursors to the Afghan mujahidin in a noble cause.[7] Now, the circle has closed, and the Basmachi are occasionally compared to the Taliban as "jihadists."[8] None of these characterizations is accurate. Peasant insurgency had a logic all its own: the Basmachi rebellion was largely local and sought to preserve order and to protect the food supply from outsiders. Basmachi leaders did not act on behalf of abstract entities such as "the nation" or "the Islamic community." Many Basmachi leaders claimed to be acting in defense of Islam, but they were clearly defending the customary way of life that was threatened equally by Russians and by urban reformist Muslims. Attempts by various urban Muslims—Jadids, Young Bukharans, and most quixotically, Enver Pasha, the disgraced former Ottoman minister of war, who showed up in Central Asia in 1921—to use the insurgency of the Basmachi for broader political purposes inevitably failed.

Ultimately, the Bolsheviks won the civil war and were able to reimpose central control over most of the former Russian empire. A Soviet government (dominated by Russian settlers) had existed in Turkestan since the autumn of 1917, but it was largely autonomous of the center, and its actions caused much consternation there. The center reintegrated Turkestan into its authority by the summer of 1920. Russian settlers were ejected from the Turkestan government, but Bolsheviks sent from Moscow to replace them knew little of local conditions and had few footholds in the region. They made a concerted effort to recruit members of the indigenous population into the new institutions of power they were building and thus opened up a space for local activists to join the regime in transforming and reshaping their society.

·   ·   ·

These conflicts defined the politics of the various actors in Turkestani urban society in the years to come. The setbacks of 1917 radicalized the Jadids, who were convinced of the futility of exhortation and gradualism and were fascinated with more robust ways of effecting change. They quickly took to the idea of revolution, if not to the class analysis on which it relied; in the coming years, many entered the Communist Party and worked to bring cultural revolution to Central Asia. They lost a great deal of their earlier fascination with the liberal civilization of Europe and turned to a radical anticolonial critique of the bourgeois order. The Bolsheviks appeared to them as agents of a new world order, an order that contained the possibility of national liberation and progress. The Bolsheviks contributed to this mood by talking incessantly in those years of "revolutionizing the East." Throughout 1917, the Bolsheviks had counted on the Russian revolution's leading to a proletarian revolution in the advanced industrial states of western Europe, such as Britain and Germany. When that revolution failed to transpire, the Bolsheviks turned their hopes to the colonies. Movements of national liberation in the colonies would destroy the economic base of bourgeois rule in Europe and thus lead to revolution. For the Jadids, "revolutionizing the East" became a mission that placed them at the center of a process of global importance. By forging revolution in Central Asia, they would help liberate Muslims of India and the Middle East from the tyranny of the British. The Jadids' infatuation with the idea of revolution brought them close to the Bolsheviks, even though ultimately the two groups' ideas of revolution were quite different. To the Jadids, revolution made sense only as a national, rather than a class, enterprise: revolution would deliver the nation, however defined, from internal and external tyranny and lead it down the road to progress.

Abdurauf Fitrat, who before the war had used an Englishman as his mouthpiece for reform, turned to an increasingly critical view of the situation. His writings from 1919 and 1920 are intensely anticolonial and specifically anti-British. To him, the British were no longer exemplars of progress; they had become unmitigated villains. Imperialism, exploitation, and oppression were now the hallmarks of Europe (and Britain in particular). In a series of essays and two plays that were staged in Tashkent, Fitrat focused on the oppressiveness of British rule in India and celebrated those who struggled against it. For Fitrat, the patriotic duty of driving the English out of India was "as great as saving the pages of the Qur'an from being trampled by an animal . . . , a worry as great as that of driving a pig out of a mosque."9 Muslims could achieve progress only by casting off the yoke of imperialism and its agents, such as the amir of Bukhara. Fitrat had not changed his mind. His earlier fascination with Europe had also been premised on the need for Bukharans and other Muslims to acquire the skills and means necessary for self-preservation and self-strengthening. The way the war turned out—with the Ottoman Empire, the last surviving Muslim power, in utter defeat and a revolutionary regime in power in Russia—had transformed the calculus on which Fitrat had based his earlier ideas. British paramountcy in the Muslim world heightened the stakes and removed all illusions of the benevolence of bourgeois Europe that Fitrat might have entertained. The Russian revolution, in contrast, with its direct challenge to the established imperial world order, offered tantalizing new hopes of achieving the same things Fitrat had desired: progress, national self-strengthening, and independence. Fitrat (and many others like him) had not given up his aspirations but had opted for different methods. Revolution represented a different route to modernity than did the gradualism inherent in emulation.

The 1920s were years of great enthusiasm for the Jadids. In Bukhara, they found themselves at the helm of an ostensibly independent people's soviet republic. For much of the republic's short life (it was abolished in 1924), it fought internal disorder. A peasant insurgency, backed by the amir and his functionaries, consumed the eastern reaches of the country and took up most of the energies of the government. Nevertheless, the Young Bukharans embarked on a program of national and cultural reform that dated from before the revolution. They set out to reform the maktabs and the madrasas and to systematize them in a network of public education. The ulama had been the main source of hostility to the Young Bukharans before 1920, and many of them suffered in the aftermath of the "revolution." Some were executed (old accounts had to be settled), and many went into exile in Afghanistan. Others supported the uprising in the mountainous regions of eastern Bukhara (present-day Tajikistan) against the Bukharan republic. But some reformist figures, such as Domla Ikram and Sharifjan Makhdum, notables and luminaries of Bukhara's literary scene, threw their support behind the new government. During its brief existence, the Bukharan government tried to organize "progressive" ulama around this core. During 1923 and 1924, these ulama held congresses (very much on the revolutionary pattern in vogue since 1917) to express support for reform of Islam and the policies the Young Bukharan government and to speak out against international imperialism.

The Young Bukharans also nationalized waqf properties, tried to establish a system of public health, and sought to establish a national economy. Fitrat returned to Bukhara from Tashkent in early 1921, where he joined the National Economic Council. He also served as minister for education, during which period he established a school of music and supervised the task of gathering information about the country's cultural heritage. The model for the Young Bukharans came not from Marx but from modernist Muslim notions of change, especially those that had been developed in the late Ottoman Empire. The years of the Bukharan republic coincided with the beginning of the nationalist movement in Turkey and the establishment of the Turkish Republic. This direction was not what the Bolsheviks had in mind, though, and they squeezed out the most "nationalist" members of the government, including Fitrat, by mid-1923.

In Turkestan, the situation was a bit different. Few Jadids got close to political power. The Bolsheviks were keen to attract members of the indigenous population into their ranks, and the earliest years of the new regime saw a substantial influx of Muslims into the Party. Many Jadids joined up, but they were upstaged by a different group of Muslims—those with Russian educations, who could function much more effort-lessly in Russian than the Jadids could. Many of them were Kazakhs from Semirech'e province, then part of Turkestan. The most prominent indigenous political figure in the early years of Soviet rule was Turar Rysqulov (1894–1938), a Kazakh who had attended a so-called Russian-native school (such schools, run by the tsarist government, provided basic literacy in Russian alongside the basic tenets of Islam) before attending a school of agronomy in Pishpek (now Bishkek). He was not a Jadid, for he had no previous connection to the reform of education or culture. His path to politics was quite direct. During the revolution, he became politically active, and he emerged in 1919 as the chairman of the Muslim Bureau of the local Communist Party, an office that was sup-posed to work for the inclusion of the Muslim population of the region into the Party. By the end of the year, he had become chair of the central executive committee of Soviet Turkestan, the highest office in the execu-tive branch of regional government under the new regime. To be sure, the executive authority of Soviet Turkestan was subordinate to the center, but Rysqulov was the first of many natives to head regional government. His passion was the revolutionary mobilization of the local population with the aim of achieving economic and political equality with Russians within the new Soviet state, and he wanted to work toward a world rev-olution that would liberate the colonial world from European rule. His enthusiasm for anticolonial revolution led him on occasion even to criti-cize Lenin for his lack of zeal in the matter.[10] Rysqulov was succeeded by a series of other figures from similar backgrounds, men comfortable with Russian and the intrigues of power but with no roots in Muslim reform.

The Jadids, however, dominated the cultural realm for much of the decade, during which time they worked to create a new *national* culture and cultural identity. What allowed the Jadids to do all this was the Soviet regime's commitment to overcoming backwardness and revolutionizing culture. The state was to play a central role in the matter of culture. If the tsarist regime had shied away from substantial intervention in local society, the Bolsheviks had the opposite agenda. The state's revolutionary goal was to "build culture." The state provided funds to open new schools; to publish newspapers, magazines, and books; and even to support theater. As we shall soon see below, the Soviets also sought to "indigenize" their regime in order to overcome the indigenous population's distrust of them as outsiders. As early as 1918, they declared Uzbek the official language of Turkestan alongside Russian (by 1921, Turkmen and Kazakh had also been elevated to this status). Although the Russian language continued to dominate until the end of the Soviet period, this official recognition of indigenous languages was important. If nothing else, it pointed to the necessity of reforming local languages and modernizing their vocabulary. The Soviets also sponsored large-scale ethnographic expeditions on the assumption that the state needed a better understanding of the land and its people if it was to incorporate the local population into the new regime. These policies opened up vast arenas of cultural work into which the Jadids stepped with gusto.

The Jadids' goals in this regard were those common to many nationalist movements in Europe and Asia of the time, which held that a nation has to have a national culture—literature, theater, journalism—that is authentically its own and expressed in its own language. Theater flourished even in the darkest days of the civil war and famine. Writers threw themselves into creating a modern literature that celebrated progress and the new life but that was also unabashedly nationalist. The 1920s were the golden age of Uzbek literature, when luminaries such as Fitrat, Cholpan, and Abdulla Qodiriy, along with a host of other writers, created works of prose, poetry, and drama that are still unrivaled.

Creating a national literature required the reform of language itself. The Jadids had long talked about simplifying the grammar and the orthography of the language. Now they tackled the matter head-on. In the radical spirit of the age, the reforms went much further than anything that had been mooted before 1917. By 1922, reformers had begun using a modified form of the Arabic alphabet that indicated all vowels. By the middle of the decade, even more radical proposals were afoot, and the proposal to adopt the Latin script for all Turkic languages in the Soviet Union gathered force, ultimately winning the day in 1928, when the

Latin script was adopted for all languages in the Turkic republics of the Soviet Union. (This reform also affected Tajik, an Indo-Iranian language.) Scripts carry enormous symbolic baggage: much more than language itself, they signify civilizational belonging. The Latinization of Turkic languages was a self-conscious cultural reorientation. To enthusiasts, the Latin script symbolized progress, modernity, and participation in a universal civilization. There was, of course, opposition to such moves, but as in much else, proponents of radical reform were able to win the argument by bringing in the power of the state to work on their behalf.[11]

The Jadids also poured a great deal of energy into the creation of modern schools. The first state-run schools for the indigenous population were new-method schools of Jadid provenance, which were taken over by local soviets (councils) and turned into Soviet schools. Teachers from Jadid schools provided the bulk of the workforce in early Soviet schools, and early primers and textbooks bore a clear Jadid imprint in their content, style, and subject.

For their part, the Bolsheviks made several concessions in the early 1920s to win the trust of the local population. During the civil war, the local Soviet government had "nationalized" all waqf property and turned over agricultural lands to the peasants who worked on them. This policy was partially revoked in 1922, when nonagricultural waqf properties were returned to the mosques or madrasas that benefited from them. (Agricultural waqf property remained under the use of those who worked it.) But this move was not a return to the prerevolutionary status quo. Waqf property was to be overseen by local waqf sections subordinate to a central waqf administration in Tashkent. Waqf was thus bureaucratized and brought within the purview of the state. The Jadids had long advocated this reform, which their counterparts in Bukhara had also put into practice. In 1920, Munavvar Qori, whom we met in chapter 2, exhorted his compatriots to reform, telling a conference of educators that madrasas had always provided a well-rounded general education and had been funded by enlightened rulers through waqfs. The despotic forces of Russian imperialism, by driving out all nonreligious subjects, were to blame for turning the madrasas into hotbeds of fanaticism.[12] This was a tendentious reading of the past, but it is telling nevertheless of the Jadid view of things. Waqfs had always been meant for educational purposes, and the community had the obligation to take them over to ensure the progress of national culture. For much of the decade, the central waqf administration, run by Muslims, presented itself

as an agent of progress and reform, an institutional arm of society helping with the upkeep of mosques and funding the fledgling network of
modern schools.

The Bolsheviks also allowed the resuscitation of the courts of qazis
and biys. These courts, which had been abolished or curtailed during the
civil war, were allowed to operate again. A decree of December 1922
allowed such courts to operate in Turkestan in parallel with Soviet courts
and to adjudicate matters of civil law if both parties were willing. The
judges were to be elected, and their decisions could be appealed in Soviet
courts. Nevertheless, the Party recognized the parallel existence of Islamic
law. In an even more radical move, also in 1922, the Party allowed the
creation of shariat administrations (*mahkama-yi shar'iyya*) in different
localities in Turkestan. These entities were religious boards, complete
with presidiums and administrative councils, whose task was to oversee
the administration of personal law, and they harked back directly to
Jadid projects of 1917. They were elected bodies charged with "dissemination among the masses of the ideas of progress, culture, and humanity." They were also to "be the link between the government and the people, to conduct the reform of religious affairs and to struggle with very
unnecessary superstructures of Islam and the incorrect interpretations of
Islam."[13] To struggle against "incorrect" interpretations of Islam, to
cleanse it of superfluous ideas, and to institutionalize and rationalize the
administration of Islamic law were objectives that had been an integral
part of the Jadid platform in 1917 and a part of the Jadids' reform project for even longer. These shariat boards appeared in several cities in
Turkestan in early 1923 and quickly became a major part of the local
cultural and political landscape. The first round of elections returned
majorities of reformist ulama to these boards, enabling them to fulfill the
goals assigned to them. The first criticisms of Sufism and of customary
practices in the Soviet era came from these boards. For the Jadids, the
establishment of the boards was only the beginning, and much remained
to be done. The religious boards had no connection to each other; the
hope was to create a centralized structure for all of Central Asia that
would bring the rural areas under the control of urban reformist ulama.
The model was the religious assembly in Ufa that continued to exist after
the revolution as the Central Religious Administration of Muslims. The
Jadids also hoped that this central organization would have access to
waqf revenues and thus take on the task of reforming Islam and building
Muslim institutions throughout Soviet Central Asia. Soviet power
seemed to have made two of the basic goals of Jadid reform possible.

·   ·   ·

The Bolsheviks were not, however, interested in helping the Jadids implement their reform program. The Bolsheviks had their own utterly utopian vision of remaking the world that they set out to implement. There was debate within the Party over questions such as how this program would be implemented, at what pace it would unfold, and so on, but not over the basic vision. In reality, the Party line zigzagged constantly, but each unexpected turn was justified by the basic underlying vision of utopian change. To the Party, cooperation with other groups was a temporary, strategic concession to political weakness but not an acceptable long-run strategy.

The Bolsheviks today are remembered for the brutality of the political order they created. In the public mind, that brutality stemmed primarily from the malevolence of the ideology behind it or from deeply entrenched political traditions unique to Russia. The issue is a deeply political one, because at its bottom lies the question of the legitimacy of Communism as an ideology and a political program, and the challenge it posed to liberalism. Yet such a characterization runs the risk of ignoring certain traits that were fundamental to Communism and that ensured its massive appeal around the globe for much of the twentieth century. Bolshevik brutality was underpinned by a deeply optimistic, utopian vision of the world that went to the heart of the Enlightenment. The idea of a classless society that transcends all conflicts, where human beings acquire their full potential through the conquest of time, nature, and all forms of superstition, was a product of the Enlightenment, even as it encompassed a critique of the social order that was then taking shape under capitalism. The utopian vision did not in itself generate the brutality—enough brutality already existed in the world, with World War I, which gave rise to the Russian revolution, being an apogee of mass violence on the European continent—but it could be used as an excuse for it.

Marx discerned in History (with a capital *h*) an evolutionary pattern. Humanity, he believed, went from one stage to another, its progress punctuated with revolutions, in each of which the oppression of man by man took ever-more-extreme forms, until capitalism produced the negation of the humanity of those oppressed by it. Yet that oppression would lead to the final revolution that would overthrow capitalism and the class relations on which it was based, and usher in the utopia of a classless society. Such was the dialectical materialism of Marx's historical vision. This vision was open to a number of interpretations, of course, and as the nineteenth century reached its culmination without the promised revolution, different Marxist schools began to crystallize. For many, Marx's vision was driven by certain iron laws of labor: the "wheel of History" turned at a rate determined by material progress; one could not hurry it along, and each new stage would arrive only when conditions were ripe for it. Others saw things differently. Lenin, for one, grafted voluntarism onto the Marxist vision. The revolution could not come about without a revolutionary party and a revolutionary consciousness, which the party would foster. Among other things, this turn to voluntarism allowed Lenin to argue that Russia, not the most highly industrialized country in Europe, could indeed have a proletarian revolution. Lenin retained the basic outline of History—as a story with a plot already known and a happy ending assured—but assigned to the Party (rather than to the proletariat) the role of executing agent. Once the Bolsheviks found themselves in power, the regime they created was in effect a party-state, in which the Party, as the vanguard of revolutionary forces and the maker of History, was ensconced as the overseer of the political life of the country and as the self-appointed watchdog. The historian Steven Kotkin has likened the Soviet Union to a theocracy in which the Party acted as the Church, the guarantor of moral purity and the guardian of purpose of the State. [14] The Soviet Union had parallel administrative structures of state and Party institutions, the former increasingly dominated by members of the Party, the latter the exclusive domain of those who were morally and politically pure enough to be admitted into the ranks of the agents of History.

But problems arose in fitting Marx's scheme of history to the Russian situation. As the Bolsheviks emerged victorious from an extremely violent civil war in 1921, they found themselves ruling a country whose economy had been devastated by seven years of continuous warfare. Large-scale industrial output stood at 13 percent of its level in 1913, grain production was down to two-thirds of prewar levels, much of the infrastructure had been destroyed, and cities had been depopulated as people fled to the countryside, where food was easier to find. The proletariat, in whose name the Bolsheviks had seized power, had shrunk significantly. Russia was more backward than it had been in 1913. The Bolsheviks had to create the preconditions of their own existence. Rebuilding the economy, especially industry, became the most urgent concern for the Bolsheviks, and the Soviet regime acquired a developmentalist orientation that it never lost. To the end of the Soviet period, the Soviet regime constantly justified and legitimated itself through its efforts and its successes in modernization: so many new factories built, so many villages electrified, so many news schools opened. As we will see, the results were mixed, but the policies of the regime cannot be understood without keeping this orientation in mind.

In giving History a push, Lenin introduced a new emphasis on consciousness over the material basis of existence and thus inverted certain key ideas in Marx. As the Soviet dissident Andrei Sinyavsky observed, "A well-known Marxist-Leninist notion is that Marx put Hegel's dialectic back on its feet. But what's remarkable is that Marxism, en route to its realization, stood itself on its head and on this head the new society was built. Henceforth, consciousness determined existence. . . . The scientific Marxist utopia materialized, but wrong side up, with its feet in the air."[15] From the beginning, the Bolsheviks sought the answer to Russia's backwardness in a *cultural* revolution. Lenin famously saw Russian workers' lack of "culture" as a major barrier to the establishment of socialism in Russia. As far as "the East" was concerned, the problem was even more straightforward. Even during the civil war, Stalin, in his capacity as people's commissar for nationalities affairs, saw "rais[ing] the cultural level of the backward peoples, [and] build[ing] a broad system of schools and educational institutions" as the foremost tasks of Soviet power in the East. This would allow Soviet agitation to be conducted in the native language of the people and thus convince indigenous groups to join the Soviet cause.[16] The emphasis on propaganda allowed the Bolsheviks to answer in the affirmative the more fundamental question (according to Marxist prescriptions) of whether Central Asia was ready for a proletarian revolution. Nothing was beyond the voluntarism that Lenin had grafted onto Marxism. If a party of professional revolutionaries could do the work of the proletariat, and by thus overcoming Russia's backwardness, lead it to revolution, then surely it could help other nations of the former empire overcome their backwardness. The answer lay in a revolution in culture to create the requisite consciousness. As materialists, the Bolsheviks also took for granted the plasticity of human culture, indeed of human nature, seeing it as a mere reflection of existing material conditions. A revolution in relations of production—the end of exploitation of man by man—would lead to new cultural forms. In practice, however, as Sinyavsky noted, the cart came before the horse, and the Bolsheviks came to see a top-down cultural revolution as the means of bringing about the revolution in social relations.

The vision was utterly universalist. All humanity was fated to tread the same path to the classless utopia of Communism. Cultural difference was significant for the practical purposes of conveying the message to each national group in its own language. Hence emerged the dictum that Soviet culture had to be "national in form, socialist in content." From the mid-1930s on, official Soviet discourse came to accept—indeed, to assert—that national and ethnic identities were real and permanent, but it still did not compromise on the basic universalism of historical progress. Although the final destination was the same for each nation, the Soviets also accepted as self-evident that different national groups had traveled different distances along that path—that some were more advanced than others. The task of the party-state was to usher all groups to the final destination. The extremely vicious policies of social engineering of the Bolsheviks were justified by these lofty ideals.

.   .   .

Both the Jadids and the Bolsheviks were committed to revolutionizing society, and in practical terms, their programs had considerable overlap. Both wanted to transform the culture, establish modern schools in the vernacular, and improve the position of women. But the basic impulses that drove them were fundamentally different. For the Bolsheviks, the accommodation with reformist Muslims had been a tactical retreat dictated by a sense of vulnerability and weakness, a concession to conditions they did not control. From the beginning, they set out to correct this situation. Lenin was acutely aware of the need to differentiate Soviet rule in the Russian empire's non-Russian borderlands from the rule of its tsarist predecessors. As he wrote to a comrade, "it is devilishly important to *conquer* the trust of the natives; to conquer it three or four times; *to show* that we are *not* imperialists, that we will *not* tolerate deviations in this direction."[17] The non-Russian peoples of the new Soviet state had to think of Soviet rule as their own. Soviet rule had to be "indigenized." In 1923, the Soviet state embarked on a much-publicized policy of *korenizatsiia,* "indigenization," which aimed to bring non-Russian peoples into the new organs of power. Terry Martin has argued persuasively that this policy was the world's first, and is still the most ambitious, program of affirmative action. The government expended substantial resources to raise the "cultural level" of the "backward" peoples of the multiethnic Soviet state, with the aim of making Soviet rule more secure.[18]

Central Asia was a prime target of this political mobilization from above. Perhaps the most significant institution was the soviet, the local council that existed at every administrative level (village, urban neigh-

borhood, city, district, and the republic as a whole). The councils had
emerged in 1917 as spontaneous expressions of self-determination, especially by underprivileged groups in society, but the Bolsheviks had
remade them into conduits for passing official policy down to the localities. In the 1920s, they served as tools for the regime's penetration of
local society. Frequently reelected, especially if the class composition of a
given council was deemed unsatisfactory, these soviets brought the local
population into the orbit of the new political power taking shape in the
region. In addition, the new regime exerted considerable effort to organize the poor into trade unions that would function as channels for reach-
ing into society. Trade unions existed for practically every craft in the
cities. Many of these organizations had sprung up in 1917 and had since
been "sovietized"; others were the creation of the Soviet period. In 1921,
the regime also established Qoshchi, a union of poor peasants and
herders with the political aim of waging class struggle against landlords,
rich peasants, and tribal aristocrats in the countryside.

The regime also focused on political education, sending out teams,
armed with posters, newspapers, film, and theater, to propagate the new
political message. The population had to be mobilized by the new institutions, but it also had to be taught new ways of thinking about politics.
A network of Red Teahouses, Red Yurts, and Red Corners sprang up at
many points in the region. These sites served as outlets for propaganda
and were showpieces for the new order the Bolsheviks hoped to establish.
Propaganda campaigns using film, music, theater, and the written word
poured forth before every policy shift. Unlike the Jadids' activities before
the revolution, this form of exhortation was well funded by state
resources. Youth organizations, such as the Young Pioneers (the Soviet
equivalent of the Boy Scouts), the Komsomol (the youth branch of the
Communist Party), and any number of "voluntary" organizations
brought people into the ambit of the new regime.

Finally, the Bolsheviks decided, in 1924, to bring to Central Asia the
countrywide pattern of making political boundaries accord with the ethnic composition of the population. The Bolsheviks had several motives
for adopting this principle. In addition to the need to indigenize Soviet
power, they had the important political motive of preempting, or rather
co-opting, nationalism, which had shown its power during the years of
revolution and civil war. Beginning in 1920, the Party began to elaborate
administrative structures that would reflect the ethnic composition of the
population and thus grant autonomy to various regions on the ethnonational, rather than the regional, principle. In the case of Central Asia, the

Bolsheviks also believed that delimiting boundaries on the ethnic principle would help consolidate the region administratively and reduce the chaos they saw in the ethnic fragmentation in the region. Creating homogeneous "national republics" would reduce interethnic conflict and help strengthen Soviet power in the region. This decision was implemented quite rapidly in 1924, and the political map of contemporary Central Asia was born. The three republics of Turkestan, Bukhara, and Khiva were reconstituted as the soviet socialist republics of Uzbekistan and Turkmenistan, which entered the Union of Soviet Socialist Republics as "union republics"—that is, as equal partners in the federation. Eventually, Kyrgyzstan, Tajikistan, and Kazakhstan also became union republics. The process of delimitation was marked by considerable debate among Central Asian Communists, as representatives of different nationalities advanced various territorial claims on behalf of their groups. Central authorities were not always happy with the ethnic conflict that the debate engendered, but they nevertheless saw the delimitation as a major achievement of Soviet rule in the region.[19]

This form of political mobilization paid off, and by the mid-1920s, the Bolsheviks had created a new political class in Central Asia. Its numbers may not have been large, and it may not have had the full confidence of the central Party leadership, but it was unmistakably a new class. Its members had entered public life after the revolution, largely through soviet and Party institutions. Unlike the Jadids, their vision of politics was entirely a product of the Soviet period. As in many other non-Russian nationalities, the new political elite was lopsided. At the top of the political pyramid, members of indigenous nationalities occupied the highest positions of authority in the region. They sat on the Central Asia Bureau of the Communist Party, the plenipotentiary organ of the Communist Party that until 1934 oversaw the functioning of power in the region; and they chaired republic-level Party organizations and governments. At the bottom of the order, they manned village neighborhood soviets and the nascent cultural institutions. They were less prominent in the middle, in midlevel jobs in the bureaucracy, and (even less so) in the technical sector, where Europeans continued to dominate until well into the Brezhnev period. To be sure, this class remained small, and it was seldom trusted fully by Party authorities. The important point, however, is that conflict did exist in Central Asian society, as did a constituency for the new regime in Central Asian society. Indigenous cadres seldom had the same comprehension of policy as the Party leadership in Moscow did, but they nevertheless were willing to act against the old and help usher in the new. The foot soldiers of the state's assault on traditional society were members of this group.

Many of the older elites found their way into the new order, but the Bolsheviks did transfer power to new groups. Fayzulla Xo'jayev (1896–1938), the former Young Bukharan who became the first prime minister of Uzbekistan and remained in office until he was arrested and executed in the Great Terror of 1937–38, was the son of one of the wealthiest merchants of Bukhara. Akmal Ikromov (1898–1938), the first secretary of the Communist Party of Uzbekistan, was the son of a mullah who entered public life in 1917 as a teacher. He joined the Party in 1919 and quickly rose in the ranks to become the first secretary of the Communist Party of Uzbekistan in 1925. But Yo'ldosh Oxunboboyev (1885–1943), the simple peasant from Ferghana, who found himself the first head of the government of Soviet Uzbekistan in 1925, exemplifies the new order most starkly. The new Soviet elite came from different sections of society. Similar patterns of recruitment were replicated in the other republics of Central Asia.

The transformation of the political elite was also replicated in the cultural realm. A new intelligentsia toppled the Jadids and others of their generation. This conflict took on an especially sharp form in Uzbekistan, where the Jadids had retained a central place in the cultural realm. Now, a new generation of fiery young men—some of them very young—began to displace them. The most vicious attacks on the Jadids, now derided as "old intellectuals," came from this new cohort. Ikromov launched the assault on the Jadids in January 1926, with a speech at the first Uzbek conference of workers in the fields of culture and education. Ikromov argued that the Jadids were the mouthpieces of the "nationalist bourgeoisie" in the region. As such, they had been revolutionary in the ("feudal") tsarist period, when they represented the interests of a more progressive class. But since the Bolsheviks had taken the Russian empire straight from feudalism to socialism, the bourgeoisie had become reactionary and had allegedly allied itself with English imperialism, the flag bearer of the interests of world capitalism. The Jadids were thus counterrevolutionary agents of English imperialism.[20] After this denunciation, the chorus of voices that accused the "old intellectuals" of all manner of political crimes—bourgeois nationalism, pan-Turkism, pan-Islamism, an inability to comprehend the new political realities, being in the pay of English, American, or Japanese imperialism—were those of the new Uzbek elite eager to assert its revolutionary credentials, even if doing so required cultural parricide. The Jadids took small comfort in the fact that many of their accusers themselves perished in the terror in the late 1930s. Ikromov was executed in the same round of terror that claimed the lives of Fayzulla Xo'jayev and Fitrat.

.   .   .

It was in the matter of religion that the Bolsheviks and indigenous reformers could never find common ground. The Jadids based their program heavily on modernization of their faith. The Bolsheviks had absolutely no need of faith. Religion represented many things to the Bolsheviks. Marx wrote, "The wretchedness of religion is at once an expression of and a protest against real wretchedness. Religion is the sigh of the oppressed creature, the heart of a heartless world, and the soul of soulless conditions. It is the opium of the people."[21] Religion was an ideological cloak that hid the exploitation of man by man and provided ideological cover to the exploiting classes. Once exploitation disappeared, so would religion. The new world the Bolsheviks were making had no place for the supernatural; that world could come about only when men and women broke all chains that kept them tied to exploitative or oppressive relationships and prevented the full realization of their humanity.[22]

Still, at the beginning of Soviet rule, there was little indication of the changes to come in a few years. Bolshevik theorists disagreed about the means the Party should use in the struggle against religion, with some arguing that religion would disappear by itself when socialism triumphed and that it could not be destroyed through coercion alone. In Central Asia, although the reformist ulama were certainly aware that the overall Soviet political framework was hostile to them, they had little fear of an all-out assault on Islam. In 1921, Nazir To'raqulov, a former Jadid who had risen high in the Party hierarchy, could write quite sincerely that "Communism [is] an ideology that works for the liberation of humanity. Without being fundamentally opposed to any religion, it explains openly and clearly the path to liberation; [but] it always respects the spiritual and religious freedoms of the people, especially those of the oppressed peoples of the East."[23] The situation changed by 1926. In the joyful world that the Bolsheviks were building, there could be (by definition) no wretchedness, no soulless conditions, and hence no need for mournful sighing. Instead, religion was now the last redoubt for ideological opposition, a cover for "counterrevolutionary elements" to wage their struggle against the Will of History. In more pragmatic terms, religious institutions were also an independent locus of power and wealth, which the new regime was loath to tolerate.

The struggle against religion took many forms. One of them was antireligious propaganda. As early as December 1921, Ne'mat Hakim, a Tatar materialist, delivered several lectures in Tashkent in which he put various aspects of Islamic belief to the test of science and disproved them to his own satisfaction. But a serious effort began only toward the end of the decade, when the Union of the Militant Godless began opening branches in Central Asia. Officially, the union was a volunteer organization of enthusiasts, but it operated in close connection with Party and state authorities. In 1928, its members began publishing *Xudosizlar* (The Godless), a journal that propagated atheistic ideas and provided a venue for discussing methods of propaganda. Atheistic propaganda posited a direct and drastic contradiction between science and religion, the latter being inherently opposed to Reason. Mannon Romiz, who wrote a manual for atheistic propaganda in Uzbekistan, quoted Friedrich Engels to argue that religion was the product of a primitive stage in human development when people, not understanding nature, attributed all of nature's workings to supernatural beings. Religion then became a tool for exploiting classes to use to maintain their power in society. It was thus harmful in many ways: "We habitually struggle with opium and hashish. It is well known that opium and other narcotics are extraordinarily dangerous poisons, which make a person stupid and crazed. Religion too poisons a person's mind, makes it believe in phantoms and suppositions, and exhausts his reason, filling it with unnatural notions, and gives rise to ideologies that stand in the way of the struggle for socialism. In sum, it is necessary to struggle with religion because it poisons people."[24] The irrationality of religion coincided neatly with its antirevolutionary and exploitative essence, and religion had to be rooted out. Stalwarts carried out atheistic propaganda throughout Central Asia, whereas all official proclamations and all acceptable art and literature had to put forth an atheistic take on life. Ultimately, the significance of atheistic propaganda lay not in its efficacy, which it did not have, but in the way in which it destabilized the terms of public debate. Atheism challenged Islam not so much at the level of individual belief but as the font of moral and ethical values that could be held in public. Islamic values were forcefully displaced from the public arena, and they never acquired that position again. The campaign for atheism tapered off by the end of the 1930s, and the Union of Militant Godless disappeared during World War II, but the "disestablishment" of Islam as the major font of moral and ethical values for society was permanent.

•   •   •

By mid-1926, Party authorities in the region felt ready to launch an assault on traditional society. All manifestations of backwardness—in everyday life (*byt*), customs and traditions, culture, and religion—had to be thrown into the dustbin of history and replaced with the bright new life the Party was creating. The new Party line held that the closer the Party came to building socialism, the more cunning its enemies—the bourgeoisie, the clergy, rich peasants (*kulak*), and capitalist powers beyond the borders of the country—became. The closer the Party came to its goal, therefore, the more merciless the struggle for the new life was going to be. In Central Asia, this view meant that the Party had to be especially wary of reformist or liberal Muslims, because they were more cunning and more dangerous than conservatives. Earlier in the decade, the Party had lent some support to reformist Muslims as a way of reforming Islam and introducing "modern culture" to the people. Now precisely these reformist Muslims posed the biggest danger to the cause of socialism. Shariat administrations that struggled against incorrect practices, the waqf administration that claimed to be doing Soviet work, and the new-method schools that pretended to be Soviet schools were all attempts by the bourgeoisie to camouflage itself in the cloak of modern civilization and support for socialism. Traditionalist ulama and the Sufis would go away once the remnants of feudalism were swept away; the real competition came from alternative visions of modernity and progress. The Jadids came to be reviled as pathetic apologists for bourgeois nationalism and as lackeys of foreign imperialism, a social order whose time had passed. The ulama, reformist and conservative alike, were now cast as "a single reactionary mass of counter revolutionaries." All of them had to be swept aside in an assault of the new revolutionary forces.

The assault was ferocious and destructive. Its epicenter was Uzbekistan (which at the time included Tajikistan as an autonomous republic), the most populous republic of Central Asia and the one that, containing the bulk of the region's sedentary population, was the most "Islamic." Here, the Russians had long held the shariat to be ascendant over the âdat, where most of Central Asia's mosques and madrasas existed, and where the ulama were more numerous and more influential than elsewhere.

The assault began modestly enough, when Uzbekistan's people's commissariats of justice and education began a "struggle against the old-style school." Clearly, now "the parallel existence of private schools cannot be permitted."[25] The struggle began with an attempt to regulate all unofficial schools to death. The schools were to meet strict requirements for hygiene and the physical plant; they were not to admit children under the age of eight, nor were they to accept students enrolled in official schools; and unofficial schools were to receive pedagogical guidance from soviet schools. They were to be denied all state funds.[26] By the middle of the following year, the government had begun closing such schools, first in the Tashkent region, where their number was smaller, and then in the rest of the republic.[27] During the following academic year, all old-method schools were shut down. The same fate was reserved for the madrasas. Their number had already shrunk, driven partly by the economic crisis and partly by the hostile political environment. Now, in 1927, they too were systematically shut down and their property confiscated. Qazi courts were similarly suppressed quickly; with its beneficiaries gone, the waqf administration was abolished and all property controlled by it was nationalized; the religious boards were abolished by 1928.

Along with schools and courts went the mosques. A few mosques had been closed earlier in the decade, and their buildings given over to "socially useful" purposes, but the years between 1927 and 1929 saw a sustained campaign of mosque closures and destruction. The closures were the job of revolutionary *troika*s, three-member teams of (often self-appointed) officials who had the authority to close down schools or mosques and confiscate their property. Members of the Komsomol, the youth wing of the Communist Party, and of the Union of Militant Godless were prominent in this movement. The campaign against mosques tended to run out of control. Indeed, as Shoshana Keller has noted, the situation was so chaotic that hardly any documentation exists in the archives until 1929. We do not have access to any individual testimony that would allow us to put a human face on this destruction.[28] Overall, we have better accounts of the destruction that Genghis Khan visited upon Islam in Central Asia than we do of the assault by the Soviets.

Yet stories of mosque closures and the persecution of the ulama crop up in practically every conversation with survivors of the period. Such tales recount Komsomol members barging into mosques during worship, throwing the imam out, and proclaiming the mosque to be communal property liberated from the clutches of oppressing classes. An imam who lay on his deathbed as his family said prayers over him was arrested for being "an enemy of the people" and hauled off to prison. No credible statistical data are available for mosques either, but the evidence of destruction was the half-destroyed or disused mosques that dotted the landscape for the rest of the Soviet era.

The same fate befell the ulama. They had long been reviled both for being relics of a superstitious past and for being class enemies of the revolution and oppressors of the toiling masses that were heroically striving to push History to its final stage. Again, we do not have eyewitness accounts to retrieve these atrocities from oblivion, but by the time the antireligious campaign slowed down in 1932, thousands of ulama had been arrested and sent off to forced-labor camps to atone for the sins of their social origin; many died or were killed, and others "fell silent." With old-method schools and madrasas destroyed, waqf property confiscated and redistributed, and qazi courts and the religious boards all abolished, the patterns through which Islam had been transmitted in Central Asia were largely destroyed. In 1929, a countrywide law on religious associations defined the scope of religious activity that the regime was willing to allow in the new conditions. Religious activity could take place only in officially recognized societies or groups of "believers," who had to register with local authorities. Religious organizations had the right to operate places of worship, although on terms dictated by the authorities. They were forbidden to form benevolent societies, render material support to members, or organize study circles or camps for children or youth.[29] The assumptions about religion that underlay the law— that it is a corporate enterprise undertaken by believers coming together in tangible organizations—derived from Christianity but were now extended in Soviet practice to all religions. This law governed the state's relationship to religious groups until the end of the Soviet era, but as we shall see in chapter 7, many of its assumptions survive to the present.

·   ·   ·

From the beginning, women occupied an important place on the Bolshevik agenda, both in Russia proper and in Central Asia. The Bolsheviks believed that only participation in productive labor could emancipate women and allow them to realize their full human potential. Overthrowing the "tyranny of the family" and the "slavery of the kitchen" was necessary if women were to become free individuals and active citizens. For the Bolsheviks, the "archaic" and "degrading" customs prevalent in Central Asia, as well as Islam itself, meant that women were no better than slaves and chattels, if they had not been turned into animals. Improving women's position, through law and revolutionary mobilization, was a matter of much importance. The issue also had great political value for the Bolsheviks, for it could help transform social bonds and cultural mores at a basic level and create a constituency loyal and grateful to the new regime. In a region where an indigenous proletariat barely existed, women might prove to be, in the words of the political scientist Gregory Massell, a "surrogate proletariat."[30]

Such hopes had to be set against social reality, of course, and in the first few years of Soviet rule, the Bolsheviks shied away from intervention in the matter. Central Asia was exempted from the sweeping transformations introduced by the new civil code of 1918, which turned marriage into a civil contract, recognized free union as equivalent to marriage, outlawed polygamy, and made divorce freely available to either party simply on demand. Nevertheless, the women's section (Zhenotdel) of the Communist Party opened branches in the region and worked to organize members for political work. Early Soviet initiatives aimed to bring women into public education, recognize their economic rights (of employment and equal inheritance of property) and emphasize companionate marriage. The leadership of the Zhenotdel came from European women sent from Russia to do "revolutionary work," but the organization attracted numerous indigenous women. Many of these women were from marginalized sections of society—girls who had run away from home, women who had abandoned abusive husbands, and so on—but then it was precisely marginal sections of society that were to destabilize the established order.

The status of women was another area in which Bolshevik aims found resonance among the Jadids. Since before the revolution, the Jadids had argued for changing the position of women in local society, using arguments from the Islamic tradition. The progress of Islam and the nation required that women be educated and that they take an active part in public life. After the revolution, the Jadids became major proponents of changing women's position in Muslim society. Their main concerns were to further education, discourage polygamy and marriage at very young ages, and, increasingly, promote unveiling.

Among the sedentary populations of Central Asia—in Uzbekistan and Tajikistan—women's seclusion was a basic fact of the social order, connected with concepts of honor, shame, respect, and hierarchy. It was marked by a dress code that required women, when outside the house, to wear a heavy cotton robe that came down to the ankles (*paranji*) and a veil of woven horsehair (*chachvon*) that completely covered the face. In the period of Russian rule, this form of dress apparently became nearly universal among the sedentary population of Central Asia, to the point that the Bolsheviks saw the paranji-chachvon as the element that defined Uzbek women. Both the Jadids and the Bolsheviks considered the paranji-chachvon to be a hazard to women's health, as well as a symbol and means of oppression and degradation. During the early 1920s, some women abandoned the veil and appeared in public places (including the theater), but most women who worked, even those doing political work, continued to wear the paranji-chachvon.

The turn to open intervention in local society in mid-1926 also meant a change in the Bolshevik policy on the question of women. Now, the liberation of women had to be accomplished in the same revolutionary way as the abolition of religion, and it was to be equated with unveiling. The campaign against the veil was to be nothing less than a *hujum*, "assault." On March 8, 1927, international women's day and the tenth anniversary of the beginning of the Russian revolution, the Zhenotdel organized a series of mass meetings, in which thousands of women cast off their veils and many burned them. Such meetings continued for the next two years, but, unlike other campaigns of the cultural revolution, the hujum was called off in 1929. It had produced a massive backlash and was turning out to be counterproductive in every way. The paranji did not disappear until the 1950s.[31]

The campaign for women's liberation extended to traditionally nomadic regions of Central Asia, where women did not veil. However, a number of other practices defined women's place in society in these regions: underage marriage, polygamy, payment of bride wealth by the groom's family (which allowed the bride's family to equip the bride with a trousseau, which thus ended up back in the groom's family but was routinely seen by Russian observers as payment for the bride, who thus became a chattel), and the abduction of brides as a way of avoiding the payment of bride wealth. In Turkmenistan and Kazakhstan, bride wealth took center place in the campaign to emancipate women.

·   ·   ·

Two years into this assault on traditional society came something even more drastic. In 1929, the state declared that a new stage in the revolu-

tion had arrived, when an all-out struggle for the achievement of socialism could be launched. The result was a campaign to collectivize agriculture and bring the rural economy under state control. Activists, mainly
young men, poured into villages and forcibly collectivized the land: land
and livestock belonging to peasants was consolidated into collective
farms, or *kolkhozes*. Collectivization was also a class war against enemies of the revolution, and an explicitly stated goal was "the liquidation
of kulaks as a class." *Kulak* was the term that Russian villagers used to
denote wealthier peasants. After the revolution, it became a generic term
for "exploiter" and "oppressor" in any peasant context. During collectivization, calling someone a kulak could be a fatal accusation. Anyone
could be accused of being a kulak and face the possibility of arrest, exile,
or execution.[32] The countryside was brought to heel, and the state was
able to dictate what peasants could grow. Central Asia was turned into a
vast cotton plantation. Cotton monoculture, which was to inflict horrific
damage on society and the environment in Central Asia, was made possible by the brutal process of collectivization.

The turmoil and the trauma created by forced collectivization are
impossible to exaggerate. In the long run, collectivization was to render
Soviet agriculture permanently dysfunctional. In the short run, it was an
absolute disaster. Rather than yield their livestock up to the state, peasants slaughtered their animals and had one last feast. The dislocation
caused by massive arrests and deportations spelled disaster for agriculture and irrigation. In nomadic areas, collectivization also entailed the
forced sedentarization of the population (for agriculture was higher on
the ladder to civilization than pastoralism)—and the consequences were
particularly devastating. In Kazakhstan, collectivization led to a demo-
graphic disaster of genocidal proportions. Nomads responded to collectivization by slaughtering their herds. Between 1929 and 1933, the number of livestock fell from 36,317,000 to 3,327,000, plunging the republic
into a famine, which killed as many as 1.5 million people, more than a
third of the Kazakh population of Kazakhstan.[33]

Collectivization dealt the deathblow to older privileged classes, whose
fortunes had drastically declined amid the destruction of the civil war
and its accompanying famine. Collectivization and the broad project of
"Soviet construction" produced new public identities for the participants. Such campaigns were thus crucial in producing a new political
elite in Central Asia, one that could identify with the "heroic" achievements of the new order. They redefined Central Asia's political terrain.
    Mosques continued to be shut down and ulama continued to be exiled

throughout the 1930s. The general turmoil was redoubled in 1937 and 1938, when the Great Terror reached its apogee. A massive wave of arrests and executions carried away two entire generations of public figures. Jadids who had not died a natural death by then perished during this period, for practically no one active in public life survived the fatal charges of ideological impurity and past errors. But the Great Terror also destroyed the first generation of Soviet cadres. Xo'jayev and Ikromov were only the most prominent of early Soviet figures to be executed. A great many people who had carried out the closures of mosques and schools and helped "liquidate the kulaks as a class" were themselves liquidated in the purges.

.   .   .

It took the Nazi invasion of the Soviet Union in 1941 for the regime to make some sort of peace with its society. The war between Nazi Germany and the Soviet Union was an apocalyptic event, a total war that required the mobilization of all resources, human and material, in both countries. Put to this test, the Stalinist regime, its hands drenched in blood, succeeded quite remarkably. Aside from a few cases of collaboration and defection to the invading side, the population remained overwhelmingly loyal in the face of massive danger. The war, with its calamitous casualties—estimates place the Soviet death toll at some 26 million—transformed the Soviet Union in many ways. With the Nazis occupying much of Ukraine, Belarus, and many western regions of Russia, entire factories—indeed, entire sectors of the economy—were evacuated eastward to Siberia and Central Asia. At the same time, universal conscription meant that not a single family in the thirteen time zones of the Soviet Union remained untouched by the war. Young and not-so-young men of all nationalities were drafted to fight "the Fascists." Prisoners volunteered from the Gulag; children of "enemies of the people" deported to far-off regions of the country less than a decade before were sent off to the front; people who had no idea what or where Germany was went off to fight. Service in the war transformed individual identities. Uzbek peasants returned from the war as Soviet citizens. Afterward, the war became a central node of pan-Soviet identity and collective memory, with Victory Day (May 9) ranking alongside Revolution Day as a major public holiday.

The regime succeeded in mobilizing the war effort partly because the war involved practically every family in the country. But the regime also made concessions. For the duration of the war, it largely put ideology on hold, and Stalin banked quite shamelessly on traditional sources of legitimacy for the war effort. The regime resurrected imperial Russian heroes, reinstated traditions of the imperial Russian army, and made peace with religion. Although the regime never justified the war effort in religious terms, and religion was absent from the front lines, it suspended the persecution of religious observance. Churches and mosques opened again, and religious organizations had leave to convene again. The regime needed all the help it could get, and religious leaders proved loyal. The Central Spiritual Administration in Ufa, the heir to the religious assembly established by Catherine II in 1788 and, miraculously, a survivor of the purges, joined the patriarch of the Russian Orthodox Church in mobilizing to support the war effort. The regime softened its tone and permitted religious observance without persecution. In 1943, it even allowed the establishment of the Spiritual Administration of the Muslims of Central Asia and Kazakhstan (known after its Russian initials as SADUM).

The initiative to establish SADUM seems to have come from surviving ulama in Uzbekistan itself, who in 1943, petitioned the central government for permission to hold a conference of the ulama of all of Central Asia with the aim of establishing a central religious organization. The ulama argued that such an organization would allow them to mobilize the region in aid of the war effort. For the ulama, this request was naturally linked to their ill-fated attempts to create a central religious board for Uzbekistan in the 1920s. Now, the regime was allowing such a board, and much more, for the jurisdiction of SADUM extended to all of Central Asia, becoming one of the few Soviet-era organizations that did not conform to the boundaries of a single republic. Similar institutions were created for Muslims of other parts of the Soviet Union, as well as for the followers of other religions. The regime hoped that by allowing limited religious activity under bureaucratic oversight, it could prevent it from going completely underground and be able to monitor and control it.[34] The authorities allowed SADUM to open a madrasa and organize higher theological education for a limited number of students, allowed it to send students abroad and establish contact with Muslims outside the Soviet Union, and granted it a budget for a limited amount of publishing. In return, they demanded support not just for the war effort and foreign-policy initiatives in the Muslim world afterward but also the issuance of fatwas on demand on issues of domestic policy. As we shall see in greater detail in the next chapter, SADUM existed in a strange situation. Its antecedents lay in Russian imperial policy (the model came from

Catherine II) rather than in the Islamic tradition, to which such an institution was quite alien. The Soviet constitution took the separation of the
church and the state as axiomatic, and the regime supported atheism; but
now the state had created a "church" for Islam that it sought to use for
monitoring religious activity and in whose activity it assumed the right to
intervene.

In his later years, Stalin tended to have a less confrontational attitude
toward religion. In 1949, he could even lecture Enver Hoxha, the
Albanian Communist leader then in the middle of an antireligious campaign in his own country, that "the question of religious beliefs must be
kept well in mind, must be handled with great care, because the religious
feelings of the people must not be offended"![35] Judging by his record at
home, Stalin was perhaps overstating the case. Nevertheless, although
the state never came to respect religious feelings, it did curtail its persecution of religious activity to a considerable degree after the war. It was
left to Khrushchev to revive the revolutionary enthusiasm of the 1920s
and lead one last antireligious campaign during 1959–62, when the government redoubled antireligious propaganda, closed unauthorized places
of worship, and persecuted unofficial clergy. Otherwise, although the
Soviet regime was ever suspicious of religious activity, it never reverted to
the ferocity of the late 1920s and 1930s.

·   ·   ·

War, revolution, famine, social upheaval, terror, and war again: the last
few pages have telescoped an amount of human suffering and destruction
so enormous that it runs the risk of incomprehensibility. Yet, these events
happened, and our task is to discern the impact of this upheaval on
society.

The regime quite wittingly caused the upheaval, but it seldom had
complete control over it. Indeed, the conflict it fostered often took on
peculiarly local meanings. Class conflict often turned into conflict
between rival kin groups or solidarity networks. Local notables or clan
elders got themselves elected to local soviets or bureaus of Qoshchi, or to
the Party itself. The land reform of 1925–26 was subverted when large
landholders (and their nomadic counterparts) divided up their property
among members of the family (including entirely fictive ones).[36] There
was a desperate shortage existed of people who were both skilled and
politically reliable, and the new organs of power built in the 1920s were
often subverted from within. Concern about the reliability and ideologi-

cal purity of local cadres was a major motive behind the purges that were a constant feature of local politics until 1938.

Overt resistance also increased dramatically. The Basmachi were a clear case of armed resistance against the new order, and the period of collectivization saw another upsurge in armed activity. Many local uprisings also took place in response to land reform and then collectivization. Thousands of Turkmen nomads voted with their feet and fled across the border to Iran or Afghanistan.

The hujum produced its own violent backlash. Women who unveiled challenged not just a dress code but the entire social and moral order that stood upon it. Many of them paid for the challenge with their lives. A spate of attacks targeted unveiled women, who were deemed to have brought shame and dishonor on their families, their neighborhoods, and Islam itself. Many were killed, others were raped, and many more wounded in vicious physical attacks. Also attacked were Party members, both local and Russian, who were associated with the unveiling campaign. The regime saw this backlash as evidence of the continuing hostility of anti-Soviet forces (an unholy combination of bourgeois nationalists, feudal exploiters, and foreign intelligence agencies) and reacted with merciless violence.

This violence produced a number of high-profile victims, who came to be memorialized as martyrs of the new life. One such victim was the actress Nurxon Yo'ldoshxo'jaeva, who was murdered by her brother for dishonoring the family. Another was the poet and dramatist Hamza Hakimzoda Niyoziy, an old Jadid who had become a wholehearted supporter of cultural revolution. In 1929, he moved to the mountain village of Shohi Mardon near Kokand, where he opened a school for girls and also began to organize Party activities. Shohi Mardon was also the site of a shrine attributed to Ali, the son-in-law of the Prophet and a foundational figure in Islamic lore. In March 1929, a number of activists, Hamza among them, decided to close the shrine and to turn it into a museum. Hamza and several others were beaten to death by a mob angry at the attempted desecration.

Society did not emerge from this turmoil unchanged and unscathed. Even by criteria that the regime would have taken seriously, the period was enormously destructive, for the regime's enthusiasm for destroying the old outran its interest in or ability to build the new. We have already noted the decline in agricultural productivity after collectivization. The disappearance of maktabs was not compensated for by the emergence of large numbers of Soviet schools. In fact, illiteracy remained a major problem until the early 1950s. Lower levels of administration remained chaotic throughout the Stalinist period. But the destruction was especially great in areas that the regime had set out to destroy. The power of older elites was largely destroyed. True, many members of the older elites found a niche for themselves in the new organs of power, but their new positions came at a cost, for now they were subject to rules and procedures over which they had little control.[37] In any case, the new political elite that took the place of those destroyed by the purges in 1937 and 1938—the cohort that the historian Donald Carlisle termed "the Class of '38"—had a rather different profile, for many of them came from humble backgrounds and were unconnected to older networks of power.[38] Among the ranks of the new elite were a remarkable number of orphans, men and women who lost their parents and were raised in foster homes or state-run orphanages and who thus stood at the margins of society. The regime had raised a new group to power and prominence, and it had this group's loyalty.

For Islam, the consequences were devastating. In the history of Central Asia, the fury of the regime's attack on Islam and its institutions is comparable perhaps only to that of Genghis Khan, whose conquest of the region seven centuries earlier had caused massive destruction and long-term transformations in religious culture. Islam had survived then, as it did now, but it was transformed in many ways. The Soviet assault destroyed the means through which Islamic knowledge was produced and transmitted. The persecution of the ulama was devastating in this respect. The ulama were in retreat already in the first half of the 1920s, with the state encroaching upon waqfs and qazi courts. Large (but undeterminable) numbers of them emigrated to Afghanistan, and others left the cities for the obscurity of the countryside. But the wholesale persecution of the ulama in the years after 1927 badly damaged the networks of learning and discipleship that had been the carriers of Islamic learning in the region. The destruction was not total, but the persecution destroyed the status and prestige of the ulama as a class. With no new religious texts being published, the amount of Islamic knowledge available locally was also vastly circumscribed. The wholesale destruction of mosques and madrasas also transformed the social and architectural landscape of the region. Mosques were not simply places of worship but also the social hubs of villages or urban neighborhoods. They ceased to be so; mosques were given over to "socially productive" uses (schools, workers' clubs, warehouses, stables for police horses) or destroyed; others fell into disrepair; a very few were recognized as "monuments of architecture" and taken under the protection of the state. The fate of the madrasas was similar.

Already in 1923, the Soviet government had established a border region twenty-two kilometers deep that ran along the entire length of the land and sea borders of the country. Initially established as a defensive measure in view of the low-level armed conflict that persisted along the borders of the country, the region was given over to the jurisdiction of the political police.[39] Throughout the 1920s, however, control of the frontier was less than effective, and in Central Asia, many nomadic tribes, and not a few bands of Basmachi, continued to go back and forth into Iran and Afghanistan. By the early 1930s, however, the government was in control of its frontier, which was effectively sealed. Foreign travel became a luxury granted only to the most trusted agents of the state, and communication in other forms was heavily censored. Central Asian Islam was cut off from developments in the rest of the Islamic world. Muslim intellectuals, modernist and traditionalist alike, lost contact with their peers abroad. If the Jadids were members of print-based communities that encompassed much of the Muslim world, now Central Asian Islam was forced into utter isolation.

Two major effects of the Soviet assault on Islam may be noted. First, Islam was localized and rendered synonymous with custom and tradition. With Muslim educational institutions abolished, the ranks of the carriers of Islamic knowledge denuded, and continuity with the past made difficult by changes in script, the family became the only site for the transmission of Islam. At the same time, because no new religious texts could be published and oral chains of transmission were often destroyed, the available religious knowledge was vastly circumscribed. This also led to a considerable homogenization of Islam, as differences in approach and interpretation were erased. The carriers of the learned tradition— those among them who survived—went underground or "fell silent." In a way, the triumph of customary Islam was a return to the situation before the arrival of Jadidism on the scene. The objectification of Islam, its separation from customary practices that the Jadids had begun, was undone. The modernization of Central Asian Islam was checked. But, of course, it was not a return to the past, for the traditions of Islamic learning were severely damaged, and Islam was faced with an intrusive state hostile to it.

The second effect was a significant de-Islamization of the terms of public discourse. No public position could be justified with reference to Islam and its moral or ethical values. The Soviet regime framed its official rhetoric in terms of universal human progress, defining progress in entirely nonreligious (indeed, antireligious) terms. At best, religion was a human construct corresponding with a certain (primitive) stage in the development of human society. At worst, it was a tool in the hands of exploiters. Although "militant atheism" proved to be a short-lived episode, over the longer term, the displacement of Islam from the public arena was quite successful. It was accomplished by official channels of socialization—most importantly, the school system and the army— which eventually reached deeply into society. Although Islamic practice was never eradicated, it now took place in an environment that was hostile to all religions. The disappearance of the social and moral authority of the carriers of Islam brought about tangible changes in actual practice: the daily routine, structured around the five-times-daily call to prayer from the mosque, was destroyed, as was the annual cycle of public celebrations of Muslim holidays; Islamic strictures against alcohol and even pork (impossible for men in military service to avoid) could now be flouted much more easily; the requirements of ritual purity (*taharat*), which help structure both private and public life to a considerable degree in Muslim society, were impossible to fulfill.

None of this is to say that Islam disappeared from Central Asia, or that more than a handful of people stopped thinking of themselves as Muslims. Rather, the meaning of being Muslim changed quite radically. Central Asian Islam, cut off from its own past and from Muslims outside the Soviet Union, became a local form of being rather than part of a global phenomenon. As we will see in greater detail in the next chapter, Islam became a marker of identity that distinguished locals from outsiders. It also became deeply intertwined with local cultural practices and with the new ethnic and cultural traditions being defined by the Soviet regime itself. Being Muslim came to mean adherence to certain local cultural norms and traditions rather than adherence to strictures that were directly validated by the learned tradition.

CHAPTER 4

Islam as National Heritage

The story of the Soviet period of Central Asian history is only half told if we stop with the destruction and trauma of the 1920s and 1930s. The destruction of the early Soviet period had lasting consequences, but it was in the relative stability of the last thirty years of Soviet rule that contemporary Central Asian societies took shape. What was the role of Islam in this period?

Plentiful evidence exists that the observance of Islamic ritual remained widespread and that it took place in the bosom of Soviet institutions. In 1961, for example, the Communist Party of Uzbekistan expelled a certain A. A'zamov from its ranks and had him fired from his job as chairman of the Navoiy kolkhoz in the Orjonikidze district of Uzbekistan. His crime had been to set aside a hectare of the collective farm's land for "servants of the cult" and to acquire sixty sheets of iron and four thousand burnt bricks from the kolkhoz's budget for the reconstruction of an old mosque and the construction of a new shed. Three years earlier, the leadership of the Bolshevik kolkhoz in the Ferghana Valley had marked Ramadan in a formal manner, with the electricity-generating station issuing a special signal at dawn to mark the beginning of the day's fast.[1] Such episodes caused a great deal of worry among Party authorities and those charged with the dissemination of atheistic propaganda, who spent much ink bemoaning the continuing hold of religion on the masses. Western observers of Soviet Islam used these statements of the atheism industry to chart the pervasiveness of Islam, which most saw as an indicator of political dissent. With hindsight and a better understanding of Islam, we can now see that pervasive Islamic ritual did not have straightforwardly political implications. Ritual was not a priori subversive or even political. Indeed, for the vast majority of Central Asians, being Muslim was *not* repugnant to being Soviet. This chapter aims to explicate these seemingly counterintuitive propositions.

Lived reality differed sharply from its official depiction. This disparity was evident throughout the Soviet Union, although perhaps the distance between the reality and its official version was greater in Central Asia than anywhere else. Official ideological formulations tended to become a mere façade , hiding a vastly different social reality that operated according to implicitly understood rules but bearing little resemblance to the way things were supposed to work. This social reality also defined Islam in its Soviet context. On the one hand, observance of Islamic ritual continued to be widespread (more so, indeed, than Western observers imagined while the Soviet Union lasted); on the other hand, Islam became a marker of ethnic identity and an aspect of national culture.

.   .   .

Although the disparity between theory and practice was perhaps more pronounced in Central Asia than elsewhere in the Soviet Union, it was hardly unique to the region. Indeed, to understand this phenomenon, we need to begin at the center, in Moscow, in the peculiarities of the era when Leonid Brezhnev presided over the country. The bloodletting stopped after Stalin's death in 1953, but Khrushchev turned out to be quite fond of shaking up things in his own way. Khrushchev was a true believer who wanted a return to the revolutionary purity of the civil war era. In 1954, for example, he launched the Virgin Lands campaign to put to the plow vast areas of steppe in northern Kazakhstan, which mobilized thousands of Russians and Ukrainians to settle the region and harness it to the needs of the Soviet economy. Khrushchev also presided over other hasty campaigns, such as the abolition of central ministries and their replacement by regional economic commissions. This enthusiasm was not shared by many in the Party hierarchy or the society at large, who were exhausted from the tumult of half a century and willing to wager on stability and peace and quiet. In 1964, a clique around Brezhnev deposed Khrushchev for his "harebrained schemes" and began a period of rule by committee that lasted into the 1980s. Gorbachev was later to term this era the "period of stagnation," but while it lasted, it was known as "the period of mature socialism," the penultimate stage to the coming of Communism—a period when all internal enemies had been vanquished and when the task at hand was simply gradual ascendance to the final goal of History. Routine and stability were the keys to consolidating historical gains.

The notion of mature socialism had been elaborated under Khrushchev, at the twenty-second congress of the Communist Party in 1962. The arrival of mature socialism meant that all contradictions within society had been resolved and that classes had been replaced by three groups—workers, peasants, and intellectuals—living in harmony. With class struggle thus rendered obsolescent, the Party restyled itself "the party of the whole Soviet people." Class struggle now gave way to Soviet patriotism—the common loyalty offered by all Soviet citizens to their homeland—with victory in World War II rising almost to the level of the revolution as one of the founding myths of the regime. Mature socialism also demanded new methods of moving forward: "stability of cadres," rather than reckless transformation, came to be the dominant theme in the Brezhnev period. The Party itself changed in character and turned into a mass party: in 1988, the Communist Party of the Soviet Union had more than 19 million members across the country, a full 8 percent of the population.[2] The vanguard party had become a political machine for the distribution of power and resources. Ultimately, the Brezhnev generation was quite successful. Those who had survived the purges and the war lived out their lives as leaders of a superpower. They celebrated this success by awarding each other medals and all manner of honors and awards and by extolling their own role in the history they were making. This celebration is clearly visible at the Novodevichy cemetery in Moscow—the burial ground of Russia's finest and greatest—where some of the gaudiest graves belong to functionaries of this generation. When Brezhnev finally died in 1982 after a long illness, his colleagues kicked his position back and forth among themselves, loath to let the glory pass to another generation. It took three deaths in two and a half years (Brezhnev, Andropov, and Chernenko) before that generation relinquished power, and Gorbachev took office in 1985.

Yet, underneath the deeply conservative politics, Soviet society underwent dramatic change. In the country at large, the years of mature socialism witnessed massive urbanization and industrialization, the achievement of universal literacy, and the emergence of an educated, white-collar urban population.[3] The accommodation of this changing society to a conservative political order produced interesting results. It is not an exaggeration to say that a new social contract emerged between the rulers and the ruled, in which the regime provided stability, international prestige, and a modicum of material comfort to the populace (housing, education, employment, practically free transportation and utilities) in return for political quiescence. Those who rocked the boat were punished but with little expenditure of blood. The dissidents, who came to define the Soviet Union for many in the West, would, after all, have been executed under Stalin. We might call this the "Brezhnevite social contract."

The system was defined by authoritarian politics and a command economy. The economy might better be termed an "economy of distribution," in which the allocation of goods took place not through market forces or cash exchange but through bureaucratic allocation. Access to scarce goods, therefore, required not cash, which could be useless in itself, but connections. A whole new social game emerged, in which informal practices came to define the way people pursued their goals in society and economy. The so-called shadow economy came about as a vast complex of private economic activity, some legal, some not. To the extent that informal relations smoothed the jagged edges of the official economy, the shadow economy was actually necessary. But its existence meant that the actual operation of Soviet society bore little resemblance to the ideological slogans that everyone had to mouth in public.

Soviet citizens of the period of mature socialism had goals in life—to get ahead, to provide the best possible opportunities for their children, to maintain social obligations, and so forth—that they had to achieve within the constraints of the system. One got ahead or improved the chances of one's children by utilizing connections and exchanging favors in vast networks of reciprocity based on personal friendships, family ties, or common origin. The official version continued to be intoned in all public or formal situations, but the number of true believers dwindled.

The Brezhnevite contract shaped the contours of local politics in Central Asia. The stability of Brezhnev's Politburo was replicated in all Central Asian republics (and in many other national republics), where the same individuals held the post of first secretary of the republic for the bulk of the Brezhnev period (see table 1). As long as these leaders did not rock the boat politically, ensured that their republics fulfilled their production quotas, and kept nationalism within certain limits, the center gave them a free hand in running "their" republics. Moreover, it used its resources to actually heighten their authority on their own turf. The tactic was quite successful: the secretaries were only too happy to comply,

TABLE I. BREZHNEV-ERA PARTY
LEADERS IN CENTRAL ASIA

Republic	First Secretary	Dates in Office
Kazakhstan	Dinmuhamed Kunaev	1964–86
Kyrgyzstan	Turdakun Usubaliev	1961–85
Tajikistan	Jabbor Rasulov	1961–82
Turkmenistan	Muhammadnazar Gapurov	1969–85
Uzbekistan	Sharaf Rashidov	1959–83

and as a result acquired for themselves the aura of national leaders with substantial support in society. Central Asian leaders were also useful to the center for foreign-policy purposes. The Soviets presented Central Asia to the Third World as an example of successful economic development by bypassing capitalism and of ethnic harmony in a multinational state. Tashkent especially hosted numerous festivals and conferences and was the destination of hundreds, if not thousands, of foreign students from other Muslim countries. Central Asian leaders traveled widely as living examples of the success of Soviet policies and routinely entertained foreign dignitaries in their capitals. Thus were Central Asians integrated into the Soviet system.

The Party secretaries sat atop vast networks of power and patronage, which took over the economy of distribution. In Central Asia, the economy meant cotton. Cotton had always been grown in Central Asia, but under tsarist rule, long-fiber varieties were introduced, and Central Asia became a major supplier of raw material for Russia's textile industry. Cotton had already displaced food crops on a great deal of irrigated land in Turkestan by the time of the revolution, but in the Soviet period, the whole region turned into a cotton plantation. "Cotton independence" was a stated goal of Soviet economic policy from the 1920s on, and in the system of regional specialization that characterized the centralized economic planning in the country, Central Asia had the task of producing all the cotton that the Soviet Union needed. Collectivization allowed the state to dictate what crops were grown and in what quantities. The state, as the monopoly buyer, could also set the prices (usually bearing no relation to world prices) at which collective farmers had to sell their produce. Cotton took up an ever-greater proportion of the region's cultivated land and spread into territory that had never before been cultivated. The central government's appetite for cotton was insatiable, and the quotas assigned to Central Asian republics constantly increased, until the region was producing (on paper at least), 8 million tons annually in the 1980s. This level of production was made possible by a relentless expansion of irrigation networks and massive application of fertilizers and pesticides. The Great Ferghana Canal, built by "volunteer" labor in 1939, was the first major Soviet project of this nature. Many others followed, culminating in the Qaraqum Canal, at thirteen hundred kilometers the longest in the world, which extended the irrigation network into Turkmenistan. By the end of the Soviet era, Central Asia had approximately 7.2 million hectares of irrigated land, a great majority of it devoted to cotton. The results were traumatic. The cotton monoculture rendered the region completely dependent on the rest of the Soviet Union for food grains and eventually resulted in environmental catastrophe. So much water was diverted from the region's rivers that the Aral Sea has dried up; so many chemicals were pumped into the land that chronic disease is the lot of many people who live on it today. In the late Soviet period, the utter domination of cotton marked the annual rhythm of life in Central Asia. The harvest was so important that children were pulled from school and sent to the villages to help pick cotton.

The cotton-production complex defined power relationships in the region. The center benefited greatly from cotton, but it did provide an array of social services and protections: free education, free health care, free water, almost-free energy, housing, and transport. By the end of the Soviet era, in 1990, social expenditures had risen to 12 percent of the gross domestic product and were largely covered by transfers from Moscow.[4] More importantly, the center made republican Party chiefs responsible for fulfilling the targets assigned to their republics. This role made the republican chiefs the dispensers of vast amounts of resources allocated for the purpose by the center. This ability to dispense patronage allowed local Party chiefs to appear as national leaders of their peoples, as arbiters of national interests at the center. Nevertheless, patronage was a system of social control that produced political quiescence and kept society in check. Noncompliance with cotton-related goals got one into trouble with the local elites, who had every incentive to play along in the deathly game of cotton monoculture.

These networks tied those in power to a home base, from which they recruited their supporters into the Party and state apparatus. Competing networks in each republic jockeyed for power within the constraints of the centralized, single-party system. This competition was the stuff of domestic politics in the Brezhnev years, but because it bore no resem-

blance to the official notions of Party life, it remained firmly behind
closed doors. The mechanisms of this system of politics have defined
post-Soviet politics in Central Asia. Unfortunately, these networks have
come to be known as *clans,* with the term's connotations of tribal primi-
tivism and the insinuation that traditional modes of political behavior
survived the Soviet era intact. This assumption then leads to essentialist
explanations of Central Asian politics that view the region as rooted in
certain primordial traits of local character that are immune even to the
most traumatic outside forces.

The networks are a more complex phenomenon that this view suggests. They arose within the new institutions of power created by the
Soviet regime, partly as a response of people to the traumatic changes
unleashed on them and partly as a result of Soviet policies. Political
"clans" are, of course, only one form of the networks of mutual (if
unequal) obligation that came to enmesh practically the whole of Soviet
society. They are rooted not so much in primordial patterns of behavior
but in a rational and logical calculus of people confronted with the brutal, impersonal machinery of a modern state *and* an economy of distribution. Networks of mutual obligation based on kinship (real or fictive)
or common places of origin provided a certain security in the face of the
state and allowed access to scarce goods. These networks were held
together by the exchange of favors, gifts, and mutual assistance, and validated by reference to "national tradition."[5]

At the political level, certainly, the "clans" were a creation of the Soviet
period. As we have seen, civil war, famine, collectivization, and the purges
destroyed a great deal in Central Asia. The new elites created in Soviet
institutions were mostly men of modest background, mainly rural, who
were entirely the products of Soviet education and beneficiaries of opportunities created by the Soviet state. They did not have networks of patronage and support waiting for them; they created these networks within the
framework of Soviet institutions. Soviet policies helped them in this
endeavor. The Soviet state had embarked on an ambitious project of indigenization *(korenizatsiia)* in the 1920s. In its most expansive form, the
project fizzled out in the 1930s, but the Party's desire to attract members
from indigenous populations was quite genuine and long lasting. In 1947,
at the height of the Stalin era, Usmon Yusupov, the Stalinist first secretary
of the Communist Party of Uzbekistan, had considered "the creation of
numerically strong national [i.e., ethnically Uzbek] Bolshevik cadres" to
be "the most important factor" in the Party's policy in the republic.[6]
Under Brezhnev, the Party hierarchy was substantially nativized, with

local leaders asserting substantial control over the recruitment of new members and the allocation of posts at the local level. In 1986, 71 percent of the people admitted to the Party in Uzbekistan were Uzbeks; the Uzbeks' share in high-ranking posts in the republic was even higher.[7] Beyond the numerical indigenization of the Party, fairly explicit programs of affirmative action ensured preferential entrance of members of indigenous nationalities into higher education and the job market.[8] This pattern was also evident in Kazakhstan and Kyrgyzstan, where Russians and other Europeans comprised a large part of the population. The Party secretaries Kunaev and Usubaliev worked out ways to include natives in the Party without alienating the local Russians. Korenizatsiia had succeeded in its own way, and Soviet power was effectively localized in Central Asia.

The Party secretaries emerged as legitimate national leaders in the eyes of the population. They wielded power locally and mediated with central authorities for access to resources. Few better examples exist of the Brezhnevite contract in operation than the career of Sharaf Rashidov (1917–83), the man who presided over Uzbekistan for twenty-four years, a third of the entire period of Soviet rule in Central Asia. Born into a humble family in the year of the revolution, Rashidov was a product of the Soviet system. He began his career as a teacher in a Soviet school in Jizzakh, near Samarqand, before entering Tashkent State University to study philology in 1937. From his schooldays, he had been writing for *Lenin yo'li* (Lenin's Path), the official newspaper of Samarqand province. After graduation from university, he became its editor. In the autumn of 1941, Rashidov was called up to the Soviet army to fight on the Northwestern front. He was decorated for bravery but demobilized after being wounded in 1942. He returned, a decorated and wounded veteran, to teaching and journalism in his native Jizzakh.

From early in his youth, Rashidov had been involved in public life, first in trade unions, then with the Communist Party, which he entered in 1939. Now, after the war, he rose quickly in both lines of work. In 1947, at the age of thirty, he became the editor of *Qizil O'zbekiston* (Red Uzbekistan), the leading Uzbek-language newspaper of Uzbekistan, and in 1949, he became the head of the Uzbekistan Writers Union, the official organization that represented those who lived by the pen and kept them in line. Rashidov continued his involvement with writing to the end of his life, producing a handful of novels on usual Soviet themes. Politically, his star had begun to rise in 1944, when he was made secretary of the Samarqand provincial organization of the Party. In 1950, he arrived in Tashkent as a member of the republic's Politburo, the highest organ of the local Party organization. He served in Party and state offices until his "election" as first secretary of the republic's Party organization in 1959. This was a time of some upheaval in Uzbekistan. Khrushchev, dissatisfied with factional struggles within the Uzbek Party apparatus, had ordered a reshuffle, and Rashidov was a compromise candidate. But Rashidov consolidated his power in the local Party organization, and once Khrushchev was out of the picture, wielded it without serious challenge until his death in 1983.

Rashidov's time at the helm was marked by all the contradictions of the Brezhnev era. Rashidov's room for maneuver was limited by the need to placate the center. Cotton, as usual, was the defining issue for the center, and the ever-increasing demand for it could not be curtailed. Evidence exists that Rashidov argued for lowering the quotas imposed on his republic, to no avail. But once the cotton was delivered, and potential dissent was curtailed, the Brezhnevite contract allowed Rashidov many blessings. He benefited personally: his chest filled up with medals and decorations showered upon him by the center, and he traveled the world as a member of Soviet delegations to various conferences and on state visits. But more important the benefits he could acquire for the republic and his followers in his "clan." Already in 1961, he had been made candidate member of the Soviet Politburo. He knew the major figures in Moscow, whom he could approach for the allocation of resources to Uzbekistan (investment in irrigation, the establishment of industrial plants, even the diversion of Siberian rivers to Central Asia). Tashkent became a showpiece city and in 1977 acquired a subway, the first in Central Asia, touted as a gift to the people of Uzbekistan to mark the sixtieth anniversary of the revolution (and, perhaps just coincidentally, to note Rashidov's birth as well). The ability to bring such "gifts" to Uzbekistan strengthened Rashidov's position not just as a patron of his own "clan," but also as a leader of the Uzbek people. Under Rashidov, the Uzbek Party elite gained political self-confidence, and the Uzbek Soviet intelligentsia, ensconced in Soviet institutions, became increasingly proud of its Uzbek identity. The fact that Rashidov himself was a writer provided a specially strong link between the political and intellectual elites in this period.[9]

One other factor helped crystallize the sense of Central Asia as indigenous space: Central Asia remained largely rural. Cities exploded in size throughout the developing world in the twentieth century, as people left the countryside in search of economic opportunity. In the slums generated by this mass movement arose all sorts of social and political move-

TABLE 2. URBAN POPULATION
AS PERCENTAGE OF TOTAL

Nationality	1959	1989
USSR total	38.2	65.85
Kazakhs	24.1	38.7
Kyrgyzes	10.8	22.2
Tajiks	20.6	28.3
Turkmens	25.4	33.4
Uzbeks	21.8	31.0

SOURCE: Robert J. Kaiser, *The Geography of Nationalism in Russia and the USSR* (Princeton, 1994), 203.
NOTE: The figures pertain to ethnic groups, not to republics.

ments that transformed many a society. In the Soviet Union as a whole, this process was more orderly. The country had no uncontrolled slums, but the population nevertheless urbanized. Central Asia bucked this trend. Throughout Central Asia, rates of urbanization remained remarkably low (see table 2). This slow pace was partly the result of official controls over migration to the cities, but it grew out of an undeniable element of choice as well. Young people chose to stay in the countryside, where life was familiar and support networks already in place.

The cities were different. There, Europeans—Russians, Jews, Ukrainians, Germans—were a major, if not a predominant presence. Nevertheless, urban Central Asians retained close contact with their kin and their networks in the countryside and re-created them in the cities. People from the same village or small town formed support networks in the cities and helped newcomers settle in. They seldom severed links with the countryside.

·   ·   ·

Along with the nativization of political power came the maturing of ethnonational identities in Central Asia. While the Soviet Union existed, Western observers held as axiomatic that nationalism and Communism were mutually exclusive and that Soviet nationality policy was aimed at the Russification of the country's non-Russians in the name of socialist internationalism. Influential authors spoke of the Soviets as "nation killers" and invested a great deal of hope in the power of nationalism to subvert the Soviet order from within.[10] Soviet reality was very different,

however; indeed, it was quite the opposite. Historians now believe that
the Soviet state itself played a crucial role in elaborating national identities in the non-Russian republics. "Soviet nationality policy," writes Yuri
Slezkine, "was devised and carried out by nationalists. Lenin's acceptance of the reality of nations and 'national rights' was one of the most
uncompromising positions he ever took." Slezkine goes on to argue that
the Soviet regime was stricken by a "chronic ethnophilia" that led it to
sponsor nation building among many (if not all) nationalities that inhabited the country. After World War II, class came to be seen as secondary
to ethnicity, and "support of nationalism in general (and not just Russian
nationalism or 'national liberation' abroad) [became] a sacred principle
of Marxism-Leninism."[11] How this came about repays close attention.

As the Bolsheviks consolidated their power in the 1920s, they were
acutely aware that they bore the burden of Russia's imperial past. They
had to overcome the distrust of the non-Russians by "indigenizing"
Soviet power. Revolutionary propaganda was most effective if conveyed
to each nation in its own language. But ultimately, the Bolsheviks were
convinced that nations were an "objective reality" that could not be
wished away.[12] Nationalism had also been a potent force in many parts
of the country during the civil war. It was a necessary evil that had to be
dealt with. If it wouldn't go away, it had to be harnessed to revolutionary
goals. Combined with other concerns about overcoming backwardness
and cultural revolution (see chapter 3), this reading of the situation led
the Soviet regime to what can only be called a nation-building project.
Each nationality had to be recognized officially and granted some degree
of territorial autonomy. Giving each nation its own homeland would
curb ethnic conflict and focus everyone's attention on the right kind of
conflict—that between social classes of the same nation. It would also,
so went the argument, make administration easier and more efficient.
Each nation would be equipped with education and publishing in its
own language, with its bureaucracy ideally staffed by its own people and
its members aware and proud of the "progressive" aspects of their own
history. Thus would arise new progressive cultures, "national in form,
socialist in content."

A wrong kind of nationalism could emerge, of course, and the Soviets
constantly struggled against "bourgeois nationalism"—the sort that provided a cloak for the exploitation of one class by another. In the purges of
the 1930s, charges of nationalism proved fatal to thousands of individuals. By the end of the 1930s, however, certain broad principles had been
worked out that were to provide an acceptable framework for national-

ity policies until the end of the Soviet era. Nations existed, and one of the achievements of socialism was to allow them to acquire ever-higher levels of progress. The celebration of one's nation was permissible but had to stay within fairly strict limits (no irredentist claims and no invocation of rivalry or animosity toward one's neighbors). The Russians had to be acknowledged as the "elder brother," whose disinterested help (in the form of leading the revolution) had made the current happiness of the other nations possible. The incorporation of the various non-Russian peoples into the Russian empire had to be seen as a union, not a conquest, so that the Russians could play the positive role scripted for them. Similarly, the Soviet Union was deemed to exist on the principle of the "friendship of the peoples," which had to be maintained at all costs, as did the idea that the Soviet system allowed for the resolution of all national conflicts. All of this necessitated a great deal of mental gymnastics and very selective, present-oriented readings of the past. Nevertheless, none of these limits brought into question the basic premises that every individual belonged to a nation defined by common origins, language, history, custom, and heritage and that each nation had a collective existence of its own that transcended history. Nationality came to be seen as a primordial aspect of one's identity.[13]

The Brezhnev period elevated these primordialist views of identity to official status with development of the notion of "ethnogenesis," which asserted that each ethnic group (or "ethnos") had a unique genesis, with the biological sense never far from the center of attention. Thus was Marxism, with its universalist message, wedded to crude primordialism. Nor was this interpretation merely a matter of academic hairsplitting. It became the dominant form of common sense that everyone used in thinking about ethnicity and difference. Thus, ethnic stereotypes—of the sort that proclaim that the women of X are the most beautiful, Y can outdrink all others, and Z are prone to violence—received academic and ideological cachet. Whereas Western observers continued to see assimilation and Russification as the main goals of Soviet policy, Soviet thinking came to take as axiomatic the distinctiveness of each nationality. Indeed, the official dictum had been stood on its head. By the late Soviet period, cultures were socialist in form but national in content.

The elaboration of national identities was made possible by a large, well-funded humanities intelligentsia created by the regime itself. Unlike their counterparts in other poor countries, where making a living from writing is difficult, if not impossible, Central Asian intellectuals could count on jobs in academe or in a large publishing industry that was immune to market forces. Every union republic had its own academy of sciences and an array of newspapers and publishing houses funded from the state budget. The Central Asian academy came to acquire a division of labor, with Russians and other Europeans dominating the technical fields and Central Asians monopolizing the humanities. Indeed, one curious aspect of Brezhnev-era cultural politics was nationalities' right to write their own histories. In 1990–91, at the fag end of the Soviet era, I was briefly an exchange student at Moscow State University as I began work on my doctoral dissertation. At that time, the university, the most prestigious in the country, could not find a scholar specializing in Central Asia to be my adviser! Only two scholars in the history department were doing work even dimly related to Central Asia: one was a specialist on tsarist foreign policy; the other studied tsarist-era Russian scholars of Central Asia. All work on Central Asian history since the Russian conquest took place in Central Asia itself.

But the history thus produced was not subversive. Many of those involved in the writing of history had close connections to the political elite (or were themselves part of it), which meant that as insiders, they had little desire to rock the boat. These humanities scholars came to see themselves as the keepers of their nations' cultures, a role they took seriously. What they achieved was to make the five nations of Central Asia look "natural," by giving them a common existence stretching back to time immemorial and by celebrating the magnificent heritage that each nation had created. This approach had its problems, because projecting the existence of contemporary nations into the distant past requires fitting the past into the categories of the present (although attempting to do so is precisely the point of Romantic nationalism). Historians from different nations squabbled over who owned what part of the common past of the region. Uzbeks tended to claim the entire heritage of the region as their own. Thus, figures such as Abu Rayhan Beruni, Ibn Sina, Alisher Navoiy, and Mirza Ulughbek were all claimed as Uzbek. Tajik intellectuals hotly contested these claims, seeing the cities of Samarqand and Bukhara, and all culture connected to them, as the patrimony of the Tajik nation instead. Turkmen scholars laid claim to the heritage of Khwarazm, and so on.[14]

Historical novels were an even more effective way of articulating and celebrating the past. (The joke was that, in Soviet conditions, historians wrote fiction, whereas the writers of fiction wrote history.) Thus, the Uzbek novelist Odil Yoqubov wrote lovingly of Mirza Ulughbek, the grandson of Timur, who was a leading astronomer of the age and the builder of an observatory in Samarqand. Pirimqul Qodirov, another Uzbek author, penned a panorama of the age of Babur, the Timurid prince who established the Mughal empire in India. Both novels take their protagonists as heroes of the Uzbek past and openly celebrate them. Both were published under official auspices and translated into several foreign languages. Other aspects of the region's heritage were similarly celebrated. In 1963, the central and republican governments both celebrated the 2500th anniversary of the founding of Samarqand; Tashkent was deemed to have reached the age of 2000 in 1983 and received its own jubilee celebration. Figures from the officially recognized pantheon of national heroes were ubiquitous: streets, squares, and parks were named after them, their works published in massive editions, and their statues strewn about the cities of Central Asia. In short, the celebration of the national past was completely legitimate under the Soviet dispensation.

National identities coexisted with quite genuine Soviet patriotism, the sense of common citizenship in a multiethnic country. Soviet patriotism was shaped by a number of powerful tools of socialization, foremost of which was universal education, achieved in the postwar decades, which shaped civic attitudes. For men, mandatory military service provided a further storehouse of common experiences that they shared with men across the length and breadth of the country. There was also an undeniable pride in being citizens of a superpower. "We had the best system of education in the world," I have been told on numerous occasions by acquaintances in Central Asia. "When our students went to Turkey after independence," a friend once claimed, with considerable scorn in his voice, "they found out they could teach the professors they found there!" No doubt such statements are a product of nostalgia in the midst of post-Soviet chaos, but they nevertheless contain a kernel of truth. When Central Asians traveled abroad or interacted with foreigners, they did so as proud citizens of a superpower who were more advanced than their brethren in the Third World. The Soviet government showcased Central Asia, especially Tashkent, as a model of development that bypassed capitalism. Central Asians may not have been posted to European parts of the Soviet Union, but they were routinely appointed to diplomatic posts abroad, especially in the Muslim world, where many Central Asians served as ambassadors. Central Asians also served willingly in the Soviet armed forces. Although conscription of Central Asians posed numerous issues for military planners (concern over the poor education of rural conscripts, the increasing proportion of fresh recruits from Central Asia), and a glass ceiling kept Central Asians underrepresented in the officer ranks, Central Asians served no more and no less willingly than any other Soviet citizens in the army. They went as military advisers to foreign countries, especially in the Muslim world, and a large number of them fought in Afghanistan.

The conjuncture of these processes created profound political conservatism in Central Asia. In an age in which the Soviet Union was defined for most Westerners by the twin phenomena of dissidence and samizdat (underground literature), Central Asia had no dissidents and no samizdat. The Party leaders came to be seen as *national* leaders, and being Uzbek or Tajik or Kazakh became inextricable from being Soviet. The elites had a vested interest in maintaining the system, and the masses, especially those in the rural majority, were tied to them too closely to want to rebel. These ties need not be romanticized, for they were unequal and involved a great deal of brutality. The elites might afford protection to their clients, but they brooked no opposition from them and were not averse to using the security apparatus of the Soviet state to deal with opposition. Nevertheless, the political order that took shape in the Brezhnev period did not threaten the stability of the Soviet order.

·   ·   ·

What does the foregoing have to do with Islam in Soviet Central Asia? Clearly, a great deal. The circumstances I describe above defined how Central Asians came to relate to Islam. That relationship was complex. On the one hand, "Muslim" became an important identity label by which people identified themselves and differentiated themselves from outsiders in their midst. Certain Islamic observances survived, and some even flourished, but they came to be seen as aspects of national culture. Moreover, they existed in the precarious space allowed by the realities of clan-based power at the grassroots level. Yet the terms of public debate were thoroughly denuded of references to Islam and any moral imperative that might emanate from it. Moreover, adherence to Islam was set against, and subjugated to, the claims of nationalism. Central Asians were Muslims by tradition and civilization, but they were also part of the modern world. Although Muslimness distinguished locals from outsiders in the Soviet context, *being Muslim was not counterposed to being Soviet.* Let us examine these propositions in concrete detail.

Customs and traditions occupied an ambiguous position in the Soviet conception of national identity. On the one hand, they were the repositories of a nation's historical experiences and an important aspect of its identity. On the other hand, they could represent backwardness and as such, were in need of revolution. As we have seen, the early Soviet period was marked by an all-out assault on "backward" traditions, an assault that succeeded to a considerable degree. Nations were to modernize in part by replacing these backward traditions with modern, enlightened Soviet ones. For several decades, many Central Asians shared the view that native tradition was a sign of backwardness. Only in the Brezhnev period, when a self-confident political elite took the helm and native cultural elites emerged—creating a sense that Central Asians were fully part of the modern world—did tradition become worthy of regular celebration. An enormous range of behavior and values were subsumed under the rubric of national traditions: they included marking births, weddings, and funerals with often lavish feasts; circumcising all boys (in opposition to the Soviet medical establishment, which saw circumcision as harmful); eating certain foods, furnishing one's living quarters in a certain way, and eating with one's hands rather than with utensils; placing a high value on families and seeing marriages as a contract between two families rather than two individuals; paying respect to elders; and providing and valuing hospitality. Many of these traditions were rooted in Islam (the fulfillment of life-cycle rituals), but all came to be seen as local, "Eastern," and Muslim. And indeed, many traditions that Muslims celebrated but that had little to do with Islam also became Muslim holidays. The clearest example of such a holiday is Navruz, the Iranian new-year holiday in late March. It had long been marked by the sedentary populations of Central Asia but was frowned upon by the Soviets as a "relic of the past," and disappeared from the annual calendar. It was revived in the 1980s, with full support of local Party elites, as a national holiday of the peoples of Central Asia, and hence a *Muslim* one.

However, talking about tradition is tricky. One can easily see tradition as an unchanging set of values or customs that remain impervious to change. Yet, it is difficult to claim that customs and traditions can remain unscathed by the kind of devastating traumas that Central Asian societies faced in the Soviet period: famine, collectivization, the destruction of social and cultural elites, the installation of universal public education and military conscription by a state bent upon transforming society. It is arrant nonsense to claim, as many do, that politics in Soviet Central Asia were "indeed a replica of the pre-Bolshevik power structure. . . . Only the names of the offices held by local politicians were changed. Rashidov . . . would previously have been the republic's khan or emir; the Party

Bureau, his vizirs; and the central Party bureaucrats, court figures along the Bukharan, Kokand or Khivan patterns."[15] Rather, tradition is highly malleable. The political culture of the Rashidov era was a local response to radically altered political circumstances that had little in common with the age of khans and emirs, but it was articulated within the new power structures.

Soviet policies themselves created a space for celebrating tradition and for making it concrete. In the 1920s, the Soviets co-opted the *mahalla*, the urban neighborhood community linked together by ties of mutual obligations and gift exchange, as the lowest rung in the new administrative system they imposed on the country. In the countryside, many new collective farms were based on preexisting village communities, which were now taken into the new bureaucratic structure and rendered concrete. In Turkmenistan, early Soviet policies crystallized existing tribal divisions by pursuing tribal parity, seeking to ensure that different Turkmen tribes were equally represented in the new organs of government. Cultural traditions became more concrete once an army of ethnographers set about documenting them. Restaurants in Central Asian cities offered either "European" or "national" cuisine (never both) and were furnished accordingly. Uzbek teahouses were so because they were furnished in the "national" fashion of low tables and cushions on the floor. This distinction produced a striking self-consciousness about tradition. More than once, I have been offered self-deprecatory excuses about the presence of "European" furniture in urban Uzbek homes. "Welcome to the home of a semi-Europeanized Uzbek," my hosts would say. (In Pakistan or India, by comparison, the modern furnishings of urban middle-class homes are not considered signs of semi-Europeanization, nor are teahouses furnished in folkloric style.) Combined with the economy of distribution, the concern with tradition also tended to flatten out differences between urban and rural populations and across income and status groups. Unlike much of the Third World, where the rich and the poor seem to inhabit different planets, so different are their lifestyles, Central Asian patterns of consumption were remarkably homogeneous in their allegiance to tradition.

But traditionalism also fed on the logic of life in Soviet conditions. The economy of distribution, with its perpetual shortages, rendered kin-based solidarities essential to procure goods and services that money alone could not obtain. Connections were crucial in jumping the queue in the wait for a car or a telephone connection, or to gain access to imported goods available only in special stores; they could also help in admission to a university, a transfer to a better job, or acceptance for a vacation in a sanatorium. These connections were based on kinship but not kinship alone—one could count on people from one's own neighborhood or village or school—and they had to be constantly maintained through reciprocity and mutual help. The extended family was the basis of these networks, and family ties and celebrations were the glue that held them together. These networks were validated in the name of tradition. Adherence to tradition thus became an absolutely essential skill for inclusion in the various solidarity networks that allowed life to be lived in the Soviet state. This system of mutual help was not an example of an "irrational" tradition's oppressing people and impeding progress, as many outsiders complained; it was a shrewd calculation of the social costs and benefits of living life in the Soviet Union.

And while certain specific traditions might be rendered sacrosanct, their actual content could change significantly. One example was the *gap* or *gashtak*, a practice in which groups of men from the same peer group got together periodically to socialize. Members took turns hosting the whole group, usually at home, for feasting and entertainment, which cemented bonds of solidarity among them and brought the expectation of mutual support. The *gap* or gashtak has a long history in Central Asia. In the early Soviet period, it experienced considerable decay, until it was revived in the 1960s. The revival transformed it in many ways: now there were women's *gap*s as well, and the peer groups could form around any number of commonalities. These associations operated as mutual support networks, in which people from different walks of life could have contact with each other. The considerable expense of hosting the *gap* (which almost invariably involved copious drinking) was seen as a form of investment in one's contacts.[16] Similarly, the *to'y*, the feast given to family, friends, and relatives to mark important life-cycle events, such as births, circumcisions, weddings, and funerals, served several purposes: it cemented social bonds between neighbors and various other relations of mutual obligation, it allowed the host to assert his status in society, and it served to distinguish Central Asians from others living in their midst. These occasions were all seen as "Muslim" celebrations, not only because they centered around religious rituals but also because non–Central Asians did not celebrate them. Nevertheless, in the Soviet period, vodka drinking became an integral part of these celebrations, as did the use of audio equipment. Indeed, vodka drinking was assimilated to national tradition through the use of "national" tea bowls for drinking the shots.

It was because of these networks that Islam survived in the Soviet period. The practice of Islam and Islamic ritual beyond the purview of the officially recognized religious directorates—the so-called unofficial Islam—existed in this realm of community-based solidarity networks that penetrated even state and Party institutions. As the episodes described at the beginning of this chapter indicate, communities supported numerous unregistered mosques and shrines using various kinds of subterfuge. The vast majority of boys were circumcised, large numbers of weddings were solemnized in religious ceremonies that supplemented the civil registration, and most people, including many Communists, continued to be buried according to Islamic rites. Sometimes the rites were conducted by official ulama affiliated with SADUM, but far more commonly, they were led by an elder esteemed locally for his knowledge. In addition, the ritual life-cycle events featured recitation of the Qur'an and other sacred texts. These recitations were usually done by women, known variously as *otin-oy, bibi-otin,* or *xalfa,* who specialized in this task. As carriers of religious knowledge and holiness, *otin*s were a feature of Central Asian life before the revolution. Traditionally, they came from learned families, and many of them taught basic religious knowledge to the girls of the neighborhood or the village. In the Soviet period, otins stood liable to the usual charges of cultural backwardness, if not antirevolutionary activity and parasitism, but they nevertheless survived. Some became teachers in the new Soviet schools, whereas others continued to teach children in secret, but their role as reciters of prayers at life-cycle events became central.[17] Older otins transmitted their knowledge and their status in private to their daughters or daughters-in-law, but their existence was a well-known secret. As long as tradition demanded the fulfillment of life-cycle rituals, there was a demand for otins.

Many other traditional practices continued as well, especially in the countryside. Shrines and holy places, whether the graves of holy men or natural sites deemed sacred, were a traditional feature of local Islamic practice. Many of them were destroyed in the antireligious campaigns of the 1920s and 1930s, and official Soviet propaganda heaped scorn on the notion of shrine worship, describing it as a form of superstition. Nevertheless, many holy places survived or were restored, while new ones continued to crop up, and all continued to attract pilgrims. Pilgrimage sites ranged from a humble grave site or a clump of sacred trees, where people would tie strips of cloth as votive offerings, to major sites, such as the mountain Takht-i Sulayman, Solomon's Throne, in southern Kyrgyzstan, where some gatherings of pilgrims in the 1950s reportedly numbered in the tens of thousands.[18]

The burden of maintaining national traditions and of preserving the honor of the community and its connection to Islam fell more heavily on women than on men. In a pattern observed in many parts of the world, women came to be seen as guardians of the faith, of the inner values of the community faced with a hostile state. This phenomenon was not specifically Islamic; it was a pattern of gender relations that persisted despite the efforts of the Soviet regime to transform it. The Soviets "liberated" women by unveiling them and bringing them into the orbit of public education and the workforce, but they no more equalized opportunity and inclusion than did many other societies. Especially in the countryside, women continued to leave school early to get married and to take jobs in a few selected areas of the labor force. Men were supposed to go out and engage in the rough and tumble of the world, whereas women were to guard the chastity of the home and of the community. They, too, performed communal rituals (such as prayer sessions to seek the intercession of Lady Tuesday [*Bibi Seshanbe*]) that were thought to benefit the whole community, whereas the otin was, as we have seen, the primary vehicle for the transmission of religious knowledge to the next generation. The British anthropologist Gillian Tett, who did fieldwork in a village in Tajikistan in the twilight years of Soviet rule, once asked a village notable whether he felt any contradiction in being both a Muslim and a Communist. "Not at all, he laughed. 'I am a communist. I cannot fast or pray at work. But my wife and *kelin* [daughter-in-law], they are sitting at home, so they must fast and pray! So we will not suffer from sins. We are a Muslim home!' "[19] This situation, of course, placed peculiar burdens on women, but it also gave Muslim women a central place in the practice of Muslim ritual.

Men had a different kind of dispensation. They could sow their wild oats and engage with the world in all its impurity, as long as they were of working age. Then, as old age approached, they were expected to turn their minds to the next world and to become observant of ritual and prohibitions. In Central Asia, the ages of forty (the age at which the Prophet received the revelation) and sixty-three (the age at which he died) have long been considered important. Upon attaining them, men often became more pious, praying more regularly, observing the fast, and participating in other forms of ritual. In doing so, they "represented" younger members of their family and indeed the community as a whole. This proxy religiosity whereby women and older men represented their community and ensured the continuation of Islam within it might have little sanction in the scriptural canons of Islam, but it had long been a customary practice in Central Asia.[20] The exigencies of the Soviet era further entrenched this aspect of tradition.

Even so, religious knowledge clearly shrank drastically in Soviet times. Muslims did not so much lose the ability to understand the literal meaning of the Qur'an or prayers as the implicit cultural knowledge, acquired in the family or the maktab during childhood and thus assimilated at the level of instinct. Maintaining this type of knowledge was no longer possible in Soviet conditions. In the face of official hostility, all religious instruction retreated into the private home, where it survived as an aspect of "national tradition." Among Uzbeks and Tajiks, for example, national tradition demanded that at the end of every meal, the eldest person at the table should pronounce "*Âmin*" ("Amen") as an expression of thanks to God. The ritual originally entailed a brief prayer in Arabic, pronounced while everyone held out their open hands to collect God's blessings, which they then splashed on the face. In Soviet conditions, the ritual came to comprise of a mumbled prayer (seldom with the original words intact) and a rather perfunctory rub of the face—and it was performed no matter what had been consumed in the meal. Similarly, very few people could perform the ritual worship (*namâz*) or even recite the proclamation of the faith (*shahâda*). Ritual provided a sense of communal belonging and a certain moral authority for a clean (uncorrupt) life, but it coexisted with a disregard for legal exactitude and indeed real skepticism about any ostentatious display of piety.

·   ·   ·

Official responses to such practices took two forms. Higher Party organs or inspectors sent from outside were often critical of such "survivals of the past" in local society, and especially the participation of local Party members in them. Indeed, a great deal of concern was expressed, both in the press and in internal Party documents, about the extent of religious observance in society (Sovietologists in the West carefully tracked such expressions and used them to back up much of their commentary on Soviet Islam). The concerns that these documents described were no doubt real, but they seldom translated into action. The state never launched a concerted campaign to close illegal mosques or destroy *mazar*s after Khrushchev's antireligious campaign in the late 1950s. Indeed, "scientific atheism" and "atheistic education," the Soviet academic specialties connected with antireligious activity, had become career paths for those who wanted to make a safe career in the Party bureaucracy. In the mid-1990s, I once invited a Kyrgyz exchange scholar to give a talk at my college. The man had received a fellowship to spend a semester studying business management at the University of Minnesota. Until the fall of the Soviet Union, he had taught dialectical materialism and scientific communism. After his talk, a student asked him how he felt about traversing the distance from dialectical materialism to business administration. His answer, delivered completely matter-of-factly, said quite a lot about late-Soviet society: "I had really wanted to study foreign languages, but it was considered a subject suitable only for women, so I went into dialectical materialism." The job of these bureaucrats was precisely to write alarm-filled reports about the religious situation in their domain; translating that concern into practice was a different matter, and not their job. Local officials, however, quite often looked the other way when people from their village or solidarity network undertook illegal religious activity. Party archives are full of complaints about local officials' inability to combat religious activity, or even about their willingness to connive in it.[21]

The authorities could take this relatively relaxed view for a number of reasons. Until the late 1970s, when the Iranian revolution and the war in Afghanistan changed the calculus drastically, officials at the highest level of Soviet power seemed to genuinely believe that neither Islam nor Muslims posed a threat to the country. Muslims (like Orthodox Christians and unlike Jews or evangelical Christians) were deemed to be loyal Soviet citizens who had collectively demonstrated their patriotism through sacrifice in the Great Patriotic War.[22] Religious observance was seen not as a political threat; it was a challenge only to the Party's mission to bring about enlightenment and a society based on rational principles. On these grounds, Party officials at the local level continued to issue resolutions highlighting the need for ever-greater vigilance in monitoring religious phenomena, producing statistics about religious observance in much the same way that they counted tons of cotton or kilowatt-hours of electricity to measure the success or otherwise of the Party's policies. "In 1956, 164,000 attended communal prayers for the two Eid celebrations, and in 1958, the number had already risen to 288,000," noted a resolution of the Central Committee of the Communist Party of Uzbekistan with characteristic alarm.[23] This kind of alarm appears in Party resolutions even at the height of Stalinism. It is best understood as a genre of internal Party correspondence, where it served as a form of self-criticism and offered proof that the Party organization was vigilant in its duty.

Above all, contrary to the hopes of Western analysts, "unofficial Islam" was completely apolitical. In part, it had to be. Local Party elites might look the other way when unofficial Islamic activity took place, but they had absolutely no patience with challenges to their position. Any political claims on behalf of Islam would have represented a challenge to the power of local political elites and threatened to rock their relationship with the center. Any expressions of Islam that went beyond the narrow, apolitical bounds defined by custom were persecuted. But fear of persecution was not the only reason "unofficial Islam" was apolitical. Although Western observers of unofficial Islam assumed that Islam had to be political, this assumption was far from reality. Central Asians tapped into the long local Hanafi tradition that disavowed political involvement. The basic instinct was to try to preserve elementary Islamic ritual in a harsh political climate. Islam was now intensely localized, a form of local pride, a part of the heritage of the nation, but it was also limited to the domestic sphere. Because the rituals and customs associated with Islamic observance were part of the culture of a given nation, they were largely immune to criticism on grounds that they contravened Islamic injunctions, for such criticism laid the critic open to claims that he was not really a member of the nation or that stricter observance of ritual was the product of foreign (Arab) culture.

We need to keep in mind one final consideration: the complete de-Islamization of public debate brought about by the upheaval of the 1920s and the 1930s. All public discourse in the Soviet period was explicitly cast in materialist terms deriving from Marxism as a philosophy of universal *human* progress, in which human fulfillment entailed the conquest of religion and superstition. All public claims were validated by appeals to universal laws of history and to socialist construction, which created its own moral imperatives. Religion was seen as a human construct corresponding to a certain (primitive) stage in the development of human society, whereas the ideological function of religion as the "opium of the masses" was constantly emphasized. Islam, along with all other religions, was excluded from the public realm. In this de-Islamized sphere, ideas of nationalism took root. Soviet ideas of nation centered on language as the most important marker of the nation, but custom and heritage were also crucially important. Clearly, Islam as a part of the national heritage could not be denied completely, but its relationship to that heritage could be rethought in various ways.

Central Asians in the late Soviet era were very conscious of being Muslims, but being Muslim meant something very specific in the Soviet context. It was a form of belonging to a local community that marked its members as different from others who lived in their midst. Being Muslim had little to do with personal belief or observance of ritual and everything to do with customs and way of life. Even so, one remained a Muslim even if one did not observe local customs or traditions. For the vast majority of Central Asians, Islam was a form of localism, a marker that opposed Muslims/Central Asians/locals to Europeans/outsiders/ Russians. In this scheme, Tatars, inhabited the very outer boundaries of Muslimness, for although they were Turkic-speaking Muslims, they did not observe local customs and were not parts of local solidarity networks. Soviet Koreans, many of whom had been forcibly resettled in Central Asia in the 1930s, counted as Europeans in this scheme. Muslims from other parts of the world who did not share Central Asian customs were not included in these boundaries of Muslimness.

Conventional wisdom in the West held that the Soviets hid "their" Muslims from foreign Muslims. Otherwise, foreign Muslims would recognize how oppressed their coreligionists were, while Soviet Muslims would forge unauthorized religious bonds. This view had little resemblance to reality. Tashkent was a common destination for large numbers of foreign students, most of whom were Muslim. Yet, little love was lost between them and their hosts. For Uzbeks, foreign Muslims were foreign because they did not observe local traditions. Many of the foreign students, for their part, were committed Russophiles, who often expressed deeply derogatory opinions about their hosts, many of them borrowed whole cloth from the Russians. More than one foreign student that I met in Tashkent's University Town when I lived there in 1991 expressed astonishment that I was learning Uzbek. "Why would you waste your time with that?" I was often asked. "They are an ignorant people. What can they have to say that's worth learning their language?"!

Finally, being a Muslim was only one aspect of one's identity; Muslimness coexisted with ethnonational identities that had become quite meaningful to many people. Indeed, one was a Muslim *because* one was an Uzbek or a Tajik or a Turkmen. Thus, common Muslimness did not exclude the possibility of antagonism to other peoples of Central Asia. Indeed, latent ethnonational tensions between Central Asian groups were a notable feature of the late-Soviet period, and they occasionally came out into the open during the Gorbachev years.

•   •   •

A comparison with the rest of the Muslim world shows the specificity of the Soviet experience of Islam. The Soviet Union was not unique in trying to control Islam and subjugate it to bureaucratic rules, and we should resist the urge to contrast Soviet control to some kind of pristine existence of Islam beyond all state control in the rest of the Muslim world. Modern states have commonly sought to reshape Islam, to institute bureaucratic controls over it, and to put it to work in garnering legitimacy and creating new forms of public morality. These attempts have varied in intensity, depending on historical peculiarities as well as the strength of the states involved, but nowhere is Islam unaffected by the reach of the modern state. The Soviet case is thus far from unique, but it is unique in the intensity of the state's assault on Islam and the longevity of the regime.

The modern map of the Middle East is the product of the disintegration of the Ottoman Empire after World War I. The Turkish Republic arose from a heroic grassroots struggle to prevent the last remnants of the Ottoman Empire from being carved up by British, French, and Greek occupiers. Upon securing victory, the new state, headed by Mustafa Kemal Atatürk, tried to sever all links with its Ottoman past, which it blamed for all the ills that had befallen Turkey. In the 1920s, Atatürk enacted a number of reforms that transformed Turkish culture in ways that paralleled the cultural revolution in Soviet Central Asia in the same decade. Although he did not launch an all-out assault on Islam, he did subjugate Islamic institutions to the state. Atatürk abolished Sufi orders, broke the connection between the shariat and civil law by enacting new civil and penal codes borrowed whole cloth from European models, and revoked all privileges enjoyed by the ulama. In 1934, the Turkish state made all Islamic religious activity subject to the supervision of a ministry of religious affairs, whose task was to regulate religious observance and education throughout the new republic. Imams thus became government functionaries, and mosques came under the control of the state. Atatürk also regularly inveighed against "primitive" religious practices, which, he thought, ought to have no place in an enlightened state. Turkey, thus, also came to have an "official Islam" with a bureaucratic structure unprecedented in Islamic history.

The shahs of the Pahlavi dynasty (1925–79) in Iran made a similar attempt to marginalize Islam and to subjugate it to a pre-Islamic national identity. Elsewhere, the anticolonial struggles in Indonesia and Algeria—the latter defined a whole era of decolonization—were fought in the name of the nation, with Islam scarcely playing a role. Egypt's national moment came in 1952, when a group of junior officers overthrew the monarchy and proclaimed a republic that was to express the will of the Egyptian people. Egypt's new leader Gamal 'Abd al-Nasser curbed the authority of the shariat and its interpreters, threw open public education to the masses, and turned the Azhar university, one of the most respected seats of Sunni learning in the world, into a state-controlled institution. The corrupt old order was responsible for the weakness of Egypt, and traditional ulama bore part of the responsibility: "The shaykh does not think of anything except the turkey and the food with which he filled his belly," Nasser once said. "He is no more than a stooge of reaction, feudalism, and capitalism."[24] The ulama and their activities had to be brought under state control, which is what Nasser proceeded to do in 1961.

But even when states have sought to control Islam, they have done so to put it to work on their behalf. Having freed up large areas of public life from the authority of Islam and its carriers, they nevertheless have used Islam to bolster their legitimacy or to found systems of public morality based on a particular reading of Islam. The Egyptian state, for instance, derives a great deal of its legitimacy from the argument that it serves Islam.[25] In Turkey, in an approved and properly nationalized form, Islam remains part of the moral education of all schoolchildren.[26] In both these countries, religious higher education is under state supervision or control, but it remains uninterrupted, and the public presence of Islam is unmistakable. The Saudi state, of course, stakes all its legitimacy on Islam, but it keeps strict control over Islamic institutions. In Pakistan, in contrast, the state was never able to institutionalize control over Islam. Rather, the military, both in and out of power, has used Islamic groups for various purposes, from sponsoring the "jihad" in Afghanistan, through instigating an insurgency in Kashmir, to fomenting sectarian violence within Pakistan itself.

Soviet policies toward Islam are thus best seen as one end of a spectrum. Here, the state stood completely outside the parameters of Islamic debate and was intensely hostile to all religions. Instances of harsher repression of Islam exist, all from socialist regimes that sought to bring about large-scale transformation of society and culture: China during the cultural revolution and Albania under Enver Hoxha, which declared itself the world's only atheistic state in 1967, are the most striking examples. Here, the public realm was de-Islamized, and patterns of the transmission of Islam to new generations were damaged. But in both these cases, the period of state persecution of Islam was shorter than the six decades of Soviet history.

•   •   •

What was the fate of the learned tradition of Islam? It survived, but only in a precarious position far away from the mainstream of public life. As we saw in chapter 3, the Soviet regime had created an official directorate (SADUM) to administer (and control) Islamic religious activity in Central Asia. SADUM and the ulama connected to it were in an unenviable position. Closely supervised by the Council for the Affairs of Religious Cults (part of the Ministry of Internal Affairs) and expected to contribute to the Soviet government's diplomatic initiatives in the Muslim world, the ulama were often seen as agents of the state by many in their own community. Western observers tended to dismiss the whole phenomenon as "official Islam," and the ulama simply as front men for the regime, opportunists lacking all credibility. The reality was a lot more complex.

SADUM's founders were bona fide ulama who had survived the horrors of the 1930s. The organization's first chairman was Eshon Babakhan ibn Abdulmajidkhan, a Naqshbandi sheikh from Tashkent. No doubt he had political approval, for the leadership of SADUM was to remain in his family until 1989. The ulama participated in the work of SADUM in the hope of preserving some semblance of a tradition of Islamic learning and perhaps of asserting some influence on local society. One of the first actions of SADUM was to establish an office to issue fatwas (legal opinions) on questions sent in by people from throughout its domain. In 1948, the Mir-i Arab madrasa in Bukhara was given over to SADUM, which was allowed to start religious instruction in it. In 1971, SADUM was allowed to open the Imam al-Bukhari Islamic Institute in Tashkent as a postgraduate adjunct to the Mir-i Arab madrasa. The number of students remained small (Mir-i Arab madrasa had an enrollment of eighty-six students in 1982, whereas the Imam al-Bukhari institute had thirty-four places, although the competition for them was intense), and matriculating students were no doubt vetted by the KGB; nevertheless, SADUM was able to ensure the continuation of higher religious learning in Soviet conditions. Even more precious, given Soviet conditions, was the opportunity to maintain contact with Muslims outside the Soviet Union. SADUM was able to arrange for a small (carefully handpicked) delegation to make the annual pilgrimage to Mecca every year, and in the 1960s, it began sending students to study at religious institutions in friendly Muslim countries (Egypt, Syria, Libya).

SADUM paid a political price, however. It was pressed into service of the government's foreign-policy agenda, especially in the Muslim world.

SADUM was supposed to prove official claims about the freedom of religion in the Soviet Union and to confirm that Muslims were active participants in the creation of the new society the Soviet leadership claimed to be building. Official ulama thus traveled the world on goodwill missions and hosted visitors from abroad. They were prominent also in Soviet efforts to court movements for independence in the colonial world, and later they played a role in Soviet campaigns for "international peace and friendship." On the domestic front, too, the state was not averse to asking SADUM for help in its struggle with phenomena it considered undesirable, and SADUM's handlers did not hesitate to ask it to issue fatwas on issues of importance to them. This practice pushed SADUM to radically modernist stances on a number of issues. In many fatwas, SADUM decreed honest work to be an Islamic virtue, the fulfillment of which required Muslims to avoid absenteeism and drunkenness (both of which were perennial problems for the state). But the fatwas went further, declaring that the fast of Ramadan was not obligatory for those involved in physical labor. Yet other fatwas declared that some forms of expense, such as the sacrifice of livestock for the Feast of Sacrifice (Qurban hayit), the celebratory breaking of the fast during Ramadan (*iftâr*), and the collection of alms for the poor were no longer obligatory in Soviet conditions. Other fatwas condemned as un-Islamic such customs as visiting shrines, seeking intercession from the dead, wearing the paranji, and spending excessive amounts at to'ys.[27]

Demands of the state were not the only force pushing official ulama toward such positions. The ulama were also motivated by a desire to provide spiritual guidance to society at large and to ensure that ritual retained a semblance of Islamic correctness. Yet their opposition to popular practices led them to take positions in defiance of the consensus of the Central Asian Hanafi tradition, which had long accepted many of the rituals they criticized. SADUM's fatwas derived their authority from other fiqh traditions, with Ibn Taymiya, the fourteenth-century purist scholar, being a particular favorite. Indeed, in their emphasis on ritual purity and the compatibility of Islam with the modern world, the official ulama shared a great deal with the Jadids and with modernist interpreters elsewhere in the Muslim world. Nevertheless, their opposition to tradition put them in a precarious position, because they criticized traditions that could be defended on both religious and national grounds: official ulama went against the consensus of local Hanafi ulama, and they criticized traditions newly valorized as national. They remained liable to marginalization on both religious and national grounds.

This reformist attitude was also visible in the kind of education SADUM provided in its two madrasas, which were very different from their pre-Soviet counterparts. Instead of studying medieval commentaries and supercommentaries on fiqh, students studied *tajwid* (the art of reciting the Qur'an), *tafsir* (the explication of the Qur'an), and hadith from primary sources. They also received intensive training in Arabic, and the curriculum included geography, history, social science, Uzbek language and literature, and physical education.[28] SADUM could not, however, publish religious texts of its own; instruction in its own institutions was based on older texts preserved in its own library, or obtained, completely legally, from abroad. This imported literature was almost entirely in Arabic, some sent from abroad, the rest left behind by visiting delegations. Much of it was reformist and modernist in its thrust.

SADUM never accounted for more than a small fraction of Islamic activity in Central Asia, and the vast majority of the activity described above went on beyond its control. During the Cold War, Western observers commonly saw this "parallel Islam" as a politically subversive force and a potential threat to the existence of the Soviet state.[29] Hindsight has proven much of this literature to be wide of the mark: we now know that ritual observance was more widespread than even the most optimistic observers had assumed during the Cold War, but also that it was not inherently political. Quite the opposite, in fact: many among the small group of learned scholars who worked illegally actively argued *against* making political claims on behalf of Islam. Nor can all of unofficial Islam be seen as a single phenomenon, existing apart from and in opposition to official Islam. The connections were much too complicated for such a simple dichotomy to explain anything.

In the Islamic tradition, the existence of official Islam is the exception. The idea of an official institution having the right to issue binding legal opinions is alien to the Islamic tradition, and although several modern states have tried to impose such structures on their Muslim populations, they have always struggled for legitimacy. SADUM could issue all the fatwas it (or its handlers) wanted, but acceptance of these opinions was not guaranteed. Unofficial Islam, in contrast, has been the rule in the history of Muslim societies. Because Islam does not require those who perform ritual to be anointed or appointed in any way, any Muslim can perform ritual (leading prayers, officiating at life-cycle events, including weddings and funerals). All Muslims are ritually self-sufficient. We need not be surprised to find that such ritual observance continued throughout the Soviet period, because it could be performed by any Muslim who could recite the necessary prayers, which could be learned in the family. Of greater interest is the fact that the world of formal Islamic learning continued to exist beyond SADUM's control. Indeed, the roots of many post-Soviet religious debates are to be found in this underground world of learning.

The destruction of the ulama in the 1930s was devastating but not total. Some survivors joined SADUM, whereas others shunned all contact with the new order. In the Brezhnev era, some of this latter group of ulama began offering lessons in secret to select students. This practice, which came to be known as *hujra* (literally, a cell in a madrasa where students lived), constituted an intellectual milieu of considerable vitality. Many of these ulama were traditionalist, their main impulse being to preserve Islamic knowledge in a hostile environment. They took self-consciously conservative positions on issues of custom and tradition. In this sense, they were much closer to the prerevolutionary tradition of learning in Central Asia than were the official ulama connected to SADUM.

The pursuit of this milieu brings us to the remarkable biography of Muhammadjon Rustamov (ca. 1892–1989), known to his students as Domla (Professor) Hindustoniy. Born in the same generation as the Jadids, Muhammadjon's life took him in a very different direction from theirs. While Abdurauf Fitrat was publishing his criticisms of the whole system of traditional education in Central Asia, Muhammadjon immersed himself in the tradition, studying in madrasas in Kokand and Bukhara. During the chaos of the revolution, he left Central Asia for Afghanistan. He found himself in India (hence his epithet), where he studied at the Usmania madrasa in Ajmer, acquiring mastery of the Hanafi tradition of Islam. He returned home in 1929 and promptly got into trouble with the state. Over the next quarter century, he spent a total of eight and a half years in jail in three stints. During World War II, he served in the Soviet army and was wounded near Minsk in Belarus. In the mid-1950s, he briefly worked as imam at the official Mavlono Charkhi mosque in Dushanbe, in Tajikistan. He returned to academic work in private, compiling, among others, a six-volume manuscript commentary on the Qur'an and teaching in a hujra from the early 1960s on. In his teaching and his writing, he took consistently conservative positions rooted in the local Hanafi tradition. He had little use for modernist reform. One of his works is *Hajviya-yi Muhammad 'Abduh,* a satire written in a Persian literary tradition of long standing, on Muhammad 'Abduh, the great Egyptian modernist theologian from the turn of the twentieth century, in which he ridicules 'Abduh's reformism as a form of conceit. Two aspects

of his conservatism are worth noting: he defended local customs and traditions against attacks from all directions, and he took a resolutely quietist stance on questions of politics. Soviet rule was a test for believers, in
which success lay in reliance on God (*tavakkul*) and patience (*sabr*)
rather than in political or military struggle.

Hindustoniy was only the most prominent of a number of such scholars in the Brezhnev era, who together constituted a religious underground in the cities and small towns of Uzbekistan and Tajikistan. The
other three republics saw little of this kind of activity. Nevertheless, the
number of participants in this underground world of Islamic learning
remained small. The scholars' relations with official Islam were complex.
Hindustani himself had briefly been an imam in an official mosque in
Dushanbe. The "underground" ulama came from the same backgrounds
as those in SADUM and were often connected to each other through ties
of initiation and common scholarly lineages. As bearers of the learned
tradition of Islam, the underground ulama had much more in common
with the "official" ulama of SADUM than with the practitioners of "customary" Islam who constituted the bulk of "parallel" Islam. SADUM
could even help its unofficial counterparts out in some ways. Although
SADUM could not publish religious literature, it had access to material
published abroad. Such material, mostly in Arabic, was collected at
SADUM's library in Tashkent, and extra copies were distributed among
unofficial ulama as well.[30]

·   ·   ·

The seven decades of Soviet rule left a deep imprint on Central Asia. The
massive social engineering undertaken by the Soviet regime left very little
unchanged. Social classes were made and unmade, the terms of cultural
debate were massively transformed, and the context in which Islam
existed was radically altered. But Soviet modernity was different from its
Western counterpart. It contained within itself a critique of many aspects
of "bourgeois" modernity, and it set out to build an alternative modernity that would avoid the alienation produced by private property in
bourgeois societies. The emphasis on community then let the nation back
in through the back door, and along with the nation came a glorification
of custom and tradition that is quite unusual in capitalist societies. The
emphasis on tradition in turn opened up the space for Islam to continue
to exist as an aspect of the national heritage of certain nations.
Conversely, the vast majority of Central Asians could conceive of Islam

only in this way. As such, Islam was not a political threat to the Soviet order. Rather, it was subordinated to the terms of public debate imposed in the Soviet era.

In the long-term perspective of Islam in Central Asia, there was nothing unusual in customary practices thus defining Islam for Muslims. Quite paradoxically, then, the forced modernization visited upon Central Asia by the Soviet regime served to preserve aspects of customary Islam that came under sustained attack in other parts of the Muslim world during the twentieth century. In the twentieth century, expanding literacy and the availability of print gave an ever-widening number of Muslims access to the textual sources of Islam and thus redefined patterns of religious authority in society. Soviet Central Asia went the other way: although the Soviets achieved near-universal literacy, they also ensured that literacy could not be used for the acquisition of religious knowledge (except by a few officially vetted students in carefully monitored institutions). Transmission of Islamic knowledge was largely oral, and Islam became synonymous with custom. The Jadid critique of customary practices was largely forgotten, as was the Jadid attempt to modernize Islamic knowledge. Islam was effectively *demodernized* in the Soviet period.

CHAPTER 5

The Revival of Islam

In 1984, during the American-sponsored jihad in Afghanistan, the CIA and its Pakistani counterparts came up with a plan. Instead of merely fighting the Soviets in Afghanistan, they would carry the battle to their own turf. There were many Muslims in Soviet Central Asia who, according to CIA's director, William Casey, "could do a lot of damage to the Soviet Union." To this end, the CIA had the Qur'an translated into Uzbek and smuggled into Soviet territory.[1] Reading the Qur'an in their own language would, it was believed, be enough to stir the Muslims up and make them rebel against the Soviet regime. This plan did not come out of the blue. Throughout the Cold War, it had been axiomatic in the West that Islam was an antidote to Communism and that the Soviet Union's own Muslims represented a "soft underbelly," an internal threat that could be exploited. Western authors spoke with much enthusiasm of the potential of Islam to pose a threat to the Soviet state.[2] Now the idea was being put into practice.

But at about the same time that the first Uzbek Qur'ans showed up in Pakistan for transshipment, another transition took place at the top of the Soviet leadership. Nikolai Chernenko, the third septuagenarian to have ruled the country in the 1980s, died, and was replaced by Mikhail Gorbachev, a man of a different generation who set out on an ambitious program of reform. He began by calling for an acceleration of growth in the Soviet economy. This campaign led him to argue for *glasnost'*, openness, as a prerequisite for change. By 1987, the emphasis was on *pere-*

stroika, the restructuring of the entire Soviet economy and polity. Gorbachev's advocacy of reform opened up processes of change that ran ahead of anyone's efforts to control them. Glasnost destroyed the monopoly of Soviet ideology, whereas perestroika opened up the political structures of the state to renegotiation. Within an astonishing seven years, the Soviet Union had ceased to exist and the Central Asian republics of the USSR were hurled into unexpected independence.

The Soviet Union collapsed without its Muslims making a lot of trouble. (The fate of the Qur'an-smuggling scheme is not known, but there is no evidence in Central Asia that it had any impact.) But no sooner had Central Asia become independent than its population ceased being "good Muslims" and became the object of fear and suspicion. The collapse of the Soviet Union and the "emergence" of Central Asia fueled fears that having escaped Communism, Central Asian Muslims would opt for Islamic fundamentalism and drift into the orbit of the Islamic Republic of Iran. The specter of fundamentalism and the need to counteract it came to define how Western observers thought about Islam in Central Asia. The result is a tendency to exaggerate all Islam-based political activism and all threats of militancy while ignoring the broader context in which they exist. That broader context, we shall see in this chapter, has changed less drastically from the late Soviet period than is often assumed. Indeed, continuities from the late Soviet era are numerous and define the political landscape of the region in far more significant ways than Islam does. Post-Soviet Central Asia has more in common with other postsocialist states in Eurasia than with the Middle East.

•   •   •

Interest in religion soared throughout the Soviet Union in the Gorbachev years. Glasnost led to a quest for moral and spiritual values that were now seen to have been corroded by Communism. There was also a very important element of the recovery of *national* memories and national legacies in the turn toward religion. Many people, Communist Party members included, rediscovered religion in its various forms. Some returned to traditional forms of ritual, whereas others experimented with denominations new to the area. Protestant missionaries, mainly from the United States, arrived in large numbers, as did proponents of other modern forms of spirituality, such as the Hare Krishnas. In 1988, the one thousandth anniversary of the conversion of Russia to Christianity was celebrated officially. By 1991, the last year of the Soviet Union, Church

leaders commonly attended official functions, while Soviet leaders jockeyed for photo ops at Christmas and Easter services.

The revival of Islam in Central Asia was quite muted in comparison.
Local Communist elites were much more circumspect about loosening
ideological control than their central counterparts were, and not until
1988 did they stop the surveillance and persecution of religious activities.
Thereafter, however, there was a rapid turn to Islam. Islam became visible in public again. Many people who had never prayed before began to
pray regularly and to observe other Islamic injunctions. It became possible again travel to Mecca for the annual pilgrimage, and every year thousands of people make the trip. New mosques began to be built, whereas
those that had long operated in disguise came out into the open and
sometimes moved to more appropriate premises. Some old landmark
mosques ("monuments of architecture") were put back into service. The
number of mosques in the region swelled, and religious education began
to be reestablished. Older ulama who had taught in secret (hujra) could
now do so in the open. A number of madrasas were opened in the first
years of independence to provide higher Islamic education. There was
also considerable interest in learning Arabic and especially the Arabic
script in which Central Asian languages had been written until the 1920s.
One could even begin to speak of an Islamic revival in the region.

Of course, this revival was not a simple return to the past. The legacy
of the Soviet era did not evaporate. It is present to this day, not just in the
social and political institutions but also in certain basic understandings
about society and politics that are widely shared by the population.
Indeed, the governments of Central Asia have had a lot to do with the
way the revival of Islam has progressed in the decade and a half since
independence in 1991. The new regimes have been wary of the power of
Islam, which they tend to view expansively. They have tried a dual strategy of attempting to co-opt Islam while controlling it.

•   •   •

For Central Asians, rediscovery of their national heritage meant, in part,
rediscovering Islam and Muslim culture and reestablishing links with the
broader Muslim world that had been severed by Soviet xenophobia.
Islam was part of the nation's ethical and spiritual values that had been
trampled on by the Soviets and that needed to be reclaimed in the new
age of national independence. The revival of Islam in contemporary
Central Asia is therefore a profoundly national phenomenon. It takes dif-

ferent forms in different countries of the region. In Uzbekistan and Tajikistan, the return to Islam takes the form of renewed interest in the achievements of the urban culture that flourished in Transoxiana in the centuries of Islam and of celebration of renowned figures of the Islamic tradition as national heroes. This celebration is, of course, not limited to Islamic figures. Poets and rulers of the Muslim past are also revered as great national heroes. In Kazakhstan and Kyrgyzstan, where the Soviet period had seen massive influxes of Russians, Islam carries a different burden. Here, a return to Islam represents an assertion of local (Kazakh or Kyrgyz) identity against the Russians, who had come to dominate local cultural life. The building of mosques has as much to do with asserting Kyrgyz or Kazakh presence in the physical landscape as anything else.

The most visible aspect of the revival of Islam was the rush to reopen disused mosques and to build new ones. During the Gorbachev years, mosques that had long operated in secret came out into the open, those that had fallen into disuse or been confiscated and put to other uses were reclaimed, and many new ones were built. The building boom receded considerably after the first couple years of independence, for two reasons. The economic crisis that accompanied the collapse of the Soviet economy made itself felt, limiting people's ability to pay for construction or repair projects. At the same time, as we will see below in greater detail, Tajikistan's slide into civil war and the deteriorating situation in Afghanistan made governments wary of all expressions of Islam and led them to curb popular enthusiasm for mosque construction. Especially in Uzbekistan, state controls were reestablished, which in many cases meant closing mosques. Still, every urban neighborhood and every sizable village in the region has a mosque now.

Central Asia was the birthplace of several Sufi orders, most notably the Naqshbandiya, which have spread all over the world. But Sufism suffered greatly from the Soviet assault on Islam. In the last years of the Soviet period, Sufis from the rest of the world flocked to Central Asia to visit the shrines of the founders of their orders, reestablish contacts with their confreres, and help resurrect their orders in their native lands. The mausoleums of Baha'uddin Naqshband outside Bukhara and of Ahmet Yesevi in the city of Turkistan in Kazakhstan receive large numbers of visitors from far afield, but national differences and language barriers have proven to be very real. Sufism has experienced a considerable revival locally—it helps that the new regimes support it as a form of "moderate," "humanist" Islam—but, as an Uzbek scholar notes, the new adepts' knowledge of the intricacies of Sufi ritual is often superficial, whereas older practices of initiation are widely disregarded.[3] Post-Soviet Sufism is not a return to the past but the creation of something new.

The region has seen a substantial amount of repair and reconstruction of local shrines. As we saw earlier in this book, shrines were what marked Central Asia as Muslim space. Visits to shrines continued throughout the Soviet period against all odds, even when shrines fell into disrepair or were destroyed. Since the Gorbachev years, interest in reopening shrines has grown steadily. The more prominent ones, such as the Naqshbandi and Yesevi shrines, have been taken over as state projects, but many others have been rebuilt through the initiative of individuals or communities. The pace of shrine reconstruction is perhaps the most hectic in Tajikistan, where despite the destructive civil war that followed independence (see chapter 6), new shrines dot the landscape and attract large numbers of pilgrims.

For most people, Islam continues to mean a "return" to national tradition, the rediscovery of a cultural heritage that was much maligned during the Soviet era. The celebration of tradition does not always sit well with the strictures of normative Islam. The celebration of weddings and funerals is, as we have seen, a central part of Islamic tradition in Central Asia. These occasions are celebrated at enormous expense that can leave the host burdened with debt. But because such celebrations are key to maintaining one's status and social obligations, and are now also legitimated as national tradition, they continue to be popular, despite the opposition of a host of critics. The Jadids, it will be remembered, faulted them for being a waste of money and for being unsanctioned by "true" Islam. To the Soviets, they were an irrational expenditure of resources. Today's authorities are wary of them for similar reasons. But when, in 2002, the official religious directorate of Kyrgyzstan declared such spendthrift practices to be against the dictates of Islam, the statement provoked outrage. "'Are we going back to [Soviet] times?' an angry inhabitant of the Kochkor region asked. 'During the Soviet dictatorship, one of our relatives was jailed for slaughtering a horse for his father's funeral. He didn't even have time to throw a lump of earth on his father's coffin.' The man's father added, 'What will happen if I die tomorrow and my son is denied the right to kill a calf? How will he be able to receive guests for several days in a dignified way? They can't go hungry! We have to preserve the traditions of our fathers.'"[4]

There remains a general suspicion of ostentatious shows of piety and a sense that the burden of piety does not fall on every individual. "Islam is a beautiful religion," a young friend of mine, a university graduate, once told me. "What it says about honesty and uprightness, the cleanliness of the heart, and respecting one's elders is, of course, beyond question. But I am still young, I have to enjoy my life, and so I can't yet live according to Islam." The Islamic revival in post-Soviet Central Asia shows little sign of affecting everyday life. There is little concern about observing the basic prohibitions of Islam against alcohol and even pork. The rhythms of everyday life remain secular in a way that is inconceivable even in other secular Muslim countries.

Pride in Islam as national heritage can coexist with complete lack of observance or indeed any belief at all, let alone a desire to live in an Islamic state. As a high school teacher of Uzbek literature said in a discussion group I used to attend in Tashkent, "Of course, I don't believe this stuff, but Islam was the religion of my forefathers, and they were not wrong either." The great figures of the region's Islamic past are great primarily because they contributed to the treasure house of human achievement. Sufism, in particular, can be seen as the region's contribution to the human spiritual quest, an indigenous humanist tradition that delivered a message of peace and that can be posited against the "scholastic" or "fanatical" traditions of "orthodox" Islam. In the Soviet era, public claims could only be made with reference to universal human values seen in materialist terms. Religion was considered a human construct, and a harmful one at that. That situation has not changed substantially. Islam is not God's binding command to humanity but an aspect of human creation. Sufism (and Islam in general) are thus being judged by external criteria. In post-Soviet Central Asia, the public space remains de-Islamized and therefore profoundly secular. Finally, there remains a substantial residue of the Soviet suspicion of religion and its potential to be put to unhealthy political uses. As we will see in chapter 7, the regimes all make use of this suspicion in their attempts to control Islam. They do not do so in a vacuum, however, for the suspicion is widely shared by large sections of the population.

The anthropologist Bruce Privratsky has called this attitude "religious minimalism." During his field research in Kazakhstan, Privratsky found that most people describe their religious life as *musïlmanshïlïq*, literally "Muslimness," or *taza jol*, "the clean path," rather than "Islam."[5] He notes that "this reflects discomfort with the abstraction of Islam as an ideology and a preference for Muslim life as an experience of the community." The community's experience of Islam need not be grounded in textual authority. Rather, as Privratsky shows, for most Kazakhs, being

Muslim is intertwined with cults of saints and holy places. Saints act as guardians of the *taza jol* for the whole community, whereas holy places (such as shrines and mosques) render the very territory on which Kazakhs live as Muslim. The community is Muslim by definition, and as long as some people (in practice, women, the elderly and certain descent groups) fulfill the ritual requirements, the rest of the population is absolved from them. Indeed, Privratsky records low levels of knowledge of Islam. Pilgrims at the shrine of Ahmet Yesevi associate the site with Islam but seldom with Sufism. They know the figure of Ahmet Yesevi only in the vaguest terms, as the man who "opened religion" in the region. Few Kazakhs know even the ritual affirmation of faith in Arabic and content themselves with the Kazakh phrase *Al-hamdulillah musïl-manmïn,* "Praise be to God, I am a Muslim."[6]

This religious minimalism does not mean, however, that Central Asians do not see themselves as Muslims; rather, it means that they see Islam as an integral part of their way of life. In a way, there is nothing new about this: historically, "customary" Islam, which ties community, custom, and tradition to Islam, has been the dominant way in which Muslims have understood Islam. In the modern world, this form of Islam has been challenged by numerous reformist movements and assaulted by secularizing states. In Central Asia, it survived in the interstices of Soviet society, but it did not remain unchanged. Today, customary Islam is wedded to modern national identities and exists in a political realm that is still de-Islamized. The traveler who flies into Central Asia from another Muslim country therefore notices a radical difference. The rhythms of everyday life in Central Asia are quite different in that the public presence of Islam is highly muted.

.   .   .

Gorbachev's easing of restrictions on travel breached the isolation of Soviet citizens from the rest of the world. For many Muslims, this represented an opportunity to reclaim Central Asia as part of the Muslim world. In 1990, the Saudi government sent one hundred thousand copies of the Qur'an to the Soviet Union to ease the severe shortage created by decades of Soviet prohibition against publishing or importing the scriptures. It also opened its coffers to pilgrims from the Soviet Union, who could now perform the hajj as guests of the Saudi state. Various Muslim organizations funded the publication of religious material in Russian and other languages, and missionaries of all stripes poured into Central Asia in those years. They came bearing different messages and with different agendas, which all added to the pluralization of Islam in the region. This honeymoon not last long, however. Central Asian regimes, wary at the best of times of the unauthorized movement of people or ideas, grew jittery after the Taliban took over Kabul in Afghanistan in 1996. Since then, activities of foreign Muslims have been greatly curbed.

Two Muslim groups are worth noting. The first is the Tablighi Jama'at, a movement founded by reformist ulama in India in 1929 with the aim of disseminating proper ritual and personal behavior among Muslims themselves. The movement focuses entirely on individual regeneration of Muslims through proper conduct modeled on the life of the Prophet as recounted in the hadith literature. Participants call other Muslims to proper conduct through *tabligh,* "proselytization." To this end, each participant is supposed to spend one night a week, three days a month, forty continuous days a year, and, ultimately, one hundred twenty days once in a lifetime, engaged in the mission. Women work among women, although occasionally they also travel with their male kin. Participants stay in mosques when on their missions. Over the years, the Tablighi Jama'at has been wildly popular, particularly in South Asia and among the South Asian diaspora, but also in many other parts of the world. There is no bureaucracy or formal organization, although annual gatherings—the biggest of which take place in Pakistan and Bangladesh—routinely attract hundreds of thousands of people. The Tablighi Jama'at eschews debate with other Muslims and is resolutely apolitical. The task of the movement is to bring about the regeneration of individuals, not the rectification of the political order. The movement does not challenge the authority of the ulama and is comfortable with Sufism. In the end, it is a self-help organization, established in a world in which physical mobility is possible, and as such, it is quintessentially modern. The historian Barbara Metcalf draws a parallel with Alcoholics Anonymous, a movement founded about the same time, which operates on similar principles of individual example and teaching of one another.[7]

Over the decades, the movement has spanned the globe, its missions crisscrossing the world, staying in a network of "tablighi mosques" and showing up in all sorts of locations with the invitation for Muslims to conduct their lives faithfully. Yet the Soviet Union had remained beyond its reach until the Gorbachev years. Since then, however, the Tablighis, as participants in the movement are called, have made their appearance in the region. They present, by their example, a vision of the good Muslim life achieved through proper fulfillment of ritual modeled on the life of the Prophet—emulating him in everything from how to pray and how to eat and sleep to what blessings to recite at various moments of the day. This approach stands in sharp contrast to local practices as they had evolved in the Soviet period. This pietism is resolutely apolitical, but it nevertheless attracts the suspicions of the regimes in the region.

A very different niche is occupied by the followers of Fethullah Gülen, a Turkish Sufi-inspired group that seeks the transformation of both individuals and society through education. Gülen (b. 1938) has articulated a vision of Islam that is at home with both the secular republic and the free market. Islam for him is both an identity and a system of morality. He draws his following from among the pious segments of the middle class that benefited from Turkey's turn to the free market in the 1980s, people who are financially successful and culturally conservative. The movement is based in a network of cultural foundations, benevolent societies, and a substantial media empire, through which it seeks to reshape the contours of public debate in Turkey. But the venue most central to the movement's program of inculcating solid moral values in the individual and society is education. The movement has established a network of private schools, in Turkey and abroad, that aim to educate a new elite that would be solidly grounded in Islamic morals and able to operate in a globalized, free-market world.

The Gülen schools arrived in Central Asia as early as 1992, in the wake of considerable Turkish investment. They have had the tacit support of the Turkish government, which sees in them a Turkish presence in the region. The schools have quickly carved a niche for themselves everywhere in Central Asia, except Uzbekistan, from which they were expelled in 2000, when relations with Turkey reached a nadir. The schools number around fifty in the remaining four countries of the region (most schools are for boys only, but girls' schools also exist). The schools are private, fee-based institutions and are thus accessible only to the elites, with whom they are popular because they offer a rigorous, world-class education and impart skills useful in the contemporary world. The language of instruction is English, though some subjects are taught in the language of the host country; the curriculum also includes Turkish and Russian. The schools possess excellent teaching materials and computer equipment and emphasize such traditional themes as respect for teachers *and* students, hygiene, personal appearance, and discipline. In keeping with local legislation, the curriculum of these schools is entirely secular, with only a few lessons in ethics (*ahlak*) presenting any moral teaching. Rather, the Gülen movement seeks to win hearts and minds by setting an example of excellence. There is nothing traditional, then, about the

Gülen school, which has little precedent in the Muslim tradition, either in Turkey or in Central Asia. In their enthusiasm for education, the followers of Gülen are heirs to the Jadids, but as the French anthropologist Bayram Balci argues, they are best understood as Muslim Jesuits in that they seek to transform society through educating the elites.[8]

Despite early fears that "Iranian-inspired fundamentalism" would sweep the region, Iranians have not had a presence on the religious scene of the region. The Sunni traditions of the region make it inhospitable to Iranian proselytism, but the Iranians have not even tried it. Iranian ambitions in the former Soviet Union have been purely "realistic"—focusing on establishing economic relations and ensuring the national security and territorial integrity of Iran. Given the geopolitical context of the region, Iran gets on better with Russia and Armenia than with its Muslim neighbors in Central Asia. The one focus of Iranian activity in Central Asia has been Tajikistan. Tajik is practically the same language as Persian, and Tajikistan sees itself as the heir to the long tradition of Persian culture in Transoxiana. It also feels threatened by its more populous Turkic-speaking neighbors. These circumstances provide the impetus for a relationship between the two countries, but the relationship remains purely cultural. The Iranian embassy in Dushanbe funds the publication of works by Tajik scholars and occasionally flies them off to conferences in Iran, but it has played no discernible role in Tajik politics or Tajik religious life.

What foreign movements do is to reintroduce Islam into the public life of the region. But these influences do not work in unison. Each movement brings its own agenda for change that is a product of the history of its country of origin. Moreover, these movements do not always fit in well with Central Asian realities. Although foreign movements have no doubt been successful in acquiring a local followings, the contacts are seldom free of friction: Sufis and Tablighis find language barriers difficult to surmount, whereas the Gülen schools are seen primarily as private schools for the elite. Finally, there remains a general sentiment that deprecates foreign Muslims (whether Arabs, Pakistanis, or Turks) who preach rigorous observance of Islam as unsuited to the temper of Central Asians.

·   ·   ·

The Islamic revival that began during the Gorbachev era was part of a much broader assertion of national identity that took place throughout the former Soviet Union in the late 1980s as glasnost broke old taboos. It involved the exploration of national and cultural legacies beyond the constraints placed on nationalist discourse by the regime. As we saw in chapter 4, the Soviet regime itself had fostered the development of national identities and provided guardians through its elaborate funding of a humanities intelligentsia. Yet, there were always limits to what could be said and what claims could be made. When glasnost allowed it, however, the intelligentsia turned on the regime and began challenging one taboo after another that had kept nationalities thinking within bounds acceptable to the regime. The Gorbachev period saw new political demands for greater rights for national groups and "their" republics. Republics and regions challenged the right of the center to legislate or to tax, but issues of culture took center stage: the use of national languages in government and education, the celebration of national heroes previously frowned upon, the filling in of blank spots in national histories, and the revival of once-outlawed national symbols. The intelligentsias of the various republics mobilized to roll back the status of Russian in the educational and bureaucratic institutions of non-Russian republics. One republic after another declared its own language to be the official language of communication. At bottom, of course, this national reassertion was very Soviet: it took for granted the basic assumptions underlying Soviet nationalities policies and challenged only the limits to Soviet discourse.

In Central Asia, the years after 1988 saw unprecedented interest in the rediscovery of the past. The mania for language reform arrived first. There were moves to exclude Russian loanwords from local languages, and, especially in Uzbekistan and Tajikistan. a renewed interest in learning the Arabic script in which these languages had been written until Latinization in 1928. Then came an attempt to fill in the blanks in national history that had been censored away in the Soviet period. Here, too, the basic outline of national history was left intact from the Soviet period—the ideas, for instance, that the five or six "nations" of Central Asia had always existed, that the region's history and heritage could be divided up among them, and that the past was only the prelude to the national present. What changed were the details: Timur went from being a villain to a hero, various figures of the early twentieth century similarly traded places, and the Russian conquest came to be called a conquest (rather than annexation, as had been obligatory since the 1930s). This shift also led to national claims and counterclaims that went beyond the limits imposed by Soviet-era common sense and censorship. Notions of ancient ethnic animosities emerged as a component of Gorbachev-era politics, as did territorial disputes between different republics.

This interest in the nation was harnessed by local Communist elites and put to good political use. It was common in the immediate aftermath of the Soviet collapse to think that it had been caused by nationalism—that the nations that the Soviets had kept in their prison house had risen up and thrown off their chains.[9] The reality was far more mundane, especially in Central Asia, where local Party elites displayed considerable agility during the final crisis of the Soviet Union and emerged firmly in control. Far from being a subversive phenomenon, nationalism had provided Party elites a way of maintaining themselves in power.

The beginning was inauspicious. The Brezhnevite contract that had kept Central Asia quiet during the late Soviet period had begun to unravel even before Gorbachev came to power. During his brief stint as general secretary, Yuri Andropov (1982–84) had made the elimination of corruption a major priority. Of course, the whole system of rule in the national republics of the Soviet Union was built on "corruption"—the exercise, sometimes furtive, sometimes not, of power beyond its formal limits—and it was corruption alone that kept the system going. As Andropov and his successors found out, however, fighting corruption could bring the roof crashing down on the whole show. Attacks by the center on "corrupt" national leaders were seen as attacks on the nation as a whole and produced nationalist backlashes.

The episode that caught the most attention at the time was the dismissal, in December 1986, of Dinmuhamed Kunaev from his long tenure as first secretary of the Communist Party of Kazakhstan. He was replaced by Gennady Kolbin, an ethnic Russian sent from Russia to put the Kazakh party in order. The announcement of these changes produced three days of rioting in Almaty, the capital of Kazakhstan, as students protested this slight to Kazakh national honor. But a deeper crisis was playing out in Uzbekistan. In September 1982, with Brezhnev still alive, authorities in Moscow had established a commission to investigate massive fraud in the reporting of cotton harvests of that republic. Systematic overreporting of cotton harvests had enabled officials to siphon off billions of rubles from the central treasury. Technically, this act was corruption, but overreporting was occasioned in part by the ridiculously high production quotas set by the center—Uzbekistan alone was expected to produce more than six million tons of cotton a year—and the center, as a monopoly buyer, paid prices well below those on the world market. Investigators revealed an elaborate web of intrigue that pervaded all levels of authority in the region and extended to figures in Moscow, including Yuri Churbanov, Brezhnev's son-in-law. The so-called cotton affair cast a long shadow over Central Asia in the 1980s, well into the Gorbachev years. It occasioned one last purge, in which thousands of members were expelled from the Party, hundreds of plant managers and kolkhoz directors were fired, and the local leadership was rearranged. Sharaf Rashidov, the first secretary of Uzbekistan's Communist Party, died suddenly just as the campaign was getting off the ground, and rumors persist that he committed suicide. He was buried with full honors but was disgraced posthumously, and his name came to be synonymous in the official press with corruption, nepotism, and greed—all that had gone wrong with the Soviet Union in the Brezhnev years (now termed "the era of stagnation").

This reassertion of central authority in Central Asia was catastrophic for local political elites, for whom the mid-1980s were a period of great disarray, as Party leaders were replaced in quick succession. As chapter 4 points out, the Party organizations in each republic had become networks for the allocation of resources in which various factions (or "clans") competed. The disarray of the 1980s altered the balance of factions and brought new faces to the fore. The leaders who found themselves heading the Party organizations in Central Asian republics were less secure in their power than their predecessors in the Brezhnev generation. Nevertheless, the reassertion of central authority had also provoked a great deal of resentment among the population. In Uzbekistan, the investigation acquired the name "Red landing" (*krasnyi desant*), an invasion by a foreign force and an affront to Uzbek national honor. The Party leadership harnessed this sense of dishonor to rebuild its authority. Leaders quickly reinvented themselves as guardians of the nation, as defenders of its interests and its honor.

Yet, for all this, the Party leaderships in Central Asia could not imagine a political framework other than that of the Soviet Union. The union's impending collapse prompted them to throw their weight behind its preservation. In March 1991, with the political structure of the Soviet Union in grave crisis, Gorbachev initiated a countrywide referendum on whether the Soviet Union should be preserved on the basis of a renegotiated union treaty between the fifteen federal republics. Six republics (Estonia, Latvia, Lithuania, Moldova, Georgia, and Armenia) refused to take part in the referendum. The republics of Central Asia not only voted but expressed near-unanimous support for the preservation of the union (see table 3). Even if the voting figures from Central Asia look suspiciously like standard Soviet-era "election" results, they nevertheless indi-

TABLE 3. RESULTS OF THE MARCH 1991
REFERENDUM ON PRESERVING THE UNION

Republic	Total Votes	Turnout (%)	"Yes"	%	"No"	%
Russia	79,701,169	75.4	56,860,783	71.3	21,030,753	26.4
Belarus	6,126,983	83.3	5,069,313	82.7	986,079	16.1
Ukraine	31,514,244	83.5	22,110,899	70.2	8,820,089	28.0
Azerbaijan	2,903,797	75.1	2,709,246	93.3	169,225	5.8
Abkhazia	166,544	52.3	164,231	98.6	1,566	0.9
Kazakhstan	8,816,543	88.2	8,295,519	94.1	436,560	5.0
Kyrgyzstan	2,174,593	92.9	2,057,971	94.6	86,245	4.0
Tajikistan	2,407,552	94.2	2,315,755	96.2	75,300	3.1
Turkmenistan	1,847,310	97.7	1,804,138	97.9	31,203	1.7
Uzbekistan	9,816,333	95.4	9,196,848	93.7	511,373	5.2

SOURCE: *Pravda,* March 27, 1991.
NOTE: Abkhazia is an autonomous republic within Georgia. Its leadership decided to participate in the referendum despite Georgia's boycott.

cate a continuity with the Soviet period that has continued to structure the interplay between state and society.

Central Asian Party leaders also supported the attempted putsch against Gorbachev in August 1991. Only when the plan failed did they hastily turn to independence, cashing in on their status as national leaders to declare their republics independent of Moscow. They retained their grip on power, which was threatened by a democratized reconstitution of the Soviet Union, by claiming it in the name of the nation. Western observers had expected nationalism to liberate the various nations of the Soviet Union from the Communist regime. Instead, nationalism became the vehicle for the Communist Party elites to retain their power. Communist *apparatchiki,* all of whom had risen to power only recently, suddenly became founding fathers of new national states.

· · ·

Central Asia inherited not just the Soviet economy and Soviet institutions but also the Soviet legal system, policing structures, and many social and official attitudes about power, politics, and the relationship between state and society. There has also been a marked continuity in the personnel who staff the institutions of power. More significantly, the networks of power, the so-called clans that took control of political and economic resources in the Soviet period, have not been dislodged from their position. Indeed, the postindependence trajectories of Central Asian states make little sense except in the context of the politics of these networks and their machinations to retain control of resources and exclude others from it. The patterns of recruitment into government service or into positions of control over the economy have not shifted dramatically. Central Asian states are run by the same elites today that were in power in the late Soviet period. Change in formal institutional structures is limited to the downgrading of the party-state, which was the conduit for the distribution of resources in the Soviet era. In the immediate aftermath of Soviet collapse, local branches of the Communist Party quickly renamed themselves, and many of them managed to stay in power as bearers of the will of the nation. But their function as a patronage machine is gone, and power has increasingly concentrated in the executive branch, which towers above all other aspects of state power.

One should not assume, however, that simply because the new regimes are corrupt, they are unpopular. All five regimes discussed above have banked on nationalism to acquire a substantial fund of legitimacy. They have all acted to "nationalize" their states—that is, to make the states ostensibly the instruments of the will of the nation, the nation being the ethnonational group from which each country takes its name. Each state presents itself as the result of centuries-long striving of its nation to unite and gain political independence, a process that was rudely interrupted by Russian conquest and then the continuation, ostensibly, of Russian rule under the Soviet guise. Although the details vary from country to country, in practical terms, nationalization of the state means the elevation of indigenous languages to official status at the expense of Russian, the promotion of members of indigenous nationality to positions of leadership in the bureaucracy and in the professions, and the constant celebration of national history.

This process of nationalization is a perfectly normal thing for new states. What is striking about Central Asia is that, the claims of the regimes notwithstanding, nationalization takes place almost entirely within Soviet parameters. Making each republic the home of a nation, in which its language would be paramount and the bureaucracy would be recruited from its own ethnic majority, was a major (unfulfilled) goal of Soviet nationalities policy. Similarly, the national history that each regime celebrates was conceptualized in the Soviet period. The only difference is that Soviet-era constraints in the celebration of national glory can now be dispensed with.

But if the new states celebrate their history, they profess to look to the future, not the past. In the official rhetoric of the regimes, the task for the present is to achieve a better tomorrow. This task is conceived in entirely worldly terms: achieving economic progress, improving educational and health indicators, and so forth. Public discourse remains entirely secular, with no attempt to use Islam to legitimize the authority of the state. The new constitutions written in the aftermath of the Soviet collapse all retain Soviet-era provisions for the separation of religion from the state and from education. State schools remain resolutely secular, with no religious education whatsoever, not even in the guise of lessons in ethics or morality, which feature prominently in the curricula of most Muslim (and non-Muslim) states. In a fundamental sense, then, the de-Islamization of public life characteristic of the Soviet period is still solidly in place.

．　．　．

The regimes' response to Islam can only be understood in this context. There is plenty of evidence from the Soviet era to indicate that local authorities were more hostile to Islam than their central counterparts were. It was one thing for weddings and funerals to be accompanied by muted forms of Islamic ritual; it was quite another for religious figures to claim any public presence. Antireligious propaganda continued to issue forth in the Central Asian press well into the era of glasnost, and Party resolutions continued to spout clichés about the need to "intensify the struggle against manifestations of religion and harmful traditions and rituals" and about the "significance of atheistic education under conditions of ever deeper democratization," as perestroika was called in official discourse.

At the same time, the political leadership had no choice but to stake its own claims to the region's Islamic revival. The result is a complex but quite logical position toward Islam. On the one hand, the new regimes celebrate the Islamic cultural heritage of the region and invoke the moral and ethical values stemming from it. In doing so, they share the sentiments of a great number of their citizens, who, as we saw above, do relate to Islam primarily as part of their national heritage and way of life. On the other hand, they make no bones about their hostility to the wrong kind of Islam, one that makes political claims of any sort, or indeed one whose expression the regimes do not control. Armed with an essentialist view of religion, they share a basic suspicion of any public activity that betrays an affiliation with Islam. Such activity is improper, being either a cover for personal ambitions or an attempt to subvert the established order. The threshold of what is considered improper is very low. Therefore, all Central Asian states take for granted the right to regulate religious life through formal bureaucratic channels, and on their terms. They can cope only with religious activity that is formally structured, and all protestations about the separation of religion and state notwithstanding, they have no hesitation in interfering in religious affairs and curtailing activity they deem undesirable.[10]

In the first years of independence, the new regimes paid considerable heed to Islamic symbols: the new presidents took their oaths of office on the Qur'an, and several of them went to Mecca as pilgrims. This ardor cooled rapidly by the mid-1990s, as Tajikistan plunged into a civil war in which Islam played a role and as the Taliban rose to ascendancy in neighboring Afghanistan. Although Islam is celebrated as part of national heritage, it must also conform to the state's vision of national heritage. The latter measure defines what aspects of Islam are celebrated. Islam is effectively nationalized. The great mosques and mausoleums are still celebrated as "architectural monuments" and national contributions to the world's cultural heritage. Similarly, Sufism has been adopted as an example of the humanist traditions of the region, an indigenous tradition of "free thought" that stood outside the "fanatical" scholasticism of the ulama. In Kazakhstan, the regime has turned Ahmet Yesevi, the founder of the Yesevi Sufi order and the "bringer of Islam" to the steppe, into a figure of national importance. In Uzbekistan, the great scholars of the Islamic tradition who hailed from cities now in Uzbekistan—men like Imam al-Bukhari, the great collector of hadith; the jurists al-Marghinani and al-Maturidi; and the Sufi master Baha'uddin Naqshband—have been co-opted as great sons of Uzbekistan and celebrated in lavish jubilees as the country's contributions to human knowledge and Islamic civilization. These jubilees are, however, entirely in the Soviet mode and celebrate the heroes from a vantage point that is completely outside the Islamic tradition.

And while the new regimes assert their respect for the spiritual heritage of their nations, they resolutely oppose the wrong kind of Islam. Such Islam, not part of the nation's traditions, denotes backwardness, obscurantism, and fanaticism and is bound to knock the nation from its path to progress. Two forces are at work here: first, a great residue of the Soviet critique of religion, and second, deep hostility to all alternative sources of power and authority. The new regimes thus present the wrong kind of Islam and its proponents in an entirely negative light. In their view, those who seek a political role for Islam are driven solely by a lust for power. For Karimov, the need exists "to make clear the difference between the spiritual values of religion and certain ambitions—political and other aggressive goals—which are far from religion."[11] The Karimov regime offers a stark choice to the people of Uzbekistan: they can have a future led by "enlightened people with a scientific world view" who are able to combine the best aspects of modern life and their heritage, or by "barbarians . . . ignorant, uneducated people who use pseudo-Islamic slogans to increase their own power."[12] The good of the nation requires that the wrong kind of Islam be kept in check.

As we will see in chapter 7, the attempt to keep the wrong kind of Islam leads to rampant persecution of all manner of unsanctioned religious activity. In Uzbekistan, particularly, the state has waged a merciless campaign against "extremism" that defines the religious landscape in the country. Everywhere, the Islamic revival is intertwined with, and limited by, the postindependent state, which remains resolutely de-Islamized.

·   ·   ·

Women's roles have changed across Central Asia since the Gorbachev years. The Soviet legacy was complex, as we have seen. The state brought all women out of the home—sometimes violently, as was the case with the hujum in Central Asia—and into the sphere of "productive labor." The Soviets took great pride in the number of women in the workforce or in school. Although Central Asia lagged behind the rest of the country in these indicators, it was far ahead of its Muslim neighbors. Bringing women into productive labor was not accompanied, however, by any serious reckoning with the issue of gender equality. Soviet social thought took for granted that gender differences were real and natural and continued to treat men and women as different categories of people. Not surprisingly, therefore, the Soviet state also pursued natalist policies, more explicitly so at some times than at others, that rewarded women for having many children. (The rewards ranged from generous maternity leaves and practically free child care to medals for women who bore five or ten children.) Women were unveiled and engaged in the workforce, but social life continued to be highly gendered.

Calls for a return to national values lead to a traditionalization of women's roles—the return to a tradition that may in fact never have existed in quite the same form but that is now valorized as authentic, and hence desirable. Many of the incumbent regimes use the rhetoric of family values to legitimate their policies. The years since independence have, therefore, seen the erosion of many of the achievements of the Soviet era. Although women are still a large part of the workforce (they have to be, in order to support themselves), they also face pressure to accord to "traditional" norms of wife and mother. This pressure has become all the more compelling as jobs have evaporated since the collapse of the Soviet economy. Although women continue to have high expectations of the state as a provider of welfare benefits, few states actually have the resources to continue to supply such benefits and therefore seek shelter in traditional values that consign women back to the house, and off the state's books.

Being a good Uzbek, for instance, means respecting one's elders, being hospitable, and thinking of the family as the bastion of the good society. The government declared 2000 to be the "Year of the Family," in which the family was to be celebrated and protected. The latter was achieved by making divorce very difficult, especially when initiated by the wife. The new model of the good Uzbek woman emphasizes the need for wives and mothers to be kind and get along. Islam is only tangentially involved here. The governments never mention Islam in their rhetoric, appealing instead to "national values." No doubt, these values have been shaped to a certain extent by Islam, but they more readily reflect local patriarchal structures that are justified, rather than created, by Islam. Likewise, in all five countries, personal law continues to derive from the civil code inherited from the Soviets. The shariat and its stipulations on the question of family law or gender relations have no legal force at all.

Nevertheless, the celebration of tradition makes certain behaviors socially acceptable (and even widespread) even though they remain illegal. Polygamy, for instance, remains illegal in all five countries, even though it is acceptable under the shariat. In practice, however, it has become increasingly common for men to take on second or third wives by marrying them only in a religious ceremony. Although illegal, such marriages are socially acceptable. The lack of state recognition, however, puts the junior wives at a disadvantage, leaving them with no recourse to the law if things go wrong. Nevertheless, the practice is accepted because it is sanctioned by tradition, and it serves the real need to provide support and protection to women without employment. Indeed, calls have arisen, often from women's groups, to legalize polygamy for precisely this reason: that polygamy is not going to go away, and the state might as well recognize it and bring it under legal supervision.[13] At the same time, desperate poverty pushes a growing number of women into sex work. Prostitution has exploded in Central Asia, where, as in the rest of the postsocialist world, the advent of the market economy is felt first and foremost in the business of sex and the selling of women's bodies. The easing of restrictions on foreign travel means that Central Asian women can work in many foreign sex markets, from Turkey, through the United Arab Emirates, to Thailand. Here, too, Central Asia's experience mirrors that of the postsocialist world. In Eastern Europe and the Baltic states, as societies seek to return to a "normal" life after the "interruption" by socialism, women's positions are being redefined both in theory and practice. "Normalization" often means a "return" to prerevolutionary gender roles, with an emphasis on domesticity and motherhood. Yet, at the same time, the market economy and the economic collapse combine to turn women into commodities. It is therefore no paradox that the glorification of women as the bearers of the nation goes hand in hand with an unprecedented rise in prostitution and pornography.[14]

·   ·   ·

A visit to a bookstore in Central Asia provides a salutary lesson in the peculiarities of the region's Islamic revival. During the decades of Soviet-imposed isolation, Central Asia diverged from the rest of the Muslim world in many respects. At the same time that Soviet education produced nearly universal literacy in the Cyrillic script, other Soviet policies led to the almost complete disappearance of religious literature from the region, which could neither be published nor imported. Islamic knowledge was confined to manuscript or oral sources. In much of the rest of the Muslim world, however, the twentieth century produced a media revolution. Although no Muslim country quite achieved the levels of literacy that Soviet Central Asia did, mass education in other countries did produce a literate audience that could consume religious knowledge through new media—most notably, the printed books mass-produced by a publishing industry that rose in the twentieth century but also, in the later decades of the century, media such as radio, television, cassette tapes, posters, and computers. These new media have transformed the way in which many Muslims relate to Islam and to religious authority.[15] Central Asia saw none of this media revolution. When glasnost finally allowed the publication of religious literature, the economic crisis produced by the collapse of the Soviet economy dampened the possibilities of a revolution in publishing. Since then, censorship and official vigilance have also set limits on the types of materials that can and cannot be published.

Although "Islamic" books have appeared in substantial numbers over the past decade, religious publishing in Central Asia differs dramatically from that in other Muslim countries. The majority of Islamic books available in the region introduce the basic tenets of Islam or provide basic Islamic knowledge that was lost during the Soviet period. Most are books of piety, acquainting the reading public with prayers and rituals. Some are newer editions of books from before the revolution, either transcribed into Cyrillic or in the original Arabic script. The choice of titles seems to be quite random, depending primarily on what older texts are at hand. Also available are "classic" texts transcribed into Cyrillic and presented with a scholarly apparatus. Although the content of these works is different from that of Soviet Orientalism, their publication is located in the same tradition. The intent behind their publication is to retrieve the cultural and spiritual heritage of the nation, although the publications are, of course, open to purely "religious" use. Works of contemporary Islamic thought, about Islamic law or jurisprudence, or about Muslim figures not connected with Central Asia can be found, ironically enough, only in Russian, and only outside Uzbekistan. In the summer of 2004, I found Russian translations of works by Sayyid Qutb, Maududi, and Khomeini available for sale in Kazakhstan. These editions had all been published by foreign Islamic foundations around the time of the Soviet collapse. Also available were manuals of Islamic conduct, including many translations of contemporary works from the Arab world, published in Russia. These materials are not available in Kazakh, and they are proscribed entirely in Uzbekistan.

What does this situation tell us about the nature of the Islamic revival in Central Asia? Censorship and the regimes' suspicion of Islamic publishing keep us from drawing unambiguous conclusions from these data. The only politically charged Islamic materials that are freely available are fliers—illegal by definition—circulated by groups such as the Hizb-ut-Tahrir (see chapter 6). Would substantial demand exist for such material were it freely available? It is difficult to tell, although the evidence in this chapter of the national character of the Islamic revival leads one to suspect that the answer would be no. The resurgence of piety does not lead directly to the politicization of Islam.

.   .   .

Finally, we must remember that Islam is not the only religion to make a comeback in the former Soviet Union. The late Soviet religious revival affected all parts of the population, especially the large European populations of Central Asia. These populations had long been used to being the "elder brothers" to the region's indigenous peoples, the heroes who would lead the natives to the millennium of Communism. With that dream destroyed, Christianity is left to serve as the marker of local Europeans' superiority over the natives. Churches have been reopened or built anew throughout Central Asia. In Kazakhstan and Kyrgyzstan, where Russians still dominate the cities, the Christian revival has a very public presence. Nevertheless, the Russian Orthodox Church has worked out a secure niche for itself in the region, by portraying itself as intimately linked with its history. It claims all of Central Asia as its canonical territory, where the church is at home. It does not, however, seek to proselytize—only to minister to the Christian population of the region. It thus presents itself as a "traditional" religion native to the region and loyal to the new political order.[16]

The main challenge, however, comes from the host of new denominations—ranging from the Hare Krishnas to the Baha'is, Falun Gong, and various evangelical Christian sects—that have appeared in the region since the collapse of the Soviet Union. These so-called new religions invariably come from the West, are well funded, and enjoy the protection afforded by their Western passports. Although some of the Christian groups are openly missionary, others operate in the guise of humanitarian, nongovernmental organizations. They benefit from the general prestige attached to foreigners in the region. Many American groups, for example, present themselves as the epitome of the American way of life. They also provide moral and material help—English lessons, health care, food aid—that attract young people.

In their rejection of local customs and traditions, Christian groups share something with the new Islamic movements in Central Asia, but, of course, they carry different baggage. Islamic reform movements claim to be purifying an indigenous tradition and returning the local community to an allegedly more pristine state. The call to evangelical Christianity, in contrast, represents a challenge to the community's sense of cultural and even national identity. Still, evangelical Christian groups have found considerable success in Kazakhstan, Kyrgyzstan, and more recently, in

Tajikistan as well. Most of the new converts are Russians, Koreans, and Ukrainians, but there have been conversions among the Muslim population as well. Most of the conversions are individual, mainly by educated youth who find that customary Islamic practices of their community lack spiritual content. Evangelical Christianity represents a different kind of religiosity than the traditional religions of the region, Islam and Orthodox Christianity alike, in that it emphasizes an intense commitment to the faith and an obligation to proselytize.

The new proselytism is widely resented, although not for religious reasons. Missionaries are routinely accused of using underhanded methods in their quest for conversion. As one young Tajik woman complained, "I am very annoyed by Christian missionaries—because they use and abuse the situation of people who are in a difficult time to manipulate them."[17] The new proselytism is also seen as an attack on *national* traditions, an affront to the people's customs. This problem has led to conflict in many places and appeals by citizens to curb the activities of "foreign" churches (even when the missionaries are local converts). For example, in 2002, the inhabitants of the tiny village of Qaynar-bulaq in southern Kazakhstan accused the local Jehovah's Witnesses of luring the village's children to services by offering them chocolates and sweets, things that few parents in the village could afford. The elders of the village told a journalist, "We are Muslims, and our children will also be Muslims. The Jehovah's Witnesses should get out of our village or we will solve the problem by force."[18] Similar incidents have occurred all over the region, and although few have come to violence, the tension remains. The governments are caught in a bit of a bind: the new constitutions adopted after independence all grant the freedom of religion and of proselytism (although, as we shall see in the following chapter, these provisions do not stop the governments from imposing strict controls on Islam), and the governments realize how sensitive interfering with foreign religious groups can be. Based in the West (or affiliated with organizations based in the West), the new religious groups can bring considerable pressure to bear on host governments in case of mistreatment. For this reason, new religious groups find it easier to register with local governments as officially recognized entities than local Muslims can. Western diplomats tend to view the governments' refusal to register mosques as a purely internal issue. Yet local governments are less than thrilled with the activities of "new religions," which they too deem an invasion of the national heritage and interference in local affairs by powerful foreigners. They also worry that the activities of such groups might incite general unrest and religious hatred and even promote radicalization of local religious traditions.

. . .

The Islamic revival in Central Asia was a grassroots movement, as non-state groups asserted their presence in the public realm. It involved the exploration of national and cultural legacies beyond the constraints placed on debate by the regime. Such activity made Soviet political elites very nervous: Central Asian Party leaders enjoyed the status of national leaders, but they were wary of any activity that challenged their monopoly over power. A great deal of the hostility toward Islam during the independence period stems from this instinctive suspicion that political elites have for unauthorized social action.

More people say their prayers than in the Soviet period, whether in private or at the mosque; more people fast during Ramadan than before; the number of those performing the hajj, the pilgrimage to Mecca, has increased massively. Births, marriages, and deaths are solemnized in more Islamic forms than before, with prayer assuming a more central role in the proceedings than before. But one should not assume that piety and stricter observance of Islamic injunctions have direct political implications. The politicization of Islam nowhere has a direct relation with piety. Rather, it is connected with how Islam is deployed in politics, how the authority of Islam is used to justify or legitimate political action, and which interpretations of Islam come to dominate the political landscape of a country. Islamic political movements are, after all, *political* phenomena, to be explained by the same analytical tools as any other political phenomenon; they do not spring simply from piety or observance of ritual.

CHAPTER 6

Islam in Opposition

In November 1991, as Central Asia lurched toward independence, Islam Karimov, the recently proclaimed president of Uzbekistan, paid a visit to the city of Namangan in the Ferghana Valley to meet local Party and government officials. Various informal groups, many of them religious, had been told that their representatives would also be able to meet Karimov and present their ideas to him. In the event, however, Karimov refused to meet them and flew back to Tashkent. As news of this snub spread through the town, a group called Adolat (Justice) organized a mass rally to demand that Karimov return to Namangan and meet with public figures. The situation became serious enough that Karimov flew back the following day to meet with the crowd. The meeting was tense: Karimov was jostled by the crowd, and the organizers of the meeting, Tohir Yo'ldoshev and Jumaboy Hojiyev, spoke to him rudely as they presented their demands, which ranged from the immediate and the concrete to the far-reaching and abstract. Adolat demanded that the building that housed the city committee of the Communist Party be turned into an Islamic center and called for the legalization of Islamic parties and the establishment of an Islamic state in Uzbekistan.

Here, finally, were Muslims who could "make trouble," as the CIA had hoped in 1984, but they had come too late and were not welcome. The episode, along with developments in neighboring Tajikistan, where an Islamic party was playing a crucial role in that country's unfolding civil war, put the threat of "Islamic fundamentalism" or "extremism" firmly on the forefront of the security agenda of the region. To many observers, the rise of movements such as Adolat seemed to confirm their view that the politicization of Islam was a logical culmination of the Islamic revival that had begun during the Gorbachev years. Today, this assessment is shared by all incumbent regimes in the region and to a large measure drives their domestic policies. Nowhere is this pattern more evident than in Uzbekistan. Karimov rode out the crisis with Adolat successfully. He accepted the first demand and promised to consider the other two, but as soon as he was able to reassert his authority, he had security agencies root out all militias in the Ferghana Valley. The Islamic center in Namangan was closed, nearly seventy activists were arrested, and other activists fled to Tajikistan.[1] But the episode was a defining moment for Karimov. A Soviet technocrat then still finding his feet at the head of the republic's government, he has since reinvented himself as the father of the nation. His instincts about religion and its place in society, as well as about opposition, are nevertheless purely Soviet. He found the confrontation with Adolat personally humiliating, but it also hardened his attitude toward opposition couched in Islamic terms. Ever since, he has been an implacable foe of all expressions of Islam that he has not expressly authorized.

Islam and Islamic sentiment have continued to feature in the opposition to the order that emerged in the aftermath of the Soviet collapse. Such opposition has taken many different forms, from worship outside of state-sanctioned institutions to the organization of secret societies such as the Hizb-ut-Tahrir al-Islami (HTI) and violent opposition to the established order. The civil war that marked Tajikistan's emergence as an independent state featured the Islamic Renaissance Party (Hizbi Nahzati Islomii Tojikiston, or IRP), whose opponents accused it of seeking the establishment of an Islamic state. The founders of Adolat ended up in Afghanistan, where they radicalized and formed the Islamic Movement of Uzbekistan, a jihadist outfit with links to al-Qaeda. Uzbekistan has seen outbursts of violence: the IMU launched incursions into Uzbekistani territory in 1999 and 2000, and there were bombings in Tashkent, the capital, in 1999 and 2004.

Radical Islamic movements do exist in post-Soviet Central Asia, but their scale and scope need more careful examination than they usually receive. All too often, authors are content to take the existence of Islamic rhetoric as proof of Islamist militancy.[2] We need to ask a number of questions: What are the differences between the various movements in their inspiration, their goals, and their base of support? Where do such movements fit in the post-Soviet religious and political landscapes of Central Asia? Are these movements seamlessly connected to transnational Islamic networks, or are they primarily expressions of domestic opposition to existing regimes? How do local activists deploy Islamic arguments? What, for instance, do they mean when they demand the promulgation of "Islamic law" or the establishment of an "Islamic state"? After all, the modern world has no single model of an Islamic state: states as diverse as the populist, constitutional, and quasi-democratic republic of Iran; the absolute monarchy of Saudi Arabia; and the military dictatorship in Pakistan have all proclaimed themselves to be Islamic. Similarly, calls to implement the shariat are never transparent. In practice, the shariat has never been a neatly codified system of canon law; it is a system of jurists' law, a legal discourse, forever in flux and often independent of state power. What is to become of the shariat when it is conceived as statutory law? Who should define it, who should interpret it, and who should implement it? These questions are of the utmost importance, but they lie latent in the proclamations of protagonists.

In Central Asia, these questions cannot always be answered precisely. As we will see in detail in chapter 7, the region's governments find the existence of an Islamic threat quite useful in justifying their authoritarian behavior. Consequently, they tend to portray all local political expressions of Islam as tied intimately to transnational networks of Islamist militancy and to exaggerate the threat posed by them. Information about the groups in question is not always easy to come by, but we also have to deal with disinformation from the region's governments. Nevertheless, we know enough to attempt a close examination of the three main Islamic groups that have appeared in post-Soviet Central Asia. Although these disparate movements operate in a new global milieu, they are rooted in local issues. To a certain extent, they are a result of the pluralization of Islam in the post-Soviet period, but they too bear the burden of the Soviet past in significant ways. Ultimately, they are a form of opposition to the political order that emerged with the demise of the Soviet Union. They give voice, each in its own way, to discontent that has plenty of reason to exist, given the inequities that abound and the repression that is commonplace. Their rise is therefore contingent upon local circumstances. Finally, we must see them in perspective. These groups do not have a monopoly on the expression of discontent or on Islam in the region. They do not have a mass following, and their message does not resonate with the population at large. I examine them at great length here not because of their popularity but because they tend to dominate discussions of Central Asian politics.

•   •   •

As the collapse of the Soviet Union redefined the world's geopolitics, the initial reaction in the West was fear that "Iranian-inspired fundamentalism" would spread and destabilize the region. Having used Islam to battle the Soviet Union in Afghanistan, American leaders were now afraid that Central Asia might fall prey to the wrong kind of Islam. During a tour of the region in February 1992, the U.S. Secretary of State, James Baker, repeatedly exhorted the leaders of the newly independent countries to follow the path of Turkey rather than that of Iran. Central Asians were Muslims, the assumption seemed to be, and must act as Muslims. As Muslims, they apparently had only two choices, "secular" Turkey or "fundamentalist" Iran, as if these two choices exhausted all possibilities and as if Central Asia's own history counted for nothing. Iran, it turned out, had little ambition to export its revolution: Iranian foreign policy toward Central Asia has been shaped by perfectly ordinary goals of ensuring national economic and security interests. Turkey's presence, too, has been much more muted than was expected. What Baker overlooked was Afghanistan.

After the Soviet withdrawal from Afghanistan in February 1989, the United States lost all interest in that unfortunate country and left. Pakistan and Saudi Arabia, which had interests of their own in the war, remained behind and continued to pour in arms and money to the various factions of the mujahidin. The enemy having vanished, the mujahidin fell out among themselves, as Afghanistan descended into anarchy and statelessness. The collapse of the Soviet Union sounded the death knell for the Communist government that had continued to exist in Kabul, thanks to financial support from Moscow, until early 1992. While Baker exhorted Central Asians to eschew fundamentalism, the United States maintained its refusal to speak to the secular Afghan government in Kabul in the hope that the mujahidin would oust it. With his foreign support cut off, Najibullah, the president of Afghanistan, pleaded with the United States to make common cause with his government against the fundamentalism represented by the mujahidin. "If fundamentalism comes to Afghanistan," he told an American journalist who was one of the few to venture to Kabul, "war will continue for many more years.

Afghanistan will turn into a center of world smuggling for narcotic drugs. Afghanistan will be turned into a center for terrorism."[3] Prophetic words, indeed. The following month, the mujahidin took Kabul and, unable to form a working government, plunged the country ever deeper into civil war and anarchy. Afghanistan became a vast stateless expanse, its territory divided up among warlords who recognized no law except their own, its economy taken over by drugs, and its infrastructure destroyed beyond recognition. The country had become a haven for terrorism—all as a by-product of an American proxy war.

This situation was to radicalize and militarize Islamic movements across a vast swath of territory. Many of the volunteers who had come from all over the Muslim world to fight the Soviets stayed behind and looked for other causes to join. They also continued to attract new recruits. The chaos in Afghanistan, combined with Saudi and Pakistani machinations, was to produce the Taliban later in the decade, but it also helped radicalize the tiny Islamic opposition in Central Asia. As we shall see, the IMU became what it did because of Afghanistan. The situation also defined the political climate in which the states of Central Asia took their first steps as independent actors on the world stage. Even if the leaders of Central Asia had needed confirmation of their hostility to Islam as a political force—and most did not—they found it aplenty in Afghanistan. Throughout the 1990s, the government of Uzbekistan explicitly used Afghanistan, torn apart by war and rife with the most militant Islamist currents, as a model of all that Uzbekistan must avoid.

•   •   •

The politicization of Islam in Central Asia began at home, however, and its first seeds were sown already in the 1970s in the milieu of underground Islamic learning (hujra) described in chapter 4. This milieu was torn asunder by a bitter dispute when some of Muhammadjon Hindustoniy's students rebelled against him and his teachings. The mere fact that such a dispute could take place is testimony to the vitality of underground Islam, although given the numbers involved, this rebellion was very much a storm in a teapot at the time. The initial impetus for the dispute was a debate about ritual: in contradiction to local customs and rituals, some students began to conduct the daily prayer in the manner of the Hanbali school dominant in the Arab lands. In disavowing traditions long dominant in Central Asia, the students were motivated by a desire to copy the ritual forms practiced in the Arab lands, which they took to be a purer form of

Islam, one uncontaminated by local traditions. The dispute soon spilled over to broader issues, and the students challenged both Hindustoniy's conservatism and his quietism.

The new reformers first took up the cudgels in defense of religious purity. They argued for ritual purism and for "cleansing" Central Asian Islam of various encrustations of custom and tradition, which they deemed identical to ignorance. Their rigorous purism led them to criticize shrine visits and the practice of asking for intercession from saints, prayers for the dead, and many basic Sufi practices. They went further, rejecting traditional fiqh, arguing for individual interpretation of sacred texts, and claiming to derive all authority from the Qur'an and the example of the Prophet. Finally, they argued that Hindustoniy was a conformist who had abdicated the responsibility to wage struggle, *jihad*, against the Soviet regime.

The dispute took the form of face-to-face disputations as well as letters of accusation that seem to have circulated in the underground. The disputations were organized enough to have been taped. The labels used by the two sides are telling. The students called themselves the *mujaddidiya*, the renovators, while calling their opponents *mushriklar*, polytheists. Hindustoniy, for his part, argued that local customs were based on a long tradition of Hanafi jurisprudence, which in itself was based on the Qur'an and the example of the Prophet, and that by forswearing accepted Hanafi dogma, his critics had placed themselves beyond the bounds of the Sunni community of Central Asia and had become "Wahhabis." Hindustoniy's use of this term owed a lot to his time in India, where such debates over ritual purity were common and where opponents of the purists had long dubbed them Wahhabis. Thus, the term *Wahhabi* entered religious debate in Central Asia, from where it was to spread throughout the lands of the former Soviet Union.

The war in Afghanistan framed this dispute, and the meaning of jihad took center stage. The reformists argued that it was incumbent upon true Muslims to "act in accordance with their knowledge" and to fight the Soviet state. Hindustoniy argued the opposite. Armed struggle was permissible only if success were certain; otherwise, taking on an unequal enemy meant only death and the destruction of Muslim lives. The attempt by Dukchi Eshon to lead a military revolt against tsarist authorities in 1898 had only led to "awful slaughter and the death of thousands," and the then-current war in Afghanistan was not a jihad but "the destruction of Muslim mosques, the murder of those who pray, the confiscation of the people's property, the murder of women and children."

Hindustoniy argued instead—and his is a conventional argument—that the greater part of jihad (*jihâd-i akbar*) is "to cleanse oneself of evil thoughts and deliver oneself from ignorance."[4] The rest is up to God's mercy. Hindustoniy argued that he had practiced this principle and that it had borne fruit: Stalinist repression had been a test of Muslims' faith, he argued, and Muslims' fortitude in sticking to their faith and their traditions had been rewarded by God in the form of the relative liberalization of the Brezhnev period. Traditional Islamic learning thus led Hindustoniy to a completely apolitical quietism.

The *mujaddids*, in contrast, had political goals in mind, no matter how quixotic these objectives might have seemed in the Brezhnev years or how vaguely they were expressed at the time. In 1977 or so, Rahmatulla Alloma, one of the most prominent figures among the first mujaddids, wrote a brief manuscript tract entitled *Musulmonobod* ("Muslimland"), in which he described an ideal country where Islam flourishes, people have equal rights, and Muslims "bow only to God, and not to any party, nor to living or dead leaders."[5] Rahmatulla Alloma died in a car accident in 1981, but the movement he represented continued. The movement even had a certain following in the countryside. Another prominent figure was Abdullah Saidov, who was arrested in Tajikistan in August 1986 on charges of "criminal violation of the law." He had evidently been arguing in public, usually at well-attended feasts marking life-cycle events, for the establishment of an Islamic state in Tajikistan. In the spring of 1986, during the buildup to the 27th Congress of the Communist Party of the Soviet Union, he had even "tried to persuade believers to submit their absurd request to the Congress"![6] Even more surprising were the events that followed his arrest. A crowd gathered outside the offices of the ministry of internal affairs in Qurghanteppa, the district center, demanded Saidov's release, and refused to disperse easily. Clearly, a constituency existed for Saidov's ideas, but one might wonder what Saidov meant by an Islamic state if it could be established through appeals to the congress of the Communist Party. Saidov was to emerge as a major figure in the IRP in the 1990s, by which time he had de-Sovietized his name to Sayyid Abdullah Nuri.

During perestroika, the schism between the mujaddids and their traditionalist opponents became public. As mosques began to open or reopen, questions of who should be the imam and what rite should be followed in a given mosque produced heated debates. As law and order broke down, vigilante groups formed across the Soviet Union. Some of the groups in the Ferghana Valley took on an Islamist coloring, although their precise programs—if any existed—remain unknown. Adolat was one such group. It fought against crime, which was skyrocketing in those years, and tried suspects in impromptu "popular courts" (a Soviet tradition). As such, Adolat was as much a product of Soviet culture as of Islam. Again, we do not know what its founders meant by the term "Islamic state" in 1991.

· · ·

In Tajikistan, the Islamic Renaissance Party emerged as a major political actor in the late Soviet period and played a crucial role in the civil war that wracked the country between 1992 and 1997. Today, activists in Tajikistan claim to have established an underground network in Tajikistan as early as 1973. Called Nahzati Javononi Islamii Tojikiston (Renewal of the Islamic Youth of Tajikistan), this organization represented hujra students who rejected the political caution of their teachers and advocated a social, if not a political status for a purified Islam. But the immediate impetus for the organization of the IRP came from outside. In July 1990, a number of Muslims, mainly lay intellectuals from the northern Caucasus, gathered in the Russian city of Astrakhan to form the Islamic Renaissance Party with the aim of struggling for freedom of conscience and freedom of practice for Muslims throughout the Soviet Union. Delegates from Tajikistan returned to Dushanbe to form a local branch of the party and succeeded, in the face of considerable hostility from the local authorities, in establishing the Islamic Renaissance Party of Tajikistan in October 1990. (A similar attempt to establish an Uzbek branch was scuttled by Uzbek authorities without much ado in January 1991.) The Tajik IRP, an alliance of unofficial reformist (mujaddid) mullahs of the countryside from the regions of Gharm and Hisor, quickly acquired a locally oriented program. Its leadership argued for the creation of an Islamic state in Tajikistan but acknowledged that this goal was a long-term one. After seven decades of Soviet rule, the main goal was to restore the basics of Islam to society and to begin the process of bringing Islamic knowledge and Islamic values back into public life. In this, the IRP differed substantially from Islamist parties of the Middle East that do not have to deal with the large scale de-Islamization that was the legacy of the Soviet past.

Tajikistan was unusual in many respects. The smallest and the poorest of the Central Asian countries, it is also the one with the shortest history. It was created in 1924 during the "national delimitation" of the region, when the mania for ethnic classification, shared by the Jadids and the Bolsheviks, led to the disaggregation of the multiethnic population of the region into ethnically defined nations. The separation of Uzbeks from Tajiks proved quite difficult conceptually and contentious politically. The sedentary Turkic-speaking population of Transoxiana had more in common with its Iranian-speaking neighbors than with other Turkic speakers, a fact complicated by widespread bilingualism. Moreover, many urban intellectuals, including those who were bilingual, considered "Turkism" more progressive than other alternatives and opted for an Uzbek identity. The monolingual Iranian-speaking population of the region could not be written out of existence, however; it was instead recognized as Tajik, a separate nation with its own language and its own history. But when it came to dividing up the territory, the Tajiks got only the sparsely populated rural, mountainous outposts of eastern Bukhara. The cities of Samarqand and Bukhara, the centers of Iranian civilization in Central Asia, were retained by the Uzbeks. By a curious twist of fortune, the Tajiks had been defined as rural, and the Uzbeks, who claimed descent from the nomadic tribes of the steppe, had ended up with all the cities.

In the Soviet era, the Tajik intelligentsia built up a glorious heritage for the nation that traced the origins of the Tajik nation, via the tenth-century Samanid state centered in Bukhara, to the ancient Sogdians. Tajik intellectuals saw their nation as the most ancient, most "civilized" people in Central Asia, heir to the wisdom of the Avesta and the glories of much of Persian poetry. But they had no modern history to lay claim to and no political references more recent than the Samanids. Tajik nationalism, for all the intellectuals' breathless claims to grandeur, proved incapable of holding the country together in the face of the severe political crisis brought on by the collapse of the Soviet Union. Alone among the countries of Central Asia, Tajikistan descended into civil war, and a particularly brutal one at that. At the time of the last Soviet census in 1989, Tajikistan had a population of 5.1 million. No unimpeachable figures are available, but estimates of casualties range from an implausibly low 25,000 to 100,000. Another half a million people fled the republic, mostly to Afghanistan. (That Afghanistan, torn apart by more than a decade of war, appeared to be a haven is an indication of the brutality of the Tajik civil war.) The bulk of the fighting took place in 1992, but the conflict rumbled on until 1997, when a U.N.-sponsored peace accord was signed.

The Tajik civil war was often portrayed as a conflict between

"Communists" and "fundamentalists," and used as a cautionary tale on the dangers of Islamic fundamentalism. The ploy worked, and the "Communist" side was able to lay claim to substantial sympathy among Western observers. With the Soviet Union gone, few in the West cared to remember that only a few years earlier, they had wagered on "fundamentalism" to fight "Communism." The facts of the Tajik civil war are, however, much more complex. The war is best explained as the result of a struggle between the forces supporting the late Soviet status quo and those that desired change; the most appropriate characterization of the two sides is as the "neo-Soviets" and "the opposition."[7] The struggle was over control of resources and of the mechanisms of power; the conflict was based on the regional networks of power that had emerged in the Soviet era. The alliances between the networks were profoundly pragmatic, and the parameters of the conflict were rooted squarely in the crisis of the end of the Soviet Union. The ulama emerged as major players in the war, but neither in their ideology nor in their conduct did they have much in common with Islamists in the rest of the Muslim world.

The way the conflict played out had everything to do with Soviet political realities. For much of its existence, the party elite (which included bureaucrats and plant managers) had been recruited from the northern province of Khujand (called Leninobod during the Soviet period and now renamed Sughd). The Leninobodi clique had learned to share the pie with some people from other parts of the republic. Its main partners came from the southern province of Kulob (sometimes rendered as Kulyab by those using Russian sources only). The opposition included members from all over the republic but especially from the regions (the provinces of Hisor and Gharm in the south, as well as the autonomous region of Mountainous Badakhshan, inhabited by people who did not speak Tajik and who were Shi'is of the Isma'ili branch) that had traditionally been excluded from power. This political issue caused the lines to be drawn the way they were. The "Islamists" of the IRP lined up alongside the reformist secular nationalists and the "unorthodox" Isma'ilis, against Soviet-era elites.

Throughout the civil war and the political crisis that preceded it, IRP spokesmen insisted that "they had no intention of establishing a theocratic fundamentalist state in Tajikistan, and that they would never strive to impose Islamic ideology and their objectives on the citizens of the country. . . . [The party's] objective was to play a role of its own in the spiritual revival and self-realization of the nation, and to defend the rights and demands of Muslims."[8] After seven decades of Soviet rule, the main goal was to restore the basics of Islam to society and to begin bringing Islamic knowledge and Islamic values back into public life. The party was also considerably invested in a specifically Tajik identity, stressing the thousand-year-old cultural legacy of the Tajik people

The Communist Party of Tajikistan was one of the most placid in the Soviet Union, and its leadership even held off on the Gorbachev reforms as long as it could. Glasnost and perestroika arrived in Tajikistan only belatedly in 1989, but once they did, the urban intelligentsia was quick to organize for reform and against the corruption of the ruling elites and their lock on political and economic power in the republic. The abiding passion of most of these intelligentsia groups was to reclaim and redefine a Tajik national identity. The urban intelligentsia established a number of political organizations (notably the Democratic Party of Tajikistan and the Rastokhez [Rebirth] organization) that pursued a secular, nationalist, democratic agenda of transforming Tajikistan into a pluralist state that would serve Tajik interests.

The main form of mobilization was the mass demonstration, and throughout the spring of 1992, supporters of the opposition—thousands of men (and women), many from the countryside—occupied one of the central squares of Dushanbe and demanded the ouster of Rahmon Nabiyev, the former first secretary of Tajikistan's Communist Party, who had become president. In April, the government mobilized its own supporters, mostly men from Kulob, who organized under the name of the Popular Front. (There was considerable irony here as well, for "popular front" was the generic name used during the Gorbachev years by public organizations mobilizing *against* the Soviet state and its lock on power.) People were bused in from Kulob to mount a counterdemonstration at another square a short distance down Dushanbe's main street from the opposition demonstration. In May, the government relented and agreed to form a coalition government of national unity until new parliamentary elections could be held. This experiment did not last long, however, and full-scale civil war erupted in June.

The war was at its most brutal in the Qurghonteppa province, where it fed off other conflicts. The province was the recipient of a large number of settlers from Gharm province, who were forced to move there to provide labor for the province's cotton fields, which expanded massively in the Brezhnev period. The Gharmis eventually came to dominate the province politically, but their new status pitted them against groups that they displaced in Qurghanteppa, as well as against the dominant factions in the neighboring Kulob province. With the Kulobis providing the bulk

of the fighting forces for the neo-Soviets, the civil war turned into a set-
tling of accounts, militarizing struggles that had hitherto been fought out
in the realm of soccer rivalries, dormitory riots, and bureaucratic competition. The conflicts became a "war of the kolkhozes," to use the terms
of the French scholar Olivier Roy, as kolkhozes dominated by one group
expelled members of the other group and mobilized militarily to defend
their territory, property, and food.[9] In Tajikistan, *mahalgaroi*, regionalism, had trumped nationalism as the main mode of solidarity.

The war also sucked in non-Tajiks living in Tajikistan. The Russians
and other Europeans emigrated en masse, but the country's biggest ethnic
minority, the Uzbeks (who constituted 23 percent of the population),
played a significant role in the war. They sided overwhelmingly with the
defenders of Soviet institutions and privilege. They had fared quite well
under the old regime and believed that the defenders of the old order
would protect their interests better. They also feared that the nationalism
of the opposition would make it anti-Uzbek. They contributed militarily
to the neo-Soviet cause, enlisting in large numbers in the Kulobi militias
and doing their part in the final victory of the neo-Soviets. But the decisive factor was military intervention by Russia (which had inherited several Soviet army units that had been stationed on the frontier with
Afghanistan) and Uzbekistan (which acted out of fear of the "Islamists,"
but which also wanted to have a pliable regime in Tajikistan). By the end
of 1992, the neo-Soviets had driven the opposition leadership into exile.
The Leninobodis and Kulobis banned all the groups that had formed the
opposition in 1991 and 1992, closed down their newspapers, and purged
their supporters from the government apparatus. The neo-Soviet victory
did not bring peace, however, as war rumbled on between armed groups
loyal to various parties in control of parts of the country and peacekeep-
ing forces from Russia and other former Soviet states stationed in
Tajikistan.

Islamization was not a central issue in the war. On the one hand, all of
Tajik society was undergoing a form of re-Islamization, in which all sides
began using Islamic symbols and references. The IRP was not the only
force for the re-Islamization of society. The secular intelligentsia's search
for national roots also led to Islam. Both groups found a mooring in the
early-twentieth-century Muslim modernism of the Jadid era, although
their heroes were not the Jadids of Central Asia (most of whom had
embraced Turkism and become Uzbeks) so much as figures from farther
afield. The greatest intellectual influence on the Tajik opposition in 1991
and 1992 was the Indian Muslim poet Iqbal (1877–1938), whose

Persian-language poetry had been available in Soviet times. Now, his "What Is to Be Done, O People of the East" (*Pas che bâyad kard, ay aqwâm-i sharq*), a poem written in 1933 in honor of the modernizing efforts of the king of Afghanistan, became the anthem of the opposition, Islamic and secular alike. Nor did the incumbent elites spurn the symbolic language of Islam. On the other hand, no political force demanded the creation of an Islamic state in Tajikistan during the conflict. The demands related to Islam were much more modest. In 1991, the *qozi kalon,* the highest-ranking official of SADUM in the republic, Hoji Akbar Turajonzoda, who was *not* a member of the IRP and remained loyal to the political order in the republic, had made the first demands: he demanded that the weekly holiday be moved to Friday, that all meat produced in the republic be slaughtered in accordance with Islamic injunctions, and that major Islamic holidays be recognized officially. When even these very modest proposals were rebuffed by the republic's government, Turajonzoda issued a fatwa forbidding Communists from being buried according to Islamic ritual.[10] The IRP's demands went further, but they nevertheless stayed focused on participation in government—that is, on breaking the hold of the incumbent elites on power—rather than on imposing Islamic law or Islamic norms on society.

Nevertheless, the neo-Soviets in Tajikistan and their backers in Tashkent and Moscow routinely depicted IRP members as the local representatives of a worldwide network of Islamist radicals. The struggle against such radicals could then be seen as a struggle to protect Central Asia and the rest of the former Soviet Union against the spread of Islamic fundamentalism, the defense of secularism against fundamentalism. Many of the leaders of the IRP ended up in northern Afghanistan, as did half a million civilians. For Tashkent and Moscow, this presence in Afghanistan was proof positive that the Islamists were at one with the mujahidin. That two civil wars in neighboring countries overlapped is hardly surprising, although evidence of material or ideological support for the IRP from Afghanistan is ambiguous. Tajik refugees received help from two mutually opposed factions of the mujahidin, the Pushtun-dominated Islamist Hizb-i Islami of Gulbuddin Hekmatyar and the Tajik Jam'iyat-i Islami of Ahmad Shah Mas'ud. Some Tajiks in exile engaged in cross-border raiding, but this activity remained on a small scale and did not prove decisive. Many of the nationalist leaders fled to Moscow, from where they continued to cooperate with the IRP, banding together as the United Tajik Opposition. A political process that began in 1994 eventually led to a peace accord in 1997, in which the government agreed to share power with the opposition. The United Tajik Opposition, including the IRP, was incorporated into the government, and its members received a number of important positions.

As the militias disbanded and the armed mobilization of the population came to an end, the IRP's influence on society shrank quite rapidly. The IRP had provided leadership to its basic constituency, the Gharmi population of Gharm and Qurghonteppa, during the war. With the war over, the ties that had bound the people of Gharm to their leaders loosened considerably, and the self-image of the Gharmis as more pious than the Kulobis was less necessary now than it had been during the war. Still, the IRP finds it impossible to organize in Kulob, even though the peace agreement legalized it. The IRP has participated in the politics of the country, running candidates for office and providing a voice in the political arena for its constituency. As we shall see in greater detail in chapter 7, however, it remains an embattled opposition, largely shut out of the structures of the state. It won only a small fraction of the vote in the parliamentary elections of 2000 and 2005, and the general atmosphere in the country betrays few signs of Islamization.

.   .   .

The ruling elites in Uzbekistan weathered the transition to independence much more comfortably. They faced challenges aplenty (of which Adolat's was only one example), along with internal factional struggles, but the elite as a whole managed to retain its grip on the structures of power.

The Gorbachev era had brought calamity to the Brezhnev-era leaders of Uzbekistan. The cotton scandal described in chapter 5 had led to a purge of the leadership not just in the Party but also in managerial spheres across the board. Other challenges came during the era of glasnost, when the intelligentsia began to organize on a secular national platform. In November 1988, a number of writers and academics formed Uzbekistan's first unofficial group, Birlik (Unity). Its central goals were cultural-nationalist: it sought to make Uzbek the sole state language, end "unjustified denigration" of Central Asian historical figures, and so forth. It also called for political reform in the Soviet Union as a whole, greater autonomy for Uzbekistan, and a guarantee of individual rights against the state. In keeping with other political trends in the Soviet Union, Birlik saw petitions, demonstrations, and the press as the basic forms of participation in public life.

Led by Abdurahim Po'lotov, a scientist, and Muhammad Solih (Salay Madaminov), a poet, the organization soon acquired a substantial urban base and made its presence felt through a series of demonstrations in 1988 and 1989, focusing largely on language issues but gradually moving to broader demands for political reform. From the beginning, however, it ran into trouble with the authorities. Unlike the authorities in Moscow, those in Tashkent were loath to loosen their hold on public life, and they tried their best to obstruct the work of the new public organizations. The official press remained implacably hostile to the new organizations, and the republic's government passed laws in the spring of 1991 protecting the dignity of the president of the republic and other top officials (infractions could result in imprisonment of up to six years) and prohibiting public organizations that worked toward "the destruction of moral foundations of society [and] universal humanistic values," advocated "the illegal change of the constitutional structure or the destruction of the unity of the USSR or the Uzbek SSR," or "inflame social hatred." Ironically, this attitude was possible largely because of Uzbekistan's growing autonomy from the center, a goal that Birlik had pursued from the beginning. The more Uzbekistan could run its own show, the more its government could dictate terms to the opposition and make life unpleasant for it.

The incessant pressure on Birlik, as well as rivalries among its leaders, led to a split, and in 1990, a "moderate" wing, led by Muhammad Solih, seceded to form the Erk (Freedom) organization. Erk argued against the utility of mass demonstrations and sought to work through persuasion. The government relented enough to allow the group to register as a political party. The concept of registration in the Gorbachev years should be properly understood, for it continues to operate in Central Asia to this day. After the Soviet regime allowed the creation of independent organizations, it still required that they be registered in order to be legal. The registration remained an administrative prerogative of the state, not a right to be exercised by all and sundry. The state could refuse to register any organization and thus condemn it to illegality.

Karimov's steady grip on power loosened briefly in the autumn of 1991. Having supported the coup against Gorbachev, Karimov scrambled to declare Uzbekistan independent on August 31, 1991. Leaving a union now dominated by Boris Yeltsin in a reformist and anti-Communist mood was a much better way of retaining power. Karimov portrayed himself as a national leader of the Uzbek people, leading them to independence. He emerged as the champion of the Uzbek people, their language, and their history. In doing so, he appropriated the cultural part of Birlik's platform, stealing much of the opposition's thunder. Nevertheless, the autumn saw a thaw in the country's politics (the emergence of Adolat was connected to this shift too). Karimov was forced to call elections for the presidency, in which he even had to face a competitor in the shape of Erk leader Muhammad Solih. The result was never, however, in doubt. Erk was no match to the Communist Party, now renamed the People's Democratic Party of Uzbekistan, in resources and the ability to mobilize. Besides, there is no reason to believe that even if the playing field had been level, Karimov would have been seriously challenged, especially in the countryside, by anyone outside the networks of power and distribution that continued to define life in Uzbekistan.

Karimov was duly elected, and took his oath of office in January 1992 with one hand on the constitution and the other on a copy of the Qur'an. He then immediately set about restoring order and recovering the control that had slipped through his fingers in the chaos of that autumn. In January 1992, students at Tashkent University went on strike to protest economic issues: in the middle of a grave economic crisis, they had not received their ration tickets to purchase basic food items. Karimov responded by sending in the police, which shot into the crowd when the demonstrators refused to disperse. When this police action gave rise to more protests, the university was closed down and the students sent home. That step was the beginning of a crackdown that quickly restored the authorities' control of the political situation in the country. Militias sent from Tashkent shut down Adolat and other vigilante groups in the Ferghana Valley, arresting nearly seventy activists and chasing others out of the country. By 1993, all opposition groups had been banned and their leaders beaten up or hounded out of the country. Karimov articulated his attitude toward the opposition in a speech to the supreme soviet in July 1992: "It is necessary to straighten out the brains of one hundred people in order to preserve the lives of thousands."[11]

"Stability" was a major virtue in Karimov's book (and one prized highly abroad as well), and, having crushed all domestic opposed, secular and Islamic, he seemingly had achieved it. For much of the 1990s, Uzbekistan was stable, if nothing else. The conflict that raged in Afghanistan throughout the decade and in Tajikistan until 1997 stopped at Uzbekistan's borders. That situation had changed by the end of the decade, with the emergence of two rather different Islamic organizations that challenged the status quo in different ways. The IMU is a militant jihadist organization that seeks the overthrow, violent if necessary, of the

Karimov regime and its replacement by an Islamic state. The HTI, in contrast, is a transnational organization that works to create, through nonviolent means, the caliphate, a universal Islamic state that would unite all of the world's Muslims. The emergence of these groups has put the struggle against "religious extremism" at the center of the regime's agenda since 1998.

·   ·   ·

The IMU shot to global prominence after September 11. It was one of the only two organizations mentioned alongside al-Qaeda in George W. Bush's speech to the joint session of Congress in the immediate aftermath of the terrorist attacks. In the ensuing war in Afghanistan, its members fought alongside the Taliban, and Juma Namangoniy, its leader, was reportedly given the command of the whole of northern Afghanistan. It is very easy, therefore, to forget just how modest the IMU's achievements had been until then.

The group was first heard of in the spring of 1999, although it had probably formed the year before. It comprised Uzbek radicals who had fled their country in the face of persecution. The two main figures in the organization, Tohir Yo'ldoshev and Juma Namangoniy, had been active in Adolat in 1991. After that group was disbanded in 1992, the two had gone to Tajikistan and fought alongside the IRP in the Tajik civil war. They had been joined by a steady creep of fresh recruits from Uzbekistan, men who had fled religious persecution (see chapter 7 for more detail) or, occasionally, grinding poverty. Many of these men ended up in jihadist madrasas or training camps in Pakistan. When the IRP signed the truce in 1997, its Uzbek fellow travelers could not follow suit and had no choice but to form a separate organization. The IMU received support from the Taliban, Pakistan's Interservices Intelligence agency, and Osama bin Laden. The Taliban provided IMU with a training base in Qunduz, where many foreign fighters also trained. Yo'ldoshev spent time in Peshawar, from whence he traveled to Saudi Arabia, the Gulf, and the Caucasus in search of funding and recruits. Uzbekistan's homegrown dissent met the jihadist culture that had emerged in Afghanistan and became entangled in its global networks.[12]

The IMU thus acquired many of the characteristic features of jihadist Islam: a fascination with armed struggle in its pursuit of an Islamic state, to the exclusion of any other political program, and a vitriolic rhetoric that mixed anti-American, anti-Jewish, and anti-Israeli motifs. But to a striking degree, the IMU was motivated by simple hatred of Karimov and his regime. This fact was clear in one of Yo'ldoshev's few interviews:

> The movement views the people of Uzbekistan as a people who prefer the Islamic outlook, who have defended Islam in hard times and who have an ancient Islamic history. Uzbekistan was considered one of the Islamic centres of the world. The history of the dark century of the Russian invaders— the Bolshevik rule—in the country has ended, but we have not achieved freedom or been able to resume our Islamic life, under which the country lived for many centuries. Instead, a despotic and apostate group have become the rulers of the country. They have waged war against Islam. They have massacred more Muslims than their Bolshevik teachers. They have sent religious scholars to jails and they have persecuted and killed. They have exerted severe oppression, particularly against young Muslims. They have closed God's mosques and forbidden the name of God to be uttered there. If it was written in the pages of history that they served the communists' interests in Uzbekistan in the past, now they are carrying out in Uzbekistan the policy of Israeli Jews and the American enemies of Islam.[13]

Although the last sentence is a boilerplate formulation of jihadist rhetoric, the rest of the paragraph is striking for its specificity. It takes the existence of Uzbekistan as a given and builds its case by attacking the actual policies of the Uzbek government.[14] There is no mention in the IMU's pronouncements of the Palestine issue, so central to the global jihadist culture, or of any other arenas of conflict, such as Kashmir, Bosnia, or even Chechnya.

What did the IMU want? Its program was simplicity itself:

> The Islamic Movement of Uzbekistan . . . has set itself the task of introducing the full meaning of Allah's shariat law to people, society and the state. The goal of the movement is to spread Islamic science and culture, as a fine example, among all the people in society; to introduce Islamic order in personal and family life, in education and in the development of conscience and also to introduce Islamic rule in public life by guiding people to do good deeds and avoid vice. The movement will fight against discord, clashes and the division of Muslims into separate parties by their enemies, which will only weaken Muslims, and will also fight for the elimination of hostility in mutual relations. The movement announces that there are solutions to all the problems of Muslims in God's book the Qur'an and in the traditions [hadith] of God's messenger Muhammad. . . . The movement believes that Islamic traditions, laws and orders are binding on every Muslim, on society and on the rulers of Muslims, and implementation of shariat instructions is the duty of every official and is the only measurement which defines whether an official is a righteous person.[15]

These formulations are vague indeed. The statement says nothing about political structures or the economy—issues central to much Islamist thought of the twentieth century—in the Islamic state that the IMU wanted to create. Namangoniy was no theorist; he was, and remained, a guerilla leader driven by intense hatred of the Karimov regime.

Although hatred of the regime might be widespread today, there is little reason to believe that the IMU's solution enjoys wide popularity in the country. As this book suggests, Islam, nation, and tradition coexist happily in Uzbekistan today. A "return" to Islam today is widely seen as a way of reclaiming the national cultural patrimony and decolonizing, but little more. The prospect of abiding by all normative injunctions of the shariat, especially as interpreted by the IMU, has no support in the country. The IMU was an organization of a thin stratum of radicalized exiles, whose radicalization took place because of the existence of the stateless expanse of Afghanistan (itself the result of a proxy war in which radical Islam was used to fight the enemy).

Could the IMU have pulled off its plan? The few operations it undertook produced very little, although the Uzbek government had reason to exaggerate the threat. On February 16, 1999, six bombs exploded within an hour in the center of Tashkent, destroying government buildings, killing sixteen people, injuring over one hundred people, and missing Karimov narrowly. No one took responsibility for the bombings, but the government quickly laid the blame at the feet of a wide assortment of exiled oppositional figures: Yo'ldoshev and Namangoniy rubbed shoulders with Muhammad Solih, the leader of Erk and the only man ever to have run against Karimov in an election, in the government's indictment. Hundreds of people were arrested, and several suspects extradited from Turkey, Ukraine, Kazakhstan, and Kyrgyzstan. In June, six suspects were duly found guilty and sentenced to death. In November 2000, a related trial led to the sentencing of Yo'ldoshev, Namangoniy, and Solih to death in absentia. In the absence of compelling proof (the confessions of the suspects were clearly extracted under torture), a number of theories were put forward to explain the bombings. Exiled opponents of the regime, pointing out that not a single official functionary was harmed in the bomb attacks, have even suggested that the bombings were staged by the government to give it a pretext for another wave of repression. Other explanations ranged from factional conflict within the Uzbekistani regime, through Russian intrigue, to retaliation on the part of the government of Tajikistan for Uzbekistan's intervention in Tajikistani affairs. Very few people in Tashkent believe that the bombs were the work of the IMU.[16]

The IMU made its debut that summer, when an armed band belonging to it entered the Batken district of Kyrgyzstan from Tajikistan and took several people, including four Japanese geologists, hostage. The insurgents demanded a ransom and passage to Uzbekistani territory, which they claimed was their real target. At the same time, the IMU issued a statement declaring that this action was the beginning of a jihad against "the tyrannical government of Uzbekistan and the puppet Islam Karimov and his henchmen." Beyond the establishment of "an Islamic state with the application of the shariat, founded upon the Qur'an and the Noble Prophetic sunnah," the statement listed as the goals of the jihad "the defence of our religion of Islam in our land against those who oppose Islam," "the defence of the Muslims in our land from those who humiliate them and spill their blood," "the release of the weak and oppressed who number some 5000 in prison," and the re-opening of "the thousands of mosques and Islamic schools that have been closed by the evil government."[17]

Kyrgyzstan's armed forces appeared powerless to expel the band, and the insurgents withdrew only when the Japanese government reportedly paid a ransom of $6 million two months later. The confrontation was repeated the following summer, when the insurgents briefly took hostage a group of American mountaineers. Although the hostages escaped, the incident moved the U.S. State Department to place the IMU on its list of terrorist organizations. The expected incursion in the summer of 2001 never came, but the IMU gained its moment of fame in Afghanistan in the autumn, when its forces fought alongside the Taliban. The war in Afghanistan also proved to be the swan song of the IMU, however. It suffered major casualties, and Namangoniy himself was killed in U.S. bombing. Although rumors persist that Yo'ldoshev is alive and the IMU is regrouping in Afghanistan or the tribal areas of Pakistan, there is little reason to believe that the IMU will ever regain the position it briefly enjoyed between 1999 and 2001.

Even the strength of that position is debatable. Two armed incursions that never reached the territory of Uzbekistan do not add to much. The number of fighters the IMU commanded also remains a matter of speculation. During the U.S. war in Afghanistan, press reports spoke of thousands of Uzbeks fighting alongside the Taliban, but the number of Uzbek fighters captured or killed in battle was in the hundreds, not thousands. No serious estimates of the number of Uzbek fighters in Afghanistan exceeded 3,500 before September 11. Whether such a force could have anything more than nuisance value is open to question, especially given that few people in Uzbekistan had any sympathy with its goals. Nevertheless, the two incursions provided the impetus for the final closing of the borders with neighboring states, affecting the livelihoods of millions of people and further constricting their movement. On the border with Tajikistan, the Uzbek government went further, mining large stretches of it. Since then, numerous civilians, usually peasants and shepherds, have been killed by the mines.

•   •   •

The Hizb-ut-Tahrir is a different kind of organization. Founded in Jerusalem in 1953, it is a transnational organization that seeks to Islamize society from the bottom up. Its avowed goals are straightforward but grandiose: to "resume the Islamic way of life and to convey the Islamic *da'wah* ["invitation," proselytism] to the world."[18] Accomplishment of this goal will bring "Muslims back to living an Islamic way of life in *Dar al-Islam* [the "Abode of Islam," a category in Islamic legal thought] and in an Islamic society such that all of life's affairs in society are administered according to the shariat rules." Such a society can only be built by "changing the society's existing thoughts to Islamic thoughts so that such thoughts become the public opinion among the people, who are then driven to implement and act upon them. Secondly the Party works to change the emotions in the society until they become Islamic emotions that accept only that which pleases Allah and rebel against and detest anything which angers Allah. Finally, the Party works to change the relationships in the society until they become Islamic relationships which proceed in accordance with the laws and solutions of Islam." The ultimate goal is the "restoration" of the *khilâfa*, the caliphate, which the Party sees as a single Islamic state encompassing all the Muslims of the world.

For all HTI's talk of return and restoration, however, the group is a thoroughly modern phenomenon, both in the conception of its goals and its organization. If the IMU is at pains to cast itself as a religious movement (backing up its call to jihad with the authority of an "agreement by the major ulama"), the HTI casts itself proudly as "a political group and not a priestly one." Typically for an Islamist party, the HTI has little interest in theological debate, seeing Islam primarily as a political system. As the party's platform puts it, "Islam is [the party's] ideology." HTI's structure is inspired by that quintessentially modern form of organization, the revolutionary party. The party is ultimately a secret society organized in semi-independent cells of only five members each, which are supposed to elect national (or, in the party's vocabulary, "provincial") executive councils, much on the Leninist model. The caliphate the HTI seeks to "restore" is a modern welfare state that has little connection to the caliphate as it existed in history.[19] HTI's caliphate will be Islamic because it will rest on an Islamic ideology. Judged by this measure, none of the regimes existing in the Muslim world are Islamic, and the HTI seeks the removal of all of them. The organization couches its critique of the present world order in both anti-imperialist and Islamist terms. Tracing the HTI's lineage takes us back not to classical Islam but to the tradition of revolutionary politics of the modern world.

HTI's members were involved in unsuccessful coup attempts in several Arab countries in the 1960s. Since then, however, the organization has not been a major factor in Islamic politics; chased out of Muslim-majority countries, it has until recently been confined to the Muslim diaspora in western Europe, where it attracts a largely educated and economically successful constituency. Its most significant activity is educational; it uses the Internet extensively (its main Web site purveys its message in seven languages) and has a substantial media presence in the West. Although it has publicly disavowed the use of violence, it has run into trouble with governments in western Europe. It was banned in Germany in 2002 for its anti-Semitic rhetoric and in Britain in 2005 as part of a crackdown on Muslim extremists in the aftermath of the bomb attacks on London transport. Nevertheless, no links between the HTI and violent action have ever been proven.

The HTI arrived in Central Asia in the mid-1990s and has enjoyed substantial growth since then. It has never sought registration and therefore remains illegal by definition. Its main activities in the region are organizing study circles and printing and distributing leaflets in local languages or Russian. But from the beginning, HTI has earned the hostility of local governments. In Uzbekistan, it is persecuted viciously by the regime, which sees no difference between it and the IMU: both are "extremists" and "Wahhabis." The mere possession of HTI literature is illegal, and thousands of people suspected of being HTI members have been imprisoned. In Kazakhstan, Kyrgyzstan, and Tajikistan, HTI is denounced by "official" ulama as an extremist organization inimical to Islam, and the governments of Uzbekistan and Kyrgyzstan have blamed it (without convincing proof) for various violent acts on their territory. The government of Uzbekistan wants the party to be listed as a terrorist organization and banned worldwide.

Despite the certitude of local governments, a number of questions remain to be answered about HTI's role in Central Asia. What makes the HTI so popular in Central Asia? Why do Central Asians join it? Is the HTI a single, monolithic organization, which matters are decided centrally and executed locally, or do wide variations exist among its local branches? How strong are the networks, personal and financial, that support it? Finally, and perhaps more important, can we take the organization's claims about itself and its avoidance of violence at face value?

The success of the HTI in Central Asia is, at first glance, surprising. Its ideologization of Islam, its emphasis on the unity of the *ummah* (the worldwide community of Muslims), and the concomitant denigration of national peculiarities all go against the way Islam and nation are generally understood in the region. In this sense, the HTI's message seems to represent a complete break from the Soviet legacy in the region. Many of the themes that obsess the HTI globally—the Arab-Israeli conflict, the relations of Arab states with the United States, the economics of oil— likewise have limited resonance in Central Asia. Questions about the level of support the party has in Central Asia are impossible to answer precisely because the HTI is persecuted and its leadership entirely invisible. With no photos or records or addresses to trace, even judging the scale of its activity is impossible. Estimates vary widely, but after careful analysis of information available in 2003, the International Crisis Group, a think tank with an established presence in Central Asia, found it "hard to imagine that there are more than 20,000 members in the whole of Central Asia."[20] The situation has not changed significantly since then. Similarly, the only indication of the composition of the party comes from the analysis of people who are arrested on charges of belonging to it. This is a hazardous exercise, for the accusation of belonging to the party does not, of course, mean that one actually belongs to the party. Nevertheless, 82 percent of those arrested in Uzbekistan in 2000 were between the ages of twenty-one and thirty-six, and 56 percent were unemployed.[21] The group appears to have a substantial stratum of educated middle- or lower-middle-class men, although women make up an increasingly large proportion of the membership.

HTI is a transnational organization, but we cannot assume that it is so efficiently centralized that all branches execute a single political program. Its activity bespeaks a substantial amount of coordination and organization of financial resources, a network of desktop presses, and people willing to take the risk of distributing leaflets. HTI members in Central Asia claim that they are funded by sympathizers locally, although transnational links no doubt exist. Indeed, critics suggest that many people join the party for material gain, for members reportedly receive money ($50 to $100 per month, a substantial sum when the average monthly salary is nearer $20) for the dangerous work of distributing leaflets. But do local members act on the same compulsions, desires, and hatreds that activists in Britain, Pakistan, or Indonesia do? Or do they have their own reasons for joining the organization? Motivations vary, no doubt. The basic unit of the organization, the circle (*doira*), educates people in the basic tenets of Islam, and many people join the circles out of a curiosity about "real" Islam. Many others are seekers, whose search for stability, moral certitude, or meaning leads them to the HTI. Although most of HTI's members are educated, few have any serious religious education. Most of the party's members are attracted not by its religious argument but by its activist political message. And women have increasingly become the visible face of the party: many have joined the party after their husbands were arrested, and on several occasions, wives and sisters of members have demonstrated in public against the detention and unfair trials of their relatives.

The party's literature does not provide a clear answer. Most of the leaflets distributed in the region are translations (apparently done on the initiative of local cells) of HTI publications posted on the party's Web site. Many of them address issues of only marginal local interest, but the political issues discussed in the majority of the leaflets—criticism of existing regimes everywhere in the Muslim world and of the "imperialism" of non-Muslim powers, mostly the United States and Israel, coupled with a call for the establishment of the caliphate—have a direct bearing on how members perceive the need for change locally. Some leaflets do address local issues directly. In HTI leaflets in Uzbekistan, Islam Karimov is a regular target of derision, being described as an agent of American and Jewish interests out to subjugate the Muslims of Uzbekistan.

Ultimately, the HTI is popular because people see its global message through the prism of local concerns. The HTI is primarily a vehicle for dissatisfaction with the current political and moral order in the region. With political life curtailed, if not outright proscribed, it is no wonder that a secret society provides the main venue for dissent. The utopian vision of a just and moral society presided over by a caliph is attractive to people living through chaotic conditions under brutal and authoritarian regimes. An Islamic order or the rule of the shariat evokes for many people nothing more concrete than a clean economy and lack of corruption. HTI's fulminations against the designs of *kufr*, of unbelief and its bearers, on Muslims resonates in a region where for decades the state assaulted Islam and sponsored atheism; and the vision of a single Islamic state appeals to those in Central Asia whose lives and movements have been constricted by the emergence, since the Soviet collapse, of international boundaries, with attendant visa and customs regimes.

HTI clearly represents dissent and discontent with the established order. What that dissent can achieve through secret organization is a separate question. We see no sign that HTI cells exist in high places in government (infiltrating regimes is the usual way in which secret societies make a grab for power); quite the contrary. The regimes in the region are implacably opposed to the organization, ever eager to pin the label of terrorism on it and to persecute its members. Short of becoming an armed organization, the HTI might achieve a transformation of the moral climate of society through grassroots action that then helps transform the way Central Asians relate to Islam, which might in its turn build up resentment against the incumbent regimes of the region. However, this task is a tall order, even without the persecution unleashed by the regimes; and, as we shall see in later in the book, the regimes might collapse for completely unrelated reasons before the HTI's long-term strategy bears fruit.

•   •   •

The three groups in this chapter—the IRP, the IMU, and the HTI—have or have had transnational links, but all have roots in domestic political realities and focus primarily on local issues. They are not implantations of a global Islamist movement with a monolithic agenda. Even the IMU, which capitalized on the transnational links its founders forged in Afghanistan, was driven primarily by its hatred of the Karimov regime. The three organizations represent forms of homegrown opposition to the political order that consolidated in the region in the aftermath of the Soviet collapse. They are also quite different from one another and do not form a single bloc of "political Islam." Not only are their ideas different, they each operate with constraints that make cooperation difficult. And while there is much in post-Soviet Central Asia that breeds discontent, from dysfunctional economies with increasingly skewed distribution of wealth to corrupt authoritarian regimes, it is difficult to see how these Islamist organizations can channel that discontent into an Islamic revolution.

The relationship of the three groups is uneasy. The IRP fought in a civil war alongside secular nationalist groups. The war led it to Afghanistan, where it came in contact with jihadist militancy, but it could never escape the clan logic of the war. Once the war was over, the IRP joined the political process and ran candidates for office. The IMU followed the IRP into Afghanistan, but lacking entrée into the political process, it sank ever deeper in the jihadist milieu of Afghanistan, before being largely destroyed by American air power in 2001. As a different kind of organization, the HTI has strained relations with both these organizations.

Individual members of the HTI have expressed mixed views of the IMU, combining admiration of the IMU's goal of toppling the regime with disdain for its use of violence and absence of a political program. "Everywhere people want to build Islam," said one member interviewed by the International Crisis Group in Kyrgyzstan. "The IMU—I also consider them brothers, the Taliban, Wahhabis, are also brothers. . . . But they don't have a program."[22] The IMU, to the extent that it had an ideological stance, objected to the peaceful tactics of the HTI, which the IMU considered irrelevant and insufficient for the task. The jihadist milieu in general is quite critical of HTI, attacking it both for its nonviolence and for its religious stance (which, as we have seen, is subordinated to political ideology).[23]

The relationship between the HTI and the IRP in Tajikistan is also quite hostile. HTI members accuse the IRP of "selling out" Islam and Muslims in its pursuit of power. The IRP, for its part, feels threatened by the HTI. Accustomed to being the only Islamic voice in the political arena, it is now loath to see its constituency raided by a more radical organization. It stakes its argument against HTI on two points. The first is legal. "This grouping does not have the right to function in Tajikistan, neither from the point of view of the shariat, nor from that of the law," says Sayyid Abdullah Nuri, the chair of the party. "From a legal point of view, this grouping is not registered and does not have the right to operate in Tajikistan."[24] To the extent that legality depends on registration, and the power to register lies with the state, this argument is specious. The invocation of the shariat is equally unconvincing, a sign perhaps that the IRP cannot offer any real competition to the HTI. The second point is Tajik nationalism. Defense of the independence and unity of Tajikistan is one of the IRP's central goals, whereas the HTI, IRP members contend, is a transnational organization that does not and cannot have the interests of Tajikistan at heart. "In practice," Qadi Akbar Turajonzoda argues, "the realization of these ideas [of HTI] means the destruction of national states. To the extent that national states and national independence are the dominant ideas of modernity, the path to the HTI's notion of the caliphate will be long and bloody. For Tajikistan, this is especially important, for the Tajik people were only recently able to establish their national independence after a thousand years, and today the construction of a national state is the main stabilizing factor in the republic."[25]

.   .   .

Events took a seemingly new turn in 2004, when Uzbekistan saw two rounds of violence. From March 28 to April 1, at least ten incidents took place in several cities of Tashkent, resulting in the deaths of forty-seven people (including thirty-three militants). A bomb went off in the apartment of a pensioner in Bukhara on March 28. The next day in Tashkent, in various encounters, assailants killed two policemen, two female suicide bombers struck a bazaar, and bombs went off near a supermarket and a historic mosque. Another explosion took place in Andijan that evening. The following morning, a shoot-out at a rural house claimed the lives of twenty suspects.[26] Then on July 30, just as the trial of those accused of involvement in these events was getting under way, three suicide bombers struck nearly simultaneously at the offices of the state prosecutor and the embassies of the United States and Israel.

These events also brought into the limelight a hitherto-unknown group calling itself Islomiy Jihod (Islamic Jihad), which claimed responsibility for the acts. The spring violence, it asserted, was a revenge for the massive arrests of Muslim activists by the Karimov regime.[27] A second message, issued after the July 30 attacks, was in Arabic and used more recognizably jihadi rhetoric: "a number of the Muslim youth carried out martyrdom operations that terrorized the apostate [Uzbek] government and her infidel allies from the Americans and the Jews. . . . These martyrdom operations that the movement carried out will not stop, God-willing, and this is a response to the injustice of the apostate [Uzbek] government and an effort to support the jihad of our Muslim brothers in Iraq, Palestine, Afghanistan, the Hijaz, and other Muslim countries that are ruled by the infidels and apostates."[28] This statement, along with the fact that this attack was the first suicide bombing in Central Asia and the first attack on targets belonging to foreign countries, seemed to indicate the involvement of global networks of Islamic militancy. Al-Qaeda, it seemed, had finally arrived in Central Asia.

The parallels with al-Qaeda, however, were mostly superficial. The

July attacks were on a much smaller scale than the al-Qaeda operations in Bali or Madrid, and they were quite amateurish in execution. Moreover, all participants were Uzbeks (although the Uzbekistani government alleged that several among them were citizens of Kazakhstan) who seemed to be acting out of local concerns. The spring events were most likely a plot gone wrong, but the fact that the violence was not directed at the public and all the victims were policemen is noteworthy. (We should also remember that thirty-three of the forty-seven people killed in the spring violence were militants or alleged militants.) Beyond confessions of those accused of participation in the spring bombings, extracted no doubt under torture, we have no evidence that would allow us to judge the extent of the ties between the perpetrators of this violence and al-Qaeda or other transnational militant groups.

A far more likely explanation is that the violence of 2004 in Uzbekistan was an expression of extreme despair about the political and economic situation in Uzbekistan and about the widespread hatred of the Karimov regime. In other words, it was likely an incipient indigenous insurgency brought on by the regime's own policies. Many reasons exist for an insurgency to arise in Uzbekistan. The Karimov regime has suppressed all opposition, refused to liberalize the economy, and (as we shall see in the next chapter) waged a merciless campaign against all expressions of Islam it does not control itself. The causes of the insurgency are local, as are those who carry it on, but presenting it as linked seamlessly to global patterns of militancy comes in handy for the regime.

CHAPTER 7

The Politics of Antiterrorism

In the National Museum of the History of Uzbekistan in Tashkent, a blown-up photograph of the World Trade Center in flames looms large over displays celebrating national achievements since independence. This display has the title "Uzbekistan: The Struggle against International Terrorism." At the foot of the photograph lies a collection of weapons confiscated from "terrorists" in Uzbekistan itself. To the left of the photograph is a tableau of scenes from the devastation caused by the bombs of February 16, 1999, along with portraits of "sons of Uzbekistan," mostly police officers, who have lost their lives in the struggle with local terrorists. To the right of the World Trade Center photograph is a picture of Islam Karimov, the president of Uzbekistan, embracing Henry Kissinger at a ceremony in New York, where he received an award "on behalf of the American public and non-governmental organizations for his outstanding contribution to the struggle against international terrorism."

Since the end of the Cold War, with ideological conflict gone (and even the Communist regime in China in a deep embrace with capitalism), opposition to religious extremism, or "fundamentalism" (the most common term used to describe the phenomenon) has come to provide a universal language that allows all kinds of regimes to position themselves on the side of Reason, Enlightenment, and Secularism, and against fanaticism, obscurantism, and reaction. Although we may recognize many fundamentalisms as threats, Islamic fundamentalism occupies a special place in our imagination and provides the new villains of the age. This anti-fundamentalist rhetoric and its ready acceptability have come in handy for a number of authoritarian regimes. In 1990, the Algerian regime annulled national elections for fear that fundamentalists would take over. In 1997, the Turkish military forced the prime minister, Necmettin Erbakan, from office for seeking to overthrow the secular order. When a nationalist protest broke out among the Uyghurs of Xinjiang province in China the same year, the Chinese government blamed it on the influence of foreign fundamentalist organizations. Throughout the 1990s, Serb nationalists justified their actions in Bosnia and Kosovo by claiming that all Balkan Muslims were fundamentalists and thus a threat not just to Serbia but to all of Europe, and to Civilization itself.

The events of September 11, 2001, immeasurably increased the power of this language, even as terrorism replaced fundamentalism as the subject of concern. The declaration by the United States of an open-ended "war on terror" raised the stakes substantially. Participation in the war of terror brings tangible benefits: military and economic aid, diplomatic support, and relief from criticism of unpalatable domestic policies. Since September 11, a number of authoritarian or oppressive regimes have shown themselves to be enthusiastic supporters of the war on terrorism. They do so by tying all domestic opposition to "international terrorism," even when no links actually exist. They thus internationalize long-running domestic disputes and justify their brutal suppression in an internationally acceptable language. The Russian president, Vladimir Putin, insists that the opposition to Russian rule in Chechnya is a phenomenon of international terrorism. The Chinese government justifies its suppression of the religious and civic rights of the Uyghur population of Xinjiang, where Chinese policies have created substantial nationalist opposition, on the grounds that the discontented Uyghurs are fundamentalists and terrorists. Other governments have ridden the bandwagon in more brazen ways. In March 2002, the government of Macedonia showed its zeal for fighting terrorism by rounding up seven Pakistani illegal immigrants on their way to western Europe, murdering them in cold blood, and announcing that police had killed "foreign militants" planning to attack "vital installations, Macedonian officials and the embassies of Germany, Great Britain and the U.S. in Skopje."[1]

The regime in Uzbekistan is an expert player at this game. Islamic militancy does exist in Uzbekistan, but if it didn't, the regime would have invented it. It provides an excellent alibi for cracking down on all dissent, religious or otherwise, by proclaiming it to be the work of "religious extremists" and "terrorists." The regime exaggerates the threat and uses it to control religious activity, even as it celebrates Islam as part of the country's heritage. Because the repression of unauthorized religious activity affects large numbers of Muslims who are pious but not politically active, the regime risks alienating a large part of the population that has no sympathy for or connection with Islamic militancy. Islam and nation coexist in Uzbekistan, but the government's policies stand a good chance of sundering the two and actually pushing people to more radical positions.

Although the bulk of this chapter focuses on Uzbekistan, where the situation is particularly bad, we will also see that the other countries of post-Soviet Central Asia are not qualitatively different in how they deal with Islam.

·   ·   ·

The government of Islam Karimov has had two overriding goals since the collapse of the Soviet Union: to suppress all domestic opposition and to achieve regional hegemony in Central Asia. The latter the government takes as its right, given that Uzbekistan is the most populous country in the region and has the largest armed forces in it. This desire, moreover, feeds off assumptions in Uzbek national mythology about the leading role of the Uzbek people in Central Asia. It also explains the seemingly erratic foreign policy the regime has pursued in the post-Soviet years, as it has moved between strategic alliances with Russia and the United States. The struggle against the wrong kind of Islam features in both these goals.

The regime defines the wrong kind of Islam expansively—to mean all unauthorized expression or observance that takes place beyond the purview of official institutions (the heirs to SADUM). The regime has produced, in effect, a category new to Islamic history, that of "independent Muslims"—that is, Muslims who practice Islam independently of the state. The state's persecution of "extremism" becomes difficult to distinguish from its persecution of Islam itself. Indeed, the jailing of "independent Muslims" and the closing of mosques are more common in Uzbekistan today than during the Brezhnev years.

As the Karimov regime strengthened its hold on the state in 1992, it brought SADUM under control as well. SADUM enjoyed a brief period of relative autonomy during the turmoil of perestroika. Despite internal upheaval, it managed to open many new mosques and to publish basic Islamic texts in large numbers between 1989 and 1992. The Soviet collapse had redefined SADUM's jurisdiction, as its branches in other republics seceded one after the other. By 1993, the organization had been renamed the Muslim Board of Uzbekistan (O'zbekiston Musulmonlari Idorasi, or MBU) and brought back under the firm control of the state. Although the law asserts that the "state shall not charge religious organizations with carrying out any state functions, and shall not interfere in their activity provided they do not contradict the law," the practice has been anything but that. The Uzbekistani state does not take kindly to voluntary organizations and independent initiative in any sphere of life. It treats MBU as an official organ and routinely interferes in its work, hiring and firing imams of mosques, controlling what is taught in the madrasas, and vigorously censoring all religious literature. It also requires unwavering loyalty of official ulama. Anyone holding an appointment in an official mosque has to pass a test in "political literacy": he needs to know the national anthem, be able to pass a test on Karimov's writings, and express support for the established constitutional order and for the services of the president in "securing stability and prosperity in the country."

Much as SADUM did in the Soviet period, the MBU issues fatwas as demanded by the state. In January 1998, for instance, it outlawed the use of loudspeakers in mosques because the practice is not "one of the fundamentals of Islam." Imams are not allowed to compose their own sermons; they must read from texts provided by MBU. More interestingly, the regime uses the MBU to counter the "extremists" on religious grounds, arguing in effect that those who seek to establish an Islamic state in Uzbekistan—or indeed, all those who practice Islam outside the framework of MBU-controlled institutions—are not good Muslims. It does so by turning to the Hanafi tradition of the region, in which the regime can find a position that validates coexistence with the state and that it can wield against the claims of those who reject local customs and traditions for not being authentically Islamic. This stance has, in effect, turned the Hanafi canon into an orthodoxy that is quite new in the history of Central Asia. In March 2000, the MBU adopted a new program "for defending our noble religion and [for the struggle] against fundamentalism and various extremist tendencies" that established Hanafi dogma as officially binding and mobilized all imams to speak out against non-Hanafi tendencies.[2] In recent years, the MBU has enjoyed a near monopoly on the publication of religious literature. Independent publishers, or those who might want to sponsor the publication of Islamic books as a pious deed, are discouraged.[3] MBU's publications present traditional Hanafi views on belief and piety. This marks a shift from the innovations SADUM undertook in the Soviet era, when many of its fatwas directly contradicted the region's Hanafi heritage. The Karimov regime has adopted the conservative Hanafi position espoused by Muhammadjan Hindustoniy.

The regime has also strengthened its control over religious education. Of the many new madrasas that emerged during the Gorbachev years, only ten remain. They are strictly regulated, and entering students must pass exams in a foreign language and in the history of Uzbekistan, in addition to submitting to a personal interview, so that authorities can gauge their political reliability. Beyond these secondary-level institutions, only the Soviet-era Tashkent Islamic Institute is available to students interested in higher Islamic education.[4] In April 1999, the government established the Tashkent Islamic University, ostensibly as a conduit for Islamic education not controlled by the ulama. The mission of the university is described in Soviet-style officialese as "the deep study of the rich and unique spiritual-cultural heritage connected to Islam . . . and to prepare highly qualified specialist cadres capable of answering the needs of the times."[5] A high university official told me when the university opened, "This is not a madrasa. We want to educate our students according to modern methods." The university has two faculties, of "fiqh, economics, and the natural sciences" (a curious combination indeed) and of "Islamic history and philosophy." "Religious studies" (dinshunoslik) is only one of the four majors offered, with fewer than one-third of incoming students able to take it. Because the university recruits students from state schools, which have no instruction in religion, its students begin from scratch. With its lavish funding, the university seems to have become yet another elite institution for well-connected urban families. As stated, state schools have no instruction in religion, but all students in middle and higher educational institutions are required to take the course "Religious Extremism and Fundamentalism: Its History, Nature, and the Present Danger." This course is often the first time students encounter religion in a school setting.[6]

Those who run afoul of the state are accused of being Wahhabis. The term Wahhabi, as we have seen, is never neutral. Hindustoniy dubbed his rebellious students, the mujaddids, "Wahhabis," even though they had little direct connection with the followers of Muhammad ibn 'Abd al-Wahhab. But in the Gorbachev years, the Soviet world began using the term as a catch-all for all nontraditional Muslims. In this usage, Wahhabi evokes a dark and sinister force of foreign origin that seeks to subvert normal life. The use of the term to label all distasteful opponents has become so routine in post-Soviet rhetoric that Feliks Kulov, then minister for national security in Kyrgyzstan could speak in 1997 of "foreign Wahhabi emissaries, from Iran in particular"![7] Accusations of Wahhabism, therefore, need to be taken with a grain of salt. Even if being a Wahhabi were a crime, most of the people caught up in the dragnet are not Wahhabi but merely pious Muslims who worship outside the parameters of official Islam. In the hands of the Uzbekistani state, the term has become synonymous with *independent Muslim,* but we must also be aware of the nativist connotations of the label. The Hanafi tradition now defended by the MBU is a national Uzbek tradition, whereas Wahhabism is an Arab import and is hence not authentic to the Uzbek people.

Official imams are expected to denounce independent Muslims for the errors of their ways and to call on them to mend their ways and seek the forgiveness of the state. They can find ammunition for such an argument in Islamic sources. "What was the greatest quality that our Prophet Muhammad possessed?" asks an imam in denouncing an independent Muslim. The Prophet, he answers, "always generously forgave guilt if a guilty person came to him with a confession and asked forgiveness. Even in cases where someone came to him intending to kill him, he called on that person with kind words to become a Muslim and forgave him. . . . Our respected President also possesses these same qualities. Even though criminals, hating our independence, slander the President and work against his policies, if they come to him and ask for forgiveness, regretting what they have done, even if they came back from abroad, the President will say, 'I forgive them!' "[8] Karimov obviously does not mind the comparison with the Prophet in such cases. Imams who refuse to go along are fired and some have been prosecuted as Wahhabis.

Ultimately, the state wants to define "true" Islam. True Islam is moderate, politically harmless, and compatible with the temper of the Uzbek people. All other forms of Islam are "extremist," "separatist," and dangerous. The MBU's job is to define the boundaries of true Islam, but occasionally the Committee on Religious Affairs, the bureaucratic organization that oversees the MBU, takes it upon itself to make these judgments. In trials of independent Muslims, it provides expert testimony on whether literature confiscated from the accused is acceptable or not. Sometimes, judges lecture those being prosecuted for belonging to "extremist" organizations and for their "incorrect" beliefs. "Real Muslims cannot join this party," the judge Mansur Ahmadjonov told defendants at the first Hizb-ut-Tahrir trial in 1998, "and people cannot believe this

is the real way of Islam. The Prophet said that the Caliphate will continue for [only] thirty years after his death and [therefore] this is not a
contemporary idea. The idea of a Caliphate and converting all people to
Islam is not the true way of Islam."[9] The following year, the head of the
MBU issued a fatwa ordering all Muslims "to break off all family relations with mercenary-minded people belonging to the Hizb-ut-Tahrir
sect, with those who have not shunned the sect's goals, words, and oaths
and have not repented. All neighborly relations should be eliminated
with them. They should not be spoken to. But extremely strict measures
should be undertaken against them in order to open their eyes."[10] He followed up this statement with another decree denying a Muslim burial to
those who do not recant oaths they have taken to support unregistered
Islamic groups.[11]

•   •   •

The control of Islam through MBU coexists with harsh persecution of all
other expressions of Islam. Even in the Gorbachev years, Uzbekistani
authorities were not fond of unauthorized expressions of Islam. An
attempt to establish a local branch of the Islamic Renaissance Party was
unceremoniously scuttled in January 1991. Controlling the Ferghana
Valley proved to be more difficult, and Islamic organizations were able to
form there. The Adolat episode later that year, however, confirmed for
the regime the danger of uncontrolled Islamic organizations. The war in
Afghanistan, which continued unabated, and Tajikistan's descent into
civil war did not help matters, and the regime continued to hold up those
two examples to make its case for stability.

As soon as the regime could do so, it banned Adolat and similar
organizations. Imam Abdulla O'tayev, the prime mover behind the
attempted organization of the IRP in Uzbekistan, "disappeared" in
1992.[12] In the autumn of 1994, Dodaxon Hasan, a popular *hofiz* (singer
of traditional songs) who had often criticized the moral shortcomings of
"bigwigs and leaders" in his songs, was arrested.[13] The following year,
the government began a systematic campaign targeting imams who did
not toe the official line. On August 29, 1995, Abduvali-qori Mirzoyev,
the popular imam of the Friday mosque in Andijan, the biggest one in the
city, disappeared. Abduvali-qori, a former student of Muhammadjan
Hindustani, had refused to heap fulsome praise on the president, as was
increasingly expected of all imams. He had, however, never been vocal in
the opposition. He was last seen boarding a plane for Moscow to attend

an international conference. The plane arrived without him. Eyewitness reports of his detention by security agents as he boarded the plane were flatly denied by the government, which later was to accuse Mirzoyev of engineering his own disappearance in order to smear the government.[14] Elders from Andijan traveled to Tashkent to petition the presidential palace and the U.N. offices in Tashkent, but to no avail. Instead, the Friday mosque was closed and turned into an art museum.

But the campaign against "extremism" began in earnest in the winter of 1997–98. In December 1997, a series of murders shook the city of Namangan. A policeman was beheaded, and his disembodied head left outside the police station where he worked. Two other people, a former chairman of a kolkhoz and his wife, were beheaded a week later, and three policemen died in a shoot-out with a criminal suspect soon after. The murders might conceivably have been the work of Muslim activists, although they were far more likely to have been connected to the world of crime. Two similar murders followed in the same month. The government seized the chance to launch a major campaign against "extremism." In the days following the murders, police swept through the town, arresting over a thousand people. Most of the detainees were men accused of being Wahhabis—those who attended mosques not controlled by the Muslim Board of Uzbekistan, supported other Islamic activities, or simply wore a beard, considered a sign of piety. In other cases, men were forced to shave their beards off, and students were expelled from educational institutions for wearing head scarves or beards. Then, on March 5, 1998, another prominent imam, Obidxon-qori Nazarov, imam of the official To'xtaboy mosque in Tashkent, disappeared. He was an official imam in an official mosque, who had refused to praise the president in his sermons or to inform on those who worshipped in his mosque. He had also spoken out against the disappearance of Abduvali-qori.[15]

Karimov used the campaign to push through a new law, On Freedom of Conscience and Religious Organizations. In true Orwellian fashion, this law imposed strict controls on religious observance, making it the purview solely of officially recognized organizations and tightening the rules for their registration. All mosques were supposed to apply for registration with the Ministry of Justice. Underlying this requirement was the assumption that all mosques were potentially dangerous spaces. "The mosques have plenty of money," Karimov told parliament in April 1998. "They do not pay any taxes in most cases. For what purposes do they use their money? They bribe the local governors or the local representatives of the justice ministry. . . . There is definitely outside influence. Someone is instructing them to manage weapons, training them as rebels and teaching them to explode their homeland."[16] The danger was extreme, and no means were to be spared in the struggle. "Such people [Islamic extremists] must be shot in the head," Karimov fulminated in parliament. "If necessary, I'll shoot them myself, if you lack the resolve."[17]

Although the ostensible purpose of the Law on Religious Freedom and Religious Organizations is "to ensure the right of every person to freedom of worship and religion, and the equality of [all] citizens irrespective of their religious convictions," the law also seeks "to regulate relations arising from the activity of religious organizations."[18] This right to regulate, justified by the state's mission to prevent "religious or other fanaticism and extremism, and actions aimed at setting off one religion against another," gives the state sweeping powers over all religious activity (defined as "the joint profession of a religion, [and the] exercise of religious services, customs and rituals") and makes a sham of the separation of religion and state entrenched in the constitution (and repeated in the law itself). Ultimately, religious freedom is not absolute but is subject to "restrictions necessary to ensure national security and public order, and life, health, morals, rights and freedoms of other citizens." Religious convictions are not an acceptable basis for refusing obligations imposed by state law.

The law requires religious activity to take place only within the purview of registered (that is, officially approved) organizations. A religious organization "is a voluntary association . . . set up at an initiative of not less than 100 citizens of the Republic of Uzbekistan aged over 18 and permanently residing on the territory of the Republic of Uzbekistan." Each organization should draw up a charter (*ustav*) indicating, among other things, the organization's sources of funding and should apply for registration with the ministry of justice. All religious activity taking place beyond the ambit of officially recognized organizations is, by definition, illegal. Failure to register a religious organization not only means that the group will not enjoy certain rights, but it also means that the group is illegal and that membership in it is criminalized. Only registered organizations have the right to impart religious education ("to train clergy and required religious personnel"); "private teaching of religious principles is prohibited," as is any religious instruction in schools. The law also prohibits citizens of Uzbekistan (except "ministers of a religious organization") from appearing in public in religious attire. The import and publishing of religious literature are permitted as long as the state does not object to the content of the material. Proselytism is prohibited, as are political parties with religious platforms. Infractions are punishable under the administrative code on the first offense and under the criminal code thereafter.

This draconian law provides legal cover for the state's persecution of all religious activity it does not control. Like its Soviet parent, this law takes the church as the model of all religious organization. Islamic observance does not require such an organizational form, but now the state mandates it. Mosques, which tended to be centers of the communities, now have to register or close. Registration is not a right but a matter of national security; it is a complicated bureaucratic procedure requiring the submission of numerous documents and a registration fee. As can easily be imagined, the authorities can find any number of pretexts for denying requests for registration. The law also severely curtails religious education and publishing and subjects these activities to government control. This restriction is particularly significant given that, historically, religious knowledge was kept alive in the Soviet period through private education. The criminal code was amended to make the possession and distribution of literature containing ideas of "religious extremism, separatism, and fundamentalism" a serious offense. The relevant terms and phrases are nowhere defined. Producing and storing materials that contain "ideas of religious extremism, separatism and fundamentalism," with the goal of distributing them, is punishable by up to three years in prison, whereas distribution of such literature carries a maximum sentence of five years in prison. In practice, courts have found the mere possession of unauthorized religious literature acceptable grounds for conviction.

The government has also made liberal use of three other articles of the criminal code in its prosecution of independent Muslims. These articles relate to subversion, organization of a criminal group, and incitement of ethnic, racial, or religious enmity. All religious activity outside the ambit of officially recognized associations can—and has been—prosecuted under any or all of these articles. Other "independent Muslims" have been prosecuted on purely criminal charges, such as the possession of drugs and weapons, which police routinely plant on suspects.

The crackdown on "extremism" reached a crescendo between 1999 and 2001 but has never stopped. Indeed, the 1998 law is written vaguely enough to make expansive application very easy. The prohibition on religious attire in public is a case in point. Islam has no clergy and no clerical attire specific to it. Rather, in each Muslim society, certain modes of dress and comportment denote piety or strict observance. In Uzbekistan, demonstrations of piety usually include a beard for men and modest dress, usually a scarf, for women. Beards and scarves can—and have been—deemed to be religious attire, and those wearing them can be prosecuted for breaking the law. Prayer outside a mosque, a perfectly normal phenomenon in Islam, can similarly be construed as an infraction of the law. In some cases, police have forcibly shaved beards off the faces of young men. The requirement to register every mosque has resulted in a huge reduction in the numbers of mosques, especially in the Ferghana Valley. Of about 2,200 mosques in and around Andijan in the mid-1990s, only 42 were able to reregister. In Namangan, a government commission stopped all but 240 of the 1,000 mosques there from operating.[19] The result has been a permanent atmosphere of harassment and persecution. Mosque attendance has fallen, as many people have stopped praying in public for fear of being taken for extremists. Others have shaved their beards for the same reason.

The campaign against "religious extremism, separatism and fundamentalism" has targeted several groups: imams who are less than willing to obey all commands of the MBU, individuals suspected of belonging to the IMU, and, increasingly, members of the HTI. But the dragnet has also swept along followers, students, and family members of the suspects, along with many others who are merely pious or who study or worship beyond the narrow limits set by the law. Human Rights Watch, the New York–based monitoring group, has maintained an office in Tashkent since 1994 and done signal work in documenting the gross violations of human rights in independent Uzbekistan. Its staff has attended hundreds of trials; gathered testimony from relatives, eyewitnesses, and local activists; and produced a meticulously documented account of this campaign. The account below reproduces only some of the evidence gathered by the organization.

The campaign has targeted the followers of particular imams. Since Obidxon Nazarov disappeared in 1998, many of his followers and family members have paid the price of having known him. His former deputy, Abduvohid Yo'ldoshev (b. 1968), was reputed to have been a popular and dynamic imam. When Nazarov was removed from his post as imam of To'xtaboy mosque in 1996, Yo'ldoshev was detained and held for fifteen days on misdemeanor charges of "hooliganism." In February 1999, he was arrested after prayer at the Ilonli Ota mosque and was convicted of drug possession. An appeals court released him on parole in August 1999, but his release was conditional and authorities kept him under tight surveillance. He was compelled to sign a statement avowing that "I, Abduvahid Yo'ldoshev, am not a member of any religious sect and do not approve of these sects," even though he had originally been arrested on drug-related charges. He was arrested again in July 2000 and, after being held incommunicado for more than five months, was sentenced to nineteen years in prison on an array of charges: conspiracy to overthrow the state; leadership of a criminal group; leadership of a religious extremist, separatist, fundamentalist or other banned organization; possession and distribution of literature containing ideas of religious extremism, separatism, and fundamentalism; and illegal acquisition of foreign currency. The state's case against Yo'ldoshev rested on the allegations that lessons he gave on the Qur'an and other Islamic texts while serving as a state-appointed imam were really lessons in Wahhabism and calls for holy war; that the defendants had distributed Wahhabi literature (which, as Human Rights Watch noted, was not produced in court) and had possessed audio- and video-cassettes of speeches made years earlier by Nazarov and Mirzoyev; and that they had recorded and distributed broadcasts of Radio Liberty and the BBC.[20]

Police arrested Ahad Barnoyev on March 15, 1999. Barnoyev had been imam of the officially registered Otavulloxon mosque in Namangan from 1991 to 1995. His crime was allowing Wahhabis to attend his mosque. Barnoyev denied the charge in court, retorting that some of his congregation were given this label only because they raised their hands during prayers and said "amen" aloud during the prayer. The state alleged, however, that those associated with the imam's mosque created an organization composed of "reactionary religious extremists." Police also claimed to have found "Wahhabi leaflets" and weapons in his home. The court found that during his time as imam of the Otavulloxon mosque, Barnoyev had "significantly contributed to the spread of Wahhabism," and "had been an instructor and leader of Wahhabis," and sentenced him to eighteen years in prison and confiscation of his property.[21] In November 2000, fifteen men were accused of having studied the Qur'an and hadith in private classes or gatherings with a man named Rahmatullo. The state charged that the classes on the Qur'an included discussions of holy war. The state's indictment of the fifteen men labeled them "Wahhabis" and "members of a Wahhabi trend." The fifteen were sentenced to prison terms ranging from six to nineteen years for "attempted overthrow of the state; organization of, or participation in, a banned religious group; and organization of, or participation in, a religious extremist, separatist, fundamentalist or other banned organization."[22]

The first trial of men accused of membership in the Hizb-ut-Tahrir took place in 1998, but since then, such trials have become routine. At the time of writing, some six thousand people are in jail for religious offenses, the majority of them accused of membership in the HTI. In such cases, the prisoners are being punished for the exchange of ideas and the study or possession of texts. Indeed, in the language of the indictments, literature that the authorities deem to be extremist is as dangerous as weapons (police have taken to planting illegal religious literature on suspects alongside arms and drugs). Although this stance bespeaks a high regard for the written word on the part of Uzbekistani authorities, it constitutes a gross violation of human rights and of the norms of civil society. For the state, however, the issues are straightforward. HTI's goal of creating a caliphate is, by definition, a call to subvert the existing government of Uzbekistan. The government conflates discussion of alternative forms of government with active attempts to overthrow the state, and it persecutes the practice. The mere possession of banned literature is proof of criminal intent.

·   ·   ·

In the way charges are framed, the way trials progress, the use of confessions as proof, and the language of indictments and judgments, these trials are reminiscent of the purge trials of the 1930s. The similarity extends to the use of tactics such as torture during pretrial detention, the targeting of family members, and the use of public humiliation and shaming. Karimov has said, "The fathers who have brought up them will be brought to account together with their children. If necessary I could sign a decree on this. The fathers are answerable. We will not fight against women, but we will take fathers by the scruff of the neck and bring them to their sons. We will take them to a certain place, interrogate and punish them. Let them know this."[23] Karimov's exemption of women from this threat has not been kept, and prisoners have routinely been threatened with the rape of female relatives if they do not confess. The brutality of a modern police apparatus is thus justified by appeal to traditional national values in which the family figures large as the hearth of morality.

The same appeal to national values has allowed the state to extend its reach into society by harnessing the mahalla, the neighborhood community, to do the work of surveillance and monitoring. As a residential community knit together with ties of mutual support and obligation, the mahalla has long been the node of social life in the cities of Central Asia.

As we saw in chapter 4, it continued to exist even during the Soviet period. The Soviet state used it as the basic unit of administration, when every mahalla had a Communist Party cell and an administrative committee. Since independence, the Karimov regime has made the "rejuvenation" of the mahalla a major plank of its agenda to make the state more Uzbek. The state has recognized mahallas as the fundamental unit of society and has divided the entire country, from villages to high-rise neighborhoods in cities, into mahalla units. Mahalla committees are now formal administrative organs of the state, responsible to regional governors and tasked with the implementation of government decrees and policies. The mahalla still continues to be the place where people lead their daily lives, but it has now been absorbed into the administrative structure of the modern state.[24]

While the state's use of the mahalla is not in itself connected to its campaign against Islam, the mahalla has fit in very well with the campaign. Speaking in the immediate aftermath of the Tashkent bombings of 1999, Karimov said, "In my opinion, every neighborhood committee should supervise the work of their local mosque. What are those mosques there for? They are there not for chief prayer-leaders but for people, for religious people, for the neighborhood. Mosques are designed to improve the life of the neighborhood, to improve people's lives and to inculcate the belief in life after death in the minds of people. They should also explain to people what it's like to have a guilty conscience, and to arouse their conscience. I repeat that if there is a mosque in the neighborhood then the local council should keep their eyes open to verify whether the mosque is fulfilling its duties."[25] In practice, the surveillance expected of mahalla committees has extended to all facets of the lives of those who live in the mahalla. Mahalla committees work in close contact with the police and have the right to go door to door to check on matters such as who prays, who has a beard, and who teaches children about Islam. According to a Human Rights Watch report on the subject, law-enforcement agencies reportedly have given mahalla committee chairmen questionnaires seeking information such as lists of the names and addresses of those who encourage women and children to pray or of those who themselves pray in unauthorized places in the city; information about "Wahhabis" who have served a prison sentence and information about their families; lists of those who have or have had a beard and those considered "authoritative," "leaders," or "unruly."[26]

Mahallas have also become the site of another Soviet ritual that the Uzbekistani state uses to control its population: public humiliation through hate rallies. These rallies are staged events, at which attendance is compulsory for both the "target" and the spectators, who are inhabitants of the mahalla summoned for the meeting. The targets, who are either accused people awaiting trial or their relatives, stand while visiting officials denounce their crimes and give warnings (to the mahalla residents as much as to the targets) against following the wrong kind of Islam and against extremism and fanaticism. When the officials finish their statements, residents take turns denouncing the target, disavowing neighborly relations and sometimes calling for incarceration or execution. The targets are branded "enemies of the state" or "enemies of the people," terms redolent of the Soviet past. Targets are called upon to repent and seek forgiveness not only of their neighbors but also of the president and of the people of Uzbekistan as a whole.[27] The purpose of the rallies is to render the targets completely vulnerable by cutting off their support networks in society, while inculcating a sense among the general populace that the "extremists" are dangerous.

The struggle against extremism also gives Uzbekistan an issue on which to assert its power against its neighbors. Ever since independence, the Uzbekistani government has pointed to Afghanistan and Tajikistan as sources of harm to and instability in the whole region. Uzbekistan intervened actively in the Tajik civil war on the side of the neo-Soviets in order to curb the influence of "Islamic extremists." The Uzbekistani government also routinely criticizes all its neighbors for not doing enough to curb the dangers posed by extremists, and its security agents operate with impunity in Kazakhstan and Kyrgyzstan. Especially in the latter, with which Uzbekistan shares the Ferghana Valley, Uzbekistani police have carried out a number of kidnappings: Uzbek-speaking suspects, even if they are citizens of Kyrgyzstan, have been abducted and brought to Uzbekistan to face trial.

•   •   •

While the Uzbekistani state's persecution of "Wahhabis" is part of a broader campaign that leaves no opposition group untouched, it clearly bears a special animus toward independent Muslims.[28] The strict-regime prison of Jaslyk, situated in the north of the country on the site of a Soviet chemical-testing ground and closed to all unauthorized individuals, has been specially designated for religious and political prisoners. Religious prisoners face lengthy sentences to strict-regime prisons. Judges show little independence in determining sentences, condemning men to roughly the number of years in prison demanded by the procurator and very rarely finding against the state.[29] And although all prisoners are treated badly in Uzbekistani prisons, plenty of evidence exists that independent Muslims are singled out for abuse. "Those who are imprisoned for practicing their faith outside state-controls are often subject to the most horrific forms of torture: electric shock, asphyxiation with gas masks or plastic bags, injections of psychotropic drugs, beatings with batons or metal rods, hanging from the ceiling by the wrists or ankles, rape and sodomy."[30] Often, these measures are punishment for trying to worship inside the prison. Although the 1998 law explicitly allows "worship and religious rites" in "detention centers, prisons and labor camps," religious observance is prohibited in several strict-regime prisons that house prisoners accused of extremism. Prison authorities take it upon themselves to break the prisoners of their extremism by forcing them to renounce their beliefs or to indulge in blasphemous behavior. In testimony before the U.S. House Committee on International Relations, a representative of Human Rights Watch cited the example of a prisoner at Navoiy prison 64/29 who, in September 2003, was beaten on the soles of his feet until he lost consciousness as punishment for praying. When he regained consciousness, the authorities sent the prisoner to a punishment cell, warned him not to make a complaint, and tried to force him to bow in prayer to the deputy head of the prison.[31] Many other reports state that guards have punished and beaten independent Muslim prisoners for religious observance in custody. One member of Hizb-ut-Tahrir told Human Rights Watch, "prison 'rules' prohibit ablution, prayer, fasting, calling (da'wa) to Islam, reciting the Qur'an and require singing the [national] anthem, [seeking] forgiveness of and glorifying the president, Karimov." At Jaslyk prison, inmates were "allegedly beaten, threatened with sexual violence, and placed in solitary confinement for refusing to renounce their religious beliefs. . . . Observance of Muslim religious rites is prohibited in the prison. Those who observed daily prayers were reportedly punished with fifteen days in isolation cells and denial of food."[32]

Then there is the case of Muzaffar Avazov, 35, who, while serving an eighteen-year sentence for involvement with the Hizb-ut-Tahrir, was beaten and put in a punishment cell for stating that nothing could stop him from performing his prayers. On August 8, 2002, his body was returned to his family. Pictures of the body showed extensive bruises and burns. Using the photographs of the body, an expert forensic examination at the University of Glasgow concluded that "the pattern of scalding shows a well-demarcated line on the lower chest/abdomen, which could well indicate the forceful application of hot water whilst the person is within some kind of bath or similar vessel. Such scalding does not have the splash pattern that is associated with random application as one would expect with accidental scalding." Avazov had been boiled alive.[33]

•   •   •

For much of the time that Uzbekistan has been independent, the West has seen it as a guarantor of stability in the region. But in 1999, the United States entered into active cooperation with the Karimov regime that did much to embolden it and provided it with a significant amount of cover from international opprobrium.

The U.S. interest in cooperation with Uzbekistan was dictated by the unfinished aftermath of the war in Afghanistan. Once Osama bin Laden found sanctuary in Afghanistan under the Taliban, the CIA began training an Uzbekistani commando force to carry out covert operations against him. The CIA also procured the use of Uzbekistani air bases from which it flew unmanned spy planes into Afghanistan.[34] (It was in this period that the IMU was placed on the State Department's list of terrorist organizations.) This cooperation became public and was turned into an alliance in the immediate aftermath of September 11. On October 5, 2001, the United States acquired the use of air bases in Khanabad and Qarshi in the south of Uzbekistan, in support of its campaign against the Taliban. Afghanistan's misfortunes had come full circle. Twenty-two years after the Soviet invasion of Afghanistan, the United States, allied with a government headed by a former Soviet functionary, was using Soviet air bases to wage war on Afghanistan, fighting groups that were a direct product of the its own proxy war.

The Uzbekistani contribution to the "war on terror" paid off. Karimov was invited to the United States for a state visit in March 2002, during which the two governments signed a Declaration of Strategic Partnership. Karimov received a standing ovation in the Senate and received the award from Henry Kissinger that is memorialized in Uzbekistan's national history museum. Relations between the two countries blossomed: in 2003, Karimov enthusiastically supported the United States in the invasion of Iraq. In 2004, the State Department described Uzbekistan as "a strong partner of the United States on foreign policy and security issues ranging from Iraq to Cuba, and nuclear proliferation to narcotics trafficking. . . . The United States," it continued, "values

Uzbekistan as a stable, moderate force in a turbulent region."[35] The alliance faltered in mid-2005, but it did so because Karimov decided to reorient Uzbekistan's strategic posture, not because of any qualms on the part of the United States.

•   •   •

In Kazakhstan, the "Islamic threat" has not loomed as large in the policies of the regime as it has in Uzbekistan. Nevertheless, Kazakhstan too has a law, dating from 1993—On the Freedom of Religion and on Religious Associations—that prohibits the formation of "parties or other political formations of a religious character and the participation of religious associations in the activity of political parties or rendering financial assistance to them."[36] This law has been expanded since then to include prohibitions against distributing printed materials that support "extremism" and against proselytism without official permission. At the same time, the Spiritual Administration for the Muslims of Kazakhstan, which split off from SADUM in 1990, functions as a quasi-official body.

The question of extremism came to the fore in the late 1990s, primarily because of the emergence of the Hizb-ut-Tahrir in the country. Although the organization was formally banned only in October 2004, it was persecuted all along (although not as harshly as in Uzbekistan). Many HTI members have been arrested for distributing leaflets or merely for their membership in the group. In December 2003, a certain Ghani Baisalbayev approached a television station and asked to speak to reporters. No sooner had he identified himself as the leader of an HTI cell than the station staff called the police and had him arrested. In April 2004, he was sentenced to four years in prison for belonging to the organization. A week later, Rahmatulla Abdullayev went on trial in Shymkent on charges of operating an underground printing press, which he used to print HTI leaflets.[37] Those arrested were charged with engaging in illegal public assembly, distributing leaflets, inciting religious strife, or attempting to overthrow the government. In early 2005, a new law, On Resisting Extremism, made membership in the party illegal.

The government has also sought to assert its control over religious education and over mosques. The only institution of Islamic learning in the country bears the awkward name of Nur-Mubarak Egyptian University of Islamic Culture. It was established in 2003 as the result of an official agreement between Kazakhstan and Egypt (and named after the two presidents, Nursultan Nazarbaev and Hosni Mubarak), and it is staffed in part by professors from Egypt who teach in Arabic. This university is clearly an attempt to control the direction and content of Islamic education in the country. With all other madrasas closed or pushed underground, the official university can ensure that the teaching is politically safe. The fact that so much of the instruction is in Arabic furthers this point, for the two hundred or so students spend the bulk of their time learning that language.[38]

In December 2004, the Spiritual Administration for the Muslims of Kazakhstan began testing all imams in questions of belief. Those who failed the test were to be removed from their position. Ostensibly, the goal was to weed out ignorant imams, but the move was clearly understood as an attempt to establish greater state control over mosques. The testing took place in tandem with a requirement that all mosques and religious associations register with the government, or be closed down. The mayor of the town of Sairam made the point quite bluntly. "We have a plan: Sairam has 26 mosques for a population of 25,000. We want to keep one mosque and close the rest down," he said. "If people pray at one mosque, and listen to the same imams, then there's less chance they will fall under the influence of missionaries from extremist organizations."[39]

Nor is Tajikistan much different. The peace agreement that ended the civil war (see chapter 6) gave the IRP a smallish share of power in the country, and Tajikistan is often touted as the land of a "secular-religious compromise." Yet the political order that emerged after the peace was really a victory of secular, neo-Soviet factions, and their basic assumptions about religion and politics described above still drive policy. Technically, Tajikistan has no official establishment akin to the Muslim Board of Uzbekistan; all Islamic organizations nevertheless report to the Islamic Center of Tajikistan, which, though not a government body, is completely subordinate to the government. The center examines imams and hires and fires them. Religious organizations are also required to register with the state, and although the constitution was amended after the peace accords to allow religious parties, political activism by religious leaders is prohibited and the government has the right to control religious education and to regulate the content of religious literature.

The Tajik state that was knit back together after the civil war is dominated by an enlarged Kulobi faction, with Emomali Rahmonov, the president, slowly consolidating his position at the expense of the various warlords who emerged during that conflict. The IRP's place in the new balance of power is quite precarious. On one side, the Kulobis have shut it out of positions of influence in the state; on the other side, it is challenged by more radical religious groups, such as HTI, but also by the aggressively proselytizing Christian groups that have suddenly become active in the country.[40] These challenges leave IRP in a quandary about how to safeguard its place in Tajikistani politics. Some in the party, such as its deputy leader, Muhiddin Kabiri, argue that the only relevant model for the party is "Euro-Islam," which could draw on the experience of Muslims living in Europe, who have had to learn how to be good Muslims while living in a non-Muslim state.[41] Others would like to work toward making Tajikistan an Islamic state, although they seem to have little clarity about what that task would entail.

The state also seeks to control education and mosques. In August 2002, the news that several Tajikistani citizens were among the inmates of the U.S. prison camp in Guantánamo Bay in Cuba was enough for the government to shut down eight mosques in the Isfara region in the north of the country. Local authorities have closed other mosques over the years for various infringements of registration-related regulations. Islamic education is in poor shape: Tajikistan has twenty-one madrasas and one advanced institute, all of which provide a deeply conservative education, "on the Bukharan model," as one critic told me. Students in these madrasas lack the wherewithal to answer the challenges posed by HTI or Christian missionaries. Indeed, one scholar has spoken of the "unfathomable institutional weakness" of Islam in Tajikistan, and argues that this weakness, rather than any strength, might be the cause of instability in the country.[42] The state harbors a deep suspicion of foreign Islamic education. Students who go abroad to study find themselves blacklisted on their return and are unable to gain legal employment.[43] Meanwhile, the IRP finds that its biggest asset is its legalized position, which allows it to side with the government in the persecution of HTI. HTI is illegal, and its members have been persecuted for several years, though again not in quite the same numbers as in Uzbekistan. The "secular-religious compromise" in Tajikistan does not keep the state from acting like any other post-Soviet state.

·   ·   ·

And then there is Saparmurat Niyazov, the eccentric leader of Turkmenistan, who has chosen a different strand of the Soviet legacy to perpetuate his rule and taken it to its most absurd extreme. He has built a cult of personality around himself that rivals that of Stalin. The first secretary of the Turkmenistan's Communist Party at the time of the collapse of the

Soviet Union, he has reinvented himself as a national leader, but one who embodies the nation and personifies the state, as expressed in the ubiquitous slogan "Halk, Watan, Türkmenbaşy" ("Nation, Homeland, Türkmenbashy"). The weakness of the opposition in the Gorbachev era meant that Niyazov did not suffer even the minor hiccups on his way to consolidating power that Karimov did. He was elected president of the republic in 1990, when he ran unopposed, and reconfirmed in that position after independence by a Soviet-style 99.5 percent vote in 1992. Since then, the parliament has bestowed on him the title of Türkmenbashy, "head Turkmen," although, in all modesty, he calls himself merely Beýik Saparmyrad Türkmenbaşy, Saparmurad Türkmenbashy the Great. The national oath is worth quoting in full: "Turkmenistan, my beloved motherland, my beloved homeland! You are always with me, in my thoughts and in my heart. For the slightest evil against you, let my hand be lost. For the slightest slander about you, let my tongue be lost. At the moment of my betrayal to my motherland, to her sacred banner, to Saparmurat Türkmenbashy the Great, let my breath stop."[44] Niyazov's presence is therefore hard to miss in the country. His profile is superimposed on the upper-right corner of all television broadcasts, his statues are everywhere (one giant, gold plated example, with arms outstretched, revolves so that it always faces the sun), and his likeness appears on billboards and the sides of buildings; on portraits in every government office, school, and hospital; on newspapers and banknotes; and on bottles of vodka and brandy produced by the national monopoly. Countless streets, squares, mosques, factories, and farms, as well as a whole city, have been named after him. He has renamed the days of the week and months of the year (January is named after him and April after his mother). Turkmenistan under Türkmenbashy seems like Soviet gallows humor come to life.

In 1991, there was talk of Turkmenistan, with its rich deposits of natural gas, becoming another Kuwait, a resource-rich autocracy in which the ruling elite purchases the political quiescence of its subjects by using some of the wealth to provide first-world comforts to all. That promise has evaporated. Niyazov has undertaken a megalomaniacal program of monumental construction in the capital, Ashgabat, which has acquired marble façades by the dozen, and rumors suggest that Niyazov's offshore personal fortune is worth $2.5 billion, but ordinary citizens live in grinding poverty, unrelieved even by the achievements of the Soviet era, which have been destroyed.[45] They are, moreover, subject to Niyazov's whimsy, which carries the force of law. In the name of rebuilding Turkmen national pride and making Turkmenistan more Turkmen, he has banned opera, ballet, cinemas, circuses (none of which are authentically Turkmen), the use of recorded music (bad for the imaginativeness of live performers), car radios, gold teeth, and long hair and beards on young men. In recent years, the whimsy has become ever more dangerous. In February 2005, Niyazov decided to close down all hospitals in the country except those in Ashgabat. "Why do we need hospitals and doctors all over the country?" he asked. "Let citizens come to the capital and be treated there." Six months later, he ordered all libraries except the national library closed. The national library had already been gutted of all its Russian-language books (which comprised the overwhelming part of the collection).

Niyazov's policies toward Islam unfold in this context. He too began by celebrating Islam as part of the nation's heritage but has increasingly sought to appropriate religious authority himself, to add a religious dimension to the national legitimacy he seeks in portraying himself as Türkmenbashy. This policy, of course, leads to strict control of religious activity and harsh repression of all unauthorized expressions of Islam. As Niyazov put it succinctly, "We keep religion pure and we will not use it for political purposes, nor will we allow anyone else to use religion for their personal ambition."[46]

Turkmenistan's early years after independence were typical enough for Central Asia. The constitution proclaimed the separation of religion and state, religious parties were outlawed, and registration was mandated for all religious organization. A council on religious affairs, directly subordinate to the president, was assigned the task of approving the appointments of all imams in the country. But Niyazov took everything one step forward in 2000, when he published the *Ruhnama* (Book of the Spirit), a rambling collection of thoughts on Turkmen history, ethics, politics, and many other things, which was "written with the help of inspiration sent to my heart by the God who created this wonderful universe."[47] Very quickly, the book acquired a sacral aura: it became "Holy Ruhnama," with government officials comparing its importance to that of the Qur'an and the Bible, neither of which were allegedly fully adequate for the spiritual needs of Turkmens. It was translated into numerous foreign languages (usually funded by foreign companies doing business in Turkmenistan, although the English edition seems to have been produced by the government itself).[48] It acquired its own monument in Ashgabat and became required reading for all citizens: government offices have study hours set aside for it, schoolchildren learn it by heart (and learn English from the English translation of the book), and aspirants to a driver's license need to pass an examination on the message of the book. September is now called Ruhnama.

In May 2001, Niyazov's press secretary declared, "Saparmurat Turkmenbashy is a national prophet, sent to the Turkmen people in the third millennium."[49] The statement is blasphemous for the vast majority of Muslims, but nevertheless amusing for its juxtaposition of the Stalinist rhetoric of Niyazov's cult of personality with Soviet-style nationalism and Islam that transforms an apparatchik into a *national* prophet sent to the Turkmen people for the third millennium of the *Christian* era! But such blasphemy was simply the unwitting result of the use of Islamic rhetoric in a de-Islamized context. Niyazov's pretensions in this regard have only increased in the years since then. Imams had long been required to recite the national oath at the end of the *namâz*. In 2004, they were ordered to place copies of the *Ruhnama* in mosques alongside those of the Qur'an.[50] A monumental mosque, built at the cost of $100 million in Niyazov's home village of Gypjak, is decorated with excerpts from the *Ruhnama* alongside quotations from the Qur'an.

This sacralization of the *Ruhnama* coincides with ruthless suppression of activity that is not completely loyal. When Nasrullah ibn Ibadullah, the long-serving chief mufti of the country, objected to the use of the *Ruhnama* in mosques, he was fired from his position, arrested, and sentenced to twenty-two years in prison. In 2004, eight mosques were demolished for having been built or operated without permission.[51] In June 2005, the Islamic theology faculty of Turkmenistan's national university, the only place left in the country to offer Islamic education once all madrasas had been closed, was shut down abruptly, and its Turkish staff sent home.

· · ·

As we have seen, few states in the Muslim world have left Islam alone, but the Soviet legacy makes Central Asia a world apart. In no other part of the Muslim world is the distance between the state and Islam so great as it is in Central Asia. To Central Asian regimes, Islam might be the religion of the majority of the population, but it is nevertheless a problem to be solved—through management and bureaucratic control at best and through repression at worst. After a brief period of flirtation with Islamic symbols at the beginning of independence, today's Central Asian regimes allow not the slightest hint of Islamic ritual to intrude on their functions. Muhammadjon Himmatzoda, a leader of the IRP, had a point when he wondered aloud at a conference, "What . . . is the reason that [leaders of Muslim-majority states in the former Soviet Union] distance themselves from a religion, that, without doubt, pertains to their national pride? Why does Mr. Putin, the President of Russia, attend Orthodox churches with pride, crosses himself, and has the Patriarch of Moscow, Aleksei II, on his side at all religious and political undertakings? And why do our leaders consider it shameful to go to a mosque or to take some Islamic authority with them to important undertakings? Does it really contradict the principles of secularism?"[52]

Central Asian regimes justify their policies toward Islam as a defense of secularism. This argument garners them considerable sympathy. Yet the evidence presented here should make abundantly clear that the threat of Islamic militancy is vastly exaggerated and is used to justify authoritarian policies that have nothing to do with Islamic militancy. Indeed, although Islamic militancy might pose some danger to the regimes, the danger the regimes pose to ordinary pious Muslims is far greater.

Andijan and Beyond

On Friday the thirteenth of May, 2005, night fell on a brutal massacre in Uzbekistan. A protest had turned violent and resulted in many deaths. The culprit, however, was the government, which had killed hundreds of its own citizens. The previous night, an armed uprising had broken out in the city of Andijan in the Ferghana Valley, as armed men, supporters of 23 men being tried on charges of religious extremism, stormed a jail and freed all prisoners. After the jailbreak, the insurgents took hostages and retreated into the building of the provincial government. As day broke on Friday, a crowd began to gather in the central square. As far as the government was concerned, Andijan was another front in the global war on terror. The jailbreak was an Islamist insurgency that had to be put down without mercy. The square was full in the afternoon when the government launched an all-out assault on the crowd, killing an unknown number of people. The government claimed that the melee that transpired was a gun battle between "terrorists" and government forces and that the final death toll was 187, and included 94 "terrorists," 20 police officers, 11 military, and 57 bystanders.[1] By all other accounts, the event was a massacre, with the death-toll estimate as high as 700, including women, children, and the elderly.

Clearly, a great deal is wrong with Central Asia today, and no one should have been surprised that the patience of citizens ran out. Two months earlier, popular protests against flawed elections in neighboring Kyrgyzstan had led to the ouster of its president, Askar Akaev, who became the first of the men who had ruled the countries of Central Asia since the Soviet collapse to be forced out. Coming on the heels of similar "revolutions" in Georgia and Ukraine, Akaev's ouster jangled nerves in the region and helped account for the brutality with which the authorities suppressed the Andijan uprising.

Given the massive problems with society, the economy, and the environment, one cannot easily be optimistic about the future of Central Asia. We should expect both political turmoil and state repression in the years to come, and for the latter to be routinely justified by the existence of an Islamic threat. The situation is clearly in flux, and as a historian, I am averse to predicting the future, but Kyrgyzstan's "revolution," in which Islam played no role whatsoever (although few observers bothered to highlight this fact) is highly likely to be a better indicator of future trends than the official version of events in Andijan.

.　　　.　　　.

For Islam Karimov, the Andijan uprising was easy to explain. It was an attempt by "extremists and fanatics" to overthrow the "constitutional order," first in Andijan and then throughout the country, and to establish in its place a caliphate based on the shariat. This operation was carefully planned and involved foreign actors (read al-Qaeda). The aim of the militants was to "repeat the events" of Kyrgyzstan.[2] (Osh and Jalalabad, where Kyrgyzstan's protests began, are in the Ferghana Valley, a short drive away from Andijan but have been cut off from it in recent years by the international border.) According to Karimov, the perpetrators belonged to a banned extremist group called the Akromiya, which, he claimed, was an offshoot of the HTI. The Andijan uprising was thus the long-awaited power grab by local extremists in cahoots with foreign elements; it also proved that the HTI is a terrorist organization.

But who were the Akromiya? The only concrete information we have is about the founder of the group, Akrom Yo'ldoshev (b. 1960), a native of Andijan who had trained as an engineer and is evidently a self-taught Muslim. In 1992, he published a booklet called *Iymonga yo'l* (The Way to Faith), which became the manifesto of a group that gathered around him. He was arrested in April 1998 on narcotics charges, released in December in a countrywide amnesty, but arrested again the day after the Tashkent bombings of February 16, 1999. He was then sentenced to seventeen years in prison for establishing an extremist religious organization that contravened not just the laws of Uzbekistan but indeed the

Universal Declaration of Human Rights![3] As to the core ideas of the group, the little available information came from official sources, which saw the Akromiya as a tight-knit secret society, whose final goal, laid out by Yol'doshev in his book, was the establishment of an Islamic state. Yo'ldoshev was supposed to have been a former member of the HTI, who "found the methods of work . . . which had developed under the conditions of the Arab countries unsuited for the conditions of Fergana. He wrote about this in his book *Iymonga yo'l* . . . where he set forth his 'Path' in 12 lessons."[4] The path passed from "secret" through "material" and "spiritual" phases, to an "organic field," before arriving at the final stage, when the existing "constitutional order" was to be overthrown and power grabbed. At the moment, however, the Akromiya were supposed to believe that because Muslims in Uzbekistan today live under the rule of an infidel state, their situation is analogous to that of the first Muslim community in Mecca immediately after the first revelation, the so-called Meccan period of Islamic history, when Muslims existed as a persecuted religious minority in the Prophet's native city. Because most of the Islamic injunctions on behavior were revealed to Muhammad only after his migration to Medina, where he was able to establish an autonomous community, they are inapplicable to today's Muslims. Therefore, for the Akromiya, neither prayer, nor fasting, nor the hajj is obligatory until an Islamic state is established. Similarly, until then, there is no restriction on the consumption of alcohol or drugs, and temporary marriage is permitted.[5]

The problem with this account is that Yo'ldoshev's book contains none of these statements. The text had long been out of print, but it was posted on the Internet by a lawyer representing the twenty-three men whose imprisonment triggered the insurgency.[6] Perusal of the work is enlightening. *Iymonga yo'l* is a discourse on religion and spirituality, clearly the work of an autodidact innocent of traditional Islamic learning. The author seeks to reconcile the search for a better life in this world with moral and spiritual imperatives derived from faith. The book is a call for individuals to take responsibility for their own actions in light of a faith derived primarily from the Qur'an and hadith. However, it contains not one word about the state or the shariat, let alone an elaborate, five-part plan to take over the state or any hint of ideological affinity with the HTI. One can only wonder how the official account came about, but this version is clearly a figment of the official imagination.

The twenty-three men who were arrested in June 2004 were successful businessmen who owned furniture factories, business-supply companies, bakeries, tailoring shops, and construction and transportation firms. They were pious individuals who reportedly acted on a self-imposed code of conduct: they made contributions to children's homes, schools, and hospitals; they calculated a genuine minimum subsistence wage in Andijan (much higher than the official figure) and agreed to pay staff more than that amount; and they helped out their employees in time of need.[7] The Akromiya had not loomed large in the regime's paranoia until the arrests; indeed, an official had declared in 2004 that upon its appearance, "the group [had] encountered sharp opposition from the people, and its activity ceased."[8] So what triggered this sudden burst of persecution? Religiously conservative businessmen who display philanthropy may be significant pillars of American society, but in independent Uzbekistan, they can be threatening to the established order. At the very least, the state saw the businessmen as ideological competitors, but it may have had other reasons for their persecution as well. As we shall see below, the regime has sought to keep the control of much of Uzbekistan's economic activity in the hands of a select few. The success of the Andijan businessmen was unacceptable to those who dominated the city's economy; the men's philanthropic activism made them suspect in the eyes of a state that seeks control over all public life; their piety provided the best possible pretext to frame them. Here is an extreme case of the state's construing unsanctioned piety as a threat and persecuting it.

The families of the accused denied involvement with religious militancy. As the trial progressed, family members organized a peaceful silent protest outside the courtroom, which was joined by many others—by many former employees of the accused, others who spent time in prison on similar charges, and their relatives, friends, and neighbors. Networks of solidarity and social obligation in the mahalla made such mobilization easy. By the time the trial neared its end, the number of demonstrators had risen to three thousand. Observers noted that the protest was well organized and entirely peaceful.[9] Similar protests had taken place in the country in the previous year, most of which had been broken up. The Andijan protest was by far the largest and best organized. As hearings in the trial ended on May 11, police began arresting those who had demonstrated outside the courthouse.[10] This action, along with the certainty that all the accused would receive long prison terms, seems to have forced motivated supporters of the accused to take more decisive action.

Reconstructing the events of the uprising is not easy. Few reporters were in Andijan as the events unfolded, and most eyewitness accounts were recorded days later.[11] Nevertheless, the events may be summarized as follows. On the night of May 12–13, a group of armed men, having seized weapons and ammunition from a police station and an army barracks, stormed the jail where the accused were being held and freed all the prisoners. The jail was not a high-security prison, and the men were able to breach it by crashing a commandeered army truck through its front gate. A number of prison guards were killed (some reports put the number of those killed as high as fifty-four) and others taken hostage. Many prisoners did not want to be freed but were forced to leave and given arms. The armed crowd then moved down the city's main avenue and took control of the building of Andijan's provincial administration. Once inside, they telephoned relatives and supporters and asked them to gather in the square outside. By dawn, a crowd had begun to form in the square, and over the course of the day, many others, both supporters and curious onlookers, joined the original group. According to cautious reports, the crowd numbered two thousand, was unarmed, and included many women, children, and the elderly. The insurgents meanwhile spoke to the minister of internal affairs, demanding that Akrom Yo'ldoshev and other prisoners be released and that Karimov come and address the crowd. Fifteen years after flying back to Namangan to face another angry crowd (see chapter 6), Karimov was in no mood to repeat the experience. The minister offered the insurgents free passage to Kyrgyzstan but otherwise refused to negotiate. In the afternoon, the government launched its assault. An armored personnel carrier drove by and fired indiscriminately into the crowd. Observers also report that a gunfight broke out as government troops retook the building. Yet a different report speaks of a confrontation with government troops, as a column containing hostages, insurgents, and unarmed supporters moved away from the square.[12] Shooting continued for a long time that evening and resulted in heavy casualties. Many of the insurgents fell victim, but some of them managed to flee across the border to Kyrgyzstan.

This event was clearly an armed uprising, but was it an Islamist putsch? The answer is clearly no. Islamic slogans and demands were absent from the protest before, during, and after the uprising. On the eve of the violence, a BBC reporter found that protestors made "a point of saying that they are not protesting against the government—they simply want justice for their relatives."[13] Without question, the demonstration on May 13 was "a massive expression of dissatisfaction with the endemic poverty, corruption, unemployment, repression, and unfair trials that plagued the area."[14] One of the demands the insurgents presented to the minister of internal affairs was that Karimov visit the city.

Human Rights Watch gathered testimony that for many in the crowd, the aim was to attract Karimov's attention and that cheers had gone up when it was wrongly announced that he was coming. "People were waiting for the president to come," a survivor told Human Rights Watch. "They wanted to meet him and explain their problems. They wanted to know if their problems came from the local [administrative] level, or if they came from the top. We wanted to ask the president to solve our problems and make our lives easier, but we were not trying to get rid of the government of Karimov."[15] A sense of the uprising's motives can also be gleaned from events that transpired in the nearby town of Qorasuv, which sits across the river from its sister town of Karasuu in Kyrgyzstan. The two towns had been the site of significant cross-border trade until Uzbekistani authorities destroyed the bridge that connected the two towns in 2003. On May 14, a crowd stormed the government building, set fire to the local police headquarters, and began rebuilding the bridge that connected the town to Kyrgyzstan. The uprising was short-lived (central authorities retook the town on May 19), but the outrage that fed it had little to do with Islam and everything to do with the state.

The fallout from the uprising was considerable. Andijan was quickly brought back under control, but several hundred Uzbekistani citizens fled to Kyrgyzstan as refugees. The initial response of Western governments was tepid, but as outrage began to mount, calls arose for an independent international investigation of the events. The Uzbekistani government flatly rejected these calls and hardened its position. Its version of events found much greater sympathy in Russia and China, both of which had been alarmed at the success of the "revolutions" in Georgia, Ukraine, and Kyrgyzstan, behind which they detected a Western agenda. The ensuing diplomatic crisis precipitated a geopolitical realignment in the region that had been in the making for the previous eighteen months. Karimov rapidly distanced his country from the United States and realigned it with Russia and China. In July 2005, Uzbekistan served notice to the United States to vacate the two air-force bases it had used since 2001. By the end of the summer, Karimov was accusing the West of aiding and abetting terrorists and seeking to destabilize the region for its own goals. The strategic alliance in place since the late 1990s evaporated overnight, but on Uzbekistan's terms. The Uzbekistani government, meanwhile, heightened its persecution of the opposition, resorting to old Soviet practices of sentencing opponents to psychiatric treatment and launching propaganda campaigns against outside forces sowing dissension in the land.[16] At the time of this writing, a show trial of fifteen men accused of plotting the uprising had concluded, with all defendants confessing to everything they had been accused of.[17]

The Andijan uprising revealed the vast storehouse of grievances that exists in Uzbekistan. The discontent that it engenders, however, is not articulated in Islamic terms. The regime, nevertheless, saw an opportunity to pin the label of "Islamic extremism" on the uprising and to quash it mercilessly. The regime's response to the uprising was a logical continuation of the policies described in chapter 7. It does not bode well for the future.

·   ·   ·

Central Asia has many potential sources of instability, and Islamic militancy ranks low on the list. The most immediate potential source of instability in the near future is the successions that loom at the top, as the first generation of leaders succumbs to mortality. Of greater long-term concern should be the dismal state of the region's economy, the ecological nightmare unfolding there, and the endemic corruption.

The Soviet Union was a party-state, in which the Party was a mechanism for allocating resources and power. The Party, with its mechanisms for recruitment and promotion, is no longer there. Instead, throughout the region, power has concentrated into the executive branch and personalized. Niyazov's Turkmenbashy cult is only the most ludicrous example of a phenomenon found elsewhere as well. Karimov too writes books whose study is mandatory in school, and his sayings appear on billboards across the length and breadth of the country. All presidents have accumulated massive fortunes, safely parked offshore. But they have done so by balancing and reconciling the interests and claims of various factions. The business of allocating resources among the clans now goes on completely behind closed doors. What will happen when the current crop of leaders succumbs to mortality? How will the region's governments manage those successions? Rumors suggest that both Islam Karimov of Uzbekistan and Nursultan Nazarbaev of Kazakhstan are grooming their daughters for the presidency. But will the daughters be able to manage the clans? The inability of major factions to agree on a candidate could lead to serious conflict, including violence, in which accusations of religious extremism are likely to play a prominent role. Kyrgyzstan's succession in 2005 was bloodless, but the situation may be different in Turkmenistan or Uzbekistan.

Of even greater concern in the long term is the region's economic situation, which, with the partial exception of Kazakhstan, is dismal. Living standards have plummeted since Soviet times, and the social infrastructure has unraveled, without much change in the economic structure. A certain amount of deindustrialization has taken place, with aviation factories lying idle and many plants and mines closing. With the public sector shrinking, petty trade is often the only avenue left for those who do not want to return to the land.

The poor economic situation stems in part from the region's underdevelopment and the generally uncompetitive nature of its economies, but corruption and poor policies are also responsible in large measure. Throughout the region, politically powerful elites, the so-called clans, have retained control over the national wealth through various means. Kazakhstan and Kyrgyzstan enacted substantial privatization, but wealth has tended to accumulate in a few hands. In Uzbekistan, private enterprise is allowed but is suspect (as the businessmen from Andijan found out). Moreover, all large-scale enterprise, whether state or private, is firmly in the hands of the dominant elites, who do not like competition. Over the past few years, the government has sought to consolidate its control over small-scale trade, with devastating consequences for those involved in it. It has curbed cross-border shuttle trade by imposing stiff tariffs on imports, requiring sellers of imported goods to have import permits and to deposit all proceeds with (government-controlled) banks, and it has periodically closed borders with its neighbors to make its point. It has required all stall owners in the country's bazaars to use cash registers to record transactions and limited them to the sale of foodstuffs. Many bazaars have been closed, their stalls demolished.[18] Much of this is done in the name of modernizing the tax structure and so forth, but most people realize that it benefits a few elites. Such policies, which provoke a sense of injustice, are far more corrosive than poverty per se.

The kleptocratic apparatus rests, in Uzbekistan, Tajikistan, and Turkmenistan at least, on the cotton monoculture that has not been transformed in any meaningful way since Soviet times. The Uzbekistani case is the starkest. The country still produces 3.5 million tons of cotton a year, is the second-largest exporter of cotton in the world, and relies on cotton as its main source of foreign exchange. In Soviet times, most of the cotton was consumed within the Soviet Union; now it is sold on the world market at world prices (which are notoriously volatile, but they at least bring in hard currency). Land is still owned by the state and leased to producers. No meaningful privatization of land has taken place;

rather, the old collective farms have been renamed cooperatives (*shirkat*). The state enters into contracts with shirkats that dictate what crops they can grow on its land, and it sets the price at which it will buy the produce. This price is a fraction of the world price (or indeed, of the price paid to producers in Kyrgyzstan or Kazakhstan). The state, in the form of cotton-trading agencies firmly controlled by dominant elites, pockets the difference. Cotton production is a labor-intensive process, and every cotton harvest is a matter of national import. Schools and universities are closed, and students are bused into the fields to help pick cotton. Public-sector employees are also expected to "volunteer" for this patriotic duty, for which they receive no reimbursement. Conditions of work are brutal, and reports surface every year of overzealous supervisors' abusing or even murdering children for not fulfilling quotas.[19] The situation is little different in Tajikistan, where the agricultural sector has nominally been liberalized. Farmers are still under enormous pressure from the state to plant cotton. The conclusion is obvious, and the International Crisis Group put it succinctly in its recent report on the subject: "The exploitative nature of cotton economics makes the repressive political systems of these states almost inevitable. Since the state and cotton elites are unwilling to pay farmers a fair price, the system can only continue through the use of coercion. States that depend on the present structure of the cotton monoculture must retain an authoritarian political system, in which the rights of individuals are suppressed, theoretically in favour of the collective good, but in practice in favour of narrow ruling elites."[20]

•   •   •

How long can this situation continue before popular discontent turns into rebellion? In Uzbekistan, every sign suggests that people's patience is running out. The past few years have seen protests of increasing magnitude. Wives and mothers of men arrested on charges of religious extremism have long protested (and been arrested or beaten up for their pains), but since 2003, economic protest has become common. In June 2004, farmers in Namangan went on strike against government orders to plant cotton rather than wheat. In November of the same year, riots broke out in several cities when tax inspectors began enforcing draconian regulations on bazaar trade, and the protests continued throughout the winter.

Does this discontent provide an opportunity for Islamists to make a play for power? Islam after Communism bears a heavy legacy of seven decades of Soviet rule, which makes such an outcome unlikely in the foreseeable future. Today, the Soviet legacy is most evident in the way that incumbent regimes understand the relationships between state, society, and religion. As chapter 7 has shown, the results are seldom salubrious. But the Soviet legacy is also reflected in ordinary people's understanding of those relationships. The Soviet period also led to the de-Islamization of public life, created strong ethnonational identities, and made Islam an integral part of the latter, all of which produced a profoundly secular understanding of politics. Such understanding is still intact. Narratives of national history and the quest to build a great *national* future still resonate with people. There is also great suspicion of ostentatious religiosity and little support for the imposition of Islamic codes of behavior. The revival of Islamic learning and piety has not in itself been subversive. Confusing piety with support for political transformation is always a mistake (although many seek to benefit by confusing the two).

Nothing is permanent, and the context of Central Asian Islam can change, of course. Much of Soviet infrastructure in the fields of health, welfare, and education is in decline, as resources are stretched and priorities redirected.[21] (In Turkmenistan, the government itself is actively gutting the infrastructure.) As Soviet patterns of socialization are transformed, Islam too will change. In the Arab world, after all, the secular nationalism of the mid-twentieth century has given way in the past few decades to the use of Islam as the dominant language of politics. Will Central Asia be different?

If the experience of the decade and a half since the end of Soviet isolation tells us anything, it is that assumptions garnered from the Middle East are not always applicable to Central Asia. The de-Islamization of the region during the Soviet period means that the authority of Islam and its carriers are much weaker than in the Middle East, as is the public presence of Islam. Central Asia is still only weakly linked to the rest of the Muslim world. The most common frame of reference for its citizens is still the countries of the former Soviet Union, to which the region is tied by the infrastructure of trade, transport, industry, and education. Links with its neighbors to the south are infinitely weaker. The same can be said of the *emotional* links that Central Asians have to the rest of the Muslim world. For the vast majority, being Muslim, whether a pious one or not, does not produce empathy or identification with other Muslims. The Palestinian issue, which produces an intense sense of outrage among Muslims in the Middle East and South Asia, has little resonance in the region. Central Asia's incorporation into the global economy, too, has its limits, and the region remains outside the flows of personnel and money that generate Islamist politics in today's world.

.   .   .

Ultimately, what the story of Islam in Central Asia shows best is the complexity of Islam as a historical phenomenon, its internal diversity, and the infinite possibilities that reside within it. Views of Islam as a monolithic phenomenon, a civilization that acts as a geopolitical entity, despite the dominance such views in the mainstream media, are simply untenable. Equally unconvincing, however, are views that see in Islam a neat binary between its "good" and "bad," "moderate" and "extremist" varieties. What is good for the regime of Islam Karimov may not be good for pious Muslims who live under it. The regime justifies its persecution in the name of fighting extremism, but clearly there is nothing moderate in the actions of a regime that boils its enemies alive.

Islam has not one, nor two, but many faces in Central Asia and in the world at large. They all exist at the same time, and they are the product of time and place and of concrete historical circumstance. The religious landscape of Saudi Arabia is different from that of Afghanistan, which is not the same as that of Indonesia, or that of Turkmenistan. Each Muslim society bears the markings of its past. Nor is Islam ever a clear given; it is what Muslims make of it. Islam is an ongoing argument in which adherents can take any number of positions and make any point, all with reference to the same set of sources. Shrine visitation by Uzbekistani peasants, women's rituals invoking the Prophet, and book learning in madrasas are all expressions of Islam. In the early twentieth century, the Jadids argued for progress and modernity through a return to "real" Islam; for their opponents, "real" Islam was something quite different. Muhammadjon Hindustoniy made an Islamic argument about the relationship between Islam and politics, as did his students, who thought he was apolitical. The think tank in Washington, D.C., that claims that Islam is the religion of the free market par excellence also makes an Islamic argument, as does Osama bin Laden. Indeed, when Islam Karimov canonizes a certain tradition of quietist Hanafi jurisprudence as the official version of good Islam (indeed, the only Islam allowed), he too takes an Islamic position, as does Saparmurad Niyazov when he, with greater audacity, takes on the mantle of the Prophet.

The United States is tied to the Muslim world in ways too numerous to count and is a significant actor in its affairs. It behooves us, therefore, to understand Islam in its full complexity, to see its many faces, and to avoid facile binaries of good and bad, moderate and extremist. Rather than emerging out of a trait inherent in Islam itself, Islamic debates take place in the here and now, using the technologies of today, and do so under political compulsions and imperatives faced by Muslims. In the aftermath of September 11, the U.S. government launched a public-relations offensive in many parts of the Muslim world, not just to sell its policies toward the region but also to promote "moderate Islam." As a result, various Central Asian countries have seen seminars galore on topics such as "religion and democracy," and for a while, Kyrgyzstan did not have enough imams to be flown to the United States to see the interaction of religion, civil society, and democracy with their own eyes. This interest is well and good, but which currents of interpretation are compelling to a given group of Muslims depends on a host of issues, and official tours or propaganda broadcasts cannot manufacture "moderate Islam." Moreover, in Central Asia, our exhortations to Muslims to be moderate put us in the company of regimes that are anything but moderate.

Islam, after all, is never a simple given, an agreed-upon set of rules or ideas. Rather, it contains infinite possibilities, and it goes where debate and contention among Muslims take it. In Central Asia, we can be sure that Muslims will invoke Islam in their struggles over the destinies of their societies. What they will mean by "Islam," however, will depend on the historical and political conditions in which Central Asians find themselves rather than on the desire to imitate other Muslim societies or to follow the injunctions of the great Islamic books. For observers, it is critical to have perspective, to discern clearly the political stakes at issue in such debates, and to separate the disinformation dished out by the regimes from the actual conduct of Muslims.

Glossary

âdat   Lit., custom. Âdat was codified in colonial times as "customary law" but is now celebrated as part of national legacy.

fatwa   Legal opinion of a mufti, issued on a specific issue, usually in response to a query.

fiqh   Islamic jurisprudence; the science of elaboration of detailed rules of conduct.

hadith   Traditions of the Prophet; a major source of authority in Islamic jurisprudence and Islamic debates in general.

HTI   Hizb-ut-Tahrir al-Islami (the Islamic Party of Liberation), a transnational Islamist party that appeared in Central Asia in the mid-1990s; see chapter 6.

hujra   Lit., [seminary] cell; the practice, peculiar to Central Asia in late Soviet times, of imparting Islamic education in secret.

hujum   Lit., assault; Soviet campaign for unveiling in Uzbekistan launched in 1927; see chapter 3.

IMU   Islamic Movement of Uzbekistan, a jihadi outfit that emerged around 1999; see chapter 6.

IRP   The Islamic Revival Party, a contender in Tajikistan's civil war (1991–97), when its opponents accused it of being "fundamentalist"; currently, a legal political party active in Tajikistani politics.

Islamism   A modern strain of political activism that treats Islam primarily or solely as a political ideology. It rejects the authority of tradi-

	tional ulama and seeks its authority in a radical reading of the Qur'an and hadith. The ultimate goal of Islamist politics is the "Islamization" of all aspects of human existence.
jihadi groups	Militant groups that interpret jihad in purely military terms and seek to use jihad as a way of establishing an Islamic order. Unlike the Islamists, they have little interest in "Islamization" beyond the imposition of Islamic law.
kolkhoz	Collective farm.
mazhab	School of fiqh. Sunni Islam has four *mazhab*s that differ in details of law and ritual but are held to be equally correct.
MBU	The Muslim Board of Uzbekistan (O'zbekiston Musulmonlari Idorasi), official body to regulate and supervise Islamic affairs in Uzbekistan; a descendent of SADUM.
mufti	A jurisconsult, a scholar able to issue legal opinions. Traditionally, a mufti's authority derived from his reputation for learning and piety, but in modern times, states have often turned the mufti's office into a formal post.
qazi	A judge ruling in accordance with the shariat.
SADUM	Spiritual Directorate for the Muslims of Central Asia and Kazakhstan, established in 1943; official body to regulate and supervise Islamic observance in the region.
shariat	The tradition of discussing the general principles that govern the elaboration of fiqh. In modern times, the shariat often tends to be seen simply as "Islamic law."
ulama	Lit., the learned; scholars of Islam.
waqf	Property endowed for specific pious purposes.

Notes

1. In this book, I use the term *Central Asia* to denote Kazakhstan, Kyrgyzstan, Tajikistan, Turkmenistan, and Uzbekistan, the five countries that emerged as sovereign states from the collapse of the Soviet Union. Now that Afghanistan is back in the news, it is often considered part of Central Asia for reasons of geographical proximity. As will become amply clear in this book, the Amu Darya represented more than the boundary between Afghanistan and the Soviet Union; it demarcated the limits of the social and cultural engineering undertaken by the Soviet regime on its own territory. Afghanistan experienced none of the transformations that make Central Asia what it is today; its virtual destruction in a quarter century of war has given it an entirely different trajectory. We would be unwise to project assumptions about one side of the Amu Darya to the other.

2. Ahmed Rashid, *Jihad: The Rise of Militant Islam in Central Asia* (New Haven, Conn., 2002), 35.

3. To say that Central Asia was transformed is not to claim that it became identical to other parts of the Soviet Union. Western observers of Central Asia, especially those whose access to the region is primarily through Russian sources, often minimize the impact of Soviet rule in the region, largely because Central Asia retained its local peculiarities and did not became an exact copy of Russia. See, for example, the essays in William Fierman, ed., *Soviet Central Asia: The Failed Transformation* (Boulder, 1991).

4. Samuel Huntington, *The Clash of Civilizations and the Remaking of the World Order* (New York, 1996). Huntington is hardly the first scholar to invoke civilizations as the building blocks of our world. Civilizational analysis has often appealed to historians trying to discern big patterns in world history, epitomized best by the twelve-volume work of Arnold Toynbee (*A Study of History,* London,

1947–57). Huntington's account distinguishes itself from this company both by the thinness of its historical research and by the argument that civilizations are primarily geopolitical phenomena primed for conflict.

5. Bernard Lewis, "The Roots of Muslim Rage," *Atlantic Monthly,* September 1990, 60.

6. Ibid., 49.

7. Ibid., 53–54.

8. Richard T. Hughes, *Myths America Lives By* (Chicago, 2004).

9. Press conference, October 11, 2001, www.whitehouse.gov/news/releases/2001/10/20011011–7.html.

10. This interest in classical thought is usually seen as "the Arabs" carrying the torch of ancient learning until they could return it to its rightful owners, the West. This view is an absurd way of looking at things. Muslim philosophers in the Hellenic traditions had the same relationship to the classical tradition that western Europeans were to have later. They did not see themselves as the caretakers of a tradition that rightfully belonged to someone else.

11. Space does not allow full development of this argument here. See, however, the essays in Emran Qureshi and Michael A. Sells, eds., *The New Crusades: Constructing the Muslim Enemy* (New York, 2003), especially the editors' introduction.

12. Marshall G. S. Hodgson, *The Venture of Islam,* 3 vols. (Chicago, 1974).

13. Dale F. Eickelman and James P. Piscatori, *Muslim Politics* (Princeton, 1996), 37–45.

14. One popular explanation for the existence of Islamic militancy is that militancy is the result of Islam's never having experienced a reformation. (For a particularly pompous recent expression of this argument, see Salman Rushdie, "The Right Time for an Islamic Reformation," *Washington Post,* August 7, 2005, B7.) According to this argument, Islamic militancy today is the result of hatreds that arise from a religious dogma untempered by humanism or doubt. Not only is the argument essentialist in deriving all political actions of Muslims back to Islam, but it also takes a seriously flawed view of the Reformation as a precursor to secularization or radical doubt. The Reformation was a critique of a church deemed to be corrupt and an argument for a return to the sources; it resulted in new, uncompromising kinds of religious and political commitments that led to immense bloodletting in Europe and beyond. The more radical heirs of the Reformation are a major political force in the United States today, and they have little truck with humanism or doubt.

15. We are wise to keep in mind that in Israel too, the 1967 war reshaped the contours of politics, as religious Jews finally reconciled themselves to the aspirations of Zionism. The settlers in the West Bank are driven by a religious zeal every bit as extremist as the Islamists', but they have the benefit of having the global status quo arrayed behind them. Moreover, for large numbers of Americans, support for Israel is driven primarily by Christian religious convictions.

16. For insights on the modernity of Islamism, I have benefited from Bruce B. Lawrence, *Defenders of God: The Fundamentalist Revolt Against the Modern Age* (San Francisco, 1989).

17. For a fascinating study of the way in which religion and modernity were

intertwined throughout the twentieth century in Iran, see Roy P. Mottehedeh, *The Mantle of the Prophet: Religion and Politics in Iran* (New York, 1986).

18. These efforts ranged from planting anti-Soviet stories in local newspapers to some truly bizarre plots. A former CIA operative relates how after the 1967 Arab-Israeli war, "the agency's skunk works had come up with the idea of filling a captured Soviet transport plane—Soviet markings and all—with live pigs and dropping them over Mecca, Islam's most holy city. The idea was to light the Middle East's fuse and direct the blast toward the Soviet Union, whose influence had been growing in the area." Robert Baer, *See No Evil: The True Story of a Ground Soldier in the CIA's War on Terrorism* (New York, 2002), 93. The plot did not, of course, come to fruition, but it does give some insight into how the CIA saw the Middle East and the role of Islam in it.

19. Nor was support for the Afghan "jihad" limited to the Reagan administration. The architect of U.S. involvement in Afghanistan was Zbignew Brzezinski, the hawkish national security adviser to Jimmy Carter. Like those in the Reagan administration, he felt the price was worth paying, and hindsight has not produced any doubts in his mind. As he asked rhetorically in an interview with a French news magazine in 1998, "What is most important to the history of the world? The Taliban or the collapse of the Soviet empire? Some stirred-up Muslims or the liberation of Central Europe and the end of the cold war?" *Le Nouvel observateur*, January 15–21, 1998, 76 (quoted from the English translation by Bill Blum at http://csf.colorado.edu/forums/isafp/2001/msg00184.html).

20. Saudi Arabia and Pakistan both have substantial Shi'i populations, which had grown restive as a result of the Iranian revolution. Not having inclusive national ideologies at their disposal, the governments of both countries countered this restiveness by fomenting sectarian hatreds. The war in Afghanistan, being next door to Iran, provided an opportunity to contain Iran geopolitically. Jihadist Islam has from the beginning been overtly sectarian and virulently anti-Shi'i. It is laughable, therefore, to assert, as many pundits have done recently in the United States, that the origins of militant Islam (and of al-Qaeda even) go back to the Iranian revolution. See, for instance, David Harris, *The Crisis: The President, the Prophet, and the Shah—1979 and the Coming of Militant Islam* (New York, 2004), or the otherwise excellent book by Stephen Kinzer, *All the Shah's Men: An American Coup and the Roots of Middle East Terror* (New York, 2003).

21. Mahmood Mamdani, *Good Muslim, Bad Muslim: America, the Cold War, and the Roots of Terror* (New York, 2004), 13. A truly comprehensive and dispassionate history of the war in Afghanistan and its role in spawning "jihadist" Islam remains to be written. The Afghan "jihad" was a popular cause in the United States during the 1980s, but the American public has maintained a studied silence about the links between that war and the rise of jihadist Islam. The *Washington Post* journalist Steve Coll has written a massive tome on the war in Afghanistan (*Ghost Wars: The Secret History of the CIA, Afghanistan, and Bin Laden, from the Soviet Invasion to September 10, 2001*, New York, 2004), but because the book's heroes are the CIA operatives in Afghanistan, it cannot, for all the wealth of detail it contains, provide the dispassionate account that is needed of U.S. policy and its intended and unintended consequences.

1. ISLAM IN CENTRAL ASIA

1. Shīr Muhammad Mirāb Munis and Muhammad Rizā Mirāb Āgahī, *Firdaws al-Iqbāl*, ed. Yuri Bregel (Leiden, 1988).

2. Quoted in 'Ala-ad-Din 'Ata Malik Juvaini, *The History of the World Conqueror*, 2 vols., trans. from the text of Mirza Muhammad Qazvini by J. A. Boyle, (Cambridge, Mass., 1958), 1:95–96.

3. Devin DeWeese, "Sacred History for a Central Asian Town: Saints, Shrines, and Legends of Origin in Histories of Sayram, 18th–19th Centuries," *Revue du monde musulman et de la Méditerranée*, no. 89–90 (2000): 245–95; Stéphane A. Dudoignon, "Local Lore, the Transmission of Learning, and Communal Identity in Late 20th-Century Tajikistan: The *Khujand-Nāma* of 'Ārifjān Yahyāzād Khujandi," in Stéphane A. Dudoignon, ed., *Devout Societies vs. Impious States? Transmitting Islamic Learning in Russia, Central Asia and China, through the Twentieth Century* (Berlin, 2004), 213–41.

4. Such conversion narratives exist all over the Muslim world and serve as a way to indigenize Islam. But such complexities of the human condition are apparently too much for Sir Vaidyanath Naipaul, the Nobel Prize–winning British novelist of Trinidadian origin, who has recently written: "Islam is in its origin an Arab religion. Everyone not an Arab who is a Muslim is a convert. Islam is not simply a matter of conscience or private belief. It makes imperial demands. A convert's worldview alters. . . . His idea of history alters. He rejects his own; he becomes, whether he likes it or not, a part of the Arab story. The convert has to turn away from everything that is his" (V. S. Naipaul, *Beyond Belief: Islamic Excursions among the Converted Peoples*, New York, 1998, xi). Apart from the fact that such a formulation is just plain wrong, it is also beyond belief that a self-proclaimed champion of cosmopolitanism would make use of such characterizations of inauthenticity at a time when forces of chauvinism and intolerance use precisely such arguments to commit unspeakable acts of barbarity. Hindu nationalism in India and Serbian nationalism in the former Yugoslavia both use such rhetoric to characterize the Muslims of India and Bosnia, respectively, as "imposters" or "traitors."

5. Devin DeWeese, *Islamization and Native Religion in the Golden Horde: Baba Tükles and Conversion to Islam in Historical and Epic Tradition* (University Park, Penn., 1994), 541–43.

6. Bernard Lewis, *The Political Language of Islam* (Chicago, 1988), 6.

7. Quoted in Bertold Spuler, *History of the Mongols, based on Eastern and Western Accounts of the Thirteenth and Fourteenth Centuries* (London, 1972), 30.

8. Juvaini, *The History of the World Conqueror*, 1:104–105

9. Ahmet T. Karamustafa, *God's Unruly Friends: Dervish Groups in the Islamic Later Middle Period, 1200–1550* (Salt Lake City, 1994).

10. Ira M. Lapidus, "State and Religion in Islamic Societies," *Past and Present*, no. 151 (1996): 19.

11. Fazl Allah b. Rûzbihân al-Isfahânî, *Kitâb-i Sulûk al-mulûk*, eds. Muhammad Nizâmuddin and Muhammad Ghaus (Hyderabad, India, 1966), 59.

12. Ibid., 60–61.

13. Ibid., 49.

14. Juvaini, *The History of the World Conqueror,* 1:97–98.

15. Research in Islamic sources has begun to show in concrete detail how intertwined the two traditions became in Central Asia in the post-Timurid period. See Qurbān-ʿAlī Khālidī, *An Islamic Biographical Dictionary of the Eastern Kazakh Steppe, 1770–1912,* eds. Allen J. Frank and Mirkasyim A. Usmanov (Leiden, 2005); see also Hamid Algar, "Shaykh Zaynullah Rasulev: The Last Great Naqshbandi Shaykh of the Volga-Urals Region," in Jo-Ann Gross, ed., *Muslims in Central Asia: Expressions of Identity and Change* (Durham, N.C., 1992), 112–33.

16. I have developed this argument at greater length in Adeeb Khalid, *The Politics of Muslim Cultural Reform: Jadidism in Central Asia* (Berkeley, 1998), 28–40.

17. Ahmad Makhdumi Donish, *Risola, yo mukhtasare az taʾrikhi saltanati khonadoni manghitiya* (Dushanbe, 1992), 11.

2. EMPIRE AND THE CHALLENGE OF MODERNITY

1. Andreas Kappeler, "Czarist Policy Toward the Muslims of the Russian Empire," in *Muslim Communities Reemerge: Historical Perspectives on Nationality, Politics, and Opposition in the Former Soviet Union and Yugoslavia,* eds. Andreas Kappeler et al. (Durham, N.C., 1992), 143.

2. Sadriddin Aynî, *Taʾrikhi amironi manghitiyai Bukhoro* (Dushanbe, 1987; orig. 1921), 96–100.

3. Adeeb Khalid, "Society and Politics in Bukhara, 1868–1920," *Central Asian Survey* 19 (2000): 367–96.

4. Munavvar Qori Abdurashidxon oʻgʻli, "Isloh ne demakdadur," *Xurshid* (Tashkent), September 28, 1906; a translation of the entire article is available as: Munawwar Qari Abdurrashid Khan oghli, "What is Reform?" in *Modernist Islam: A Sourcebook, 1840–1940,* ed. Charles Kurzman (New York, 2002), 227–28.

5. On Jadidism, see Adeeb Khalid, *The Politics of Muslim Cultural Reform: Jadidism in Central Asia* (Berkeley, 1998).

6. Fitrat Bukhârâyî, *Munâzara-yi mudarris-i bukhârâyî bâ yak nafar-i farangî dar Hindustân dar bâra-yi makâtib-i jadîda* (Istanbul, 1910), 67.

7. ʿAbd al-Raʾûf [Fitrat], *Bayânât-i sayyâh-i hindî* (Istanbul, 1911).

8. Hence the term *Salafi.* Today, when the term has been discovered by the media and is often used as a synonym for *fundamentalism* or *Wahhabism,* it is worth remembering that it was first coined by modernists at the turn of the twentieth century.

9. Hamid Algar, *Wahhabism: A Critical Essay* (Oneonta, N.Y., 2002), 10.

10. Surprisingly, the episode still lacks a full-scale study, although a large number of archival documents have been published. The most accessible accounts are in Edward Sokol, *The Revolt of 1916 in Russian Central Asia* (Baltimore, 1954); Khalid, *Politics of Muslim Cultural Reform,* 239–42, 272–73; Daniel R. Brower, "Kyrgyz Nomads and Russian Pioneers: Colonization and

Ethnic Conflict in the Turkestan Revolt of 1916," *Jahrbücher für Geschichte Osteuropas* 44 (1996): 41–53.

3. THE SOVIET ASSAULT ON ISLAM

1. Mark D. Steinberg and Vladimir M. Khrustalëv, eds., *The Fall of the Romanovs: Political Dreams and Personal Struggles in a Time of Revolution* (New Haven, Conn., 1995), 73. The royal couple corresponded in English, and the quote here retains the idiosyncrasies of the original text. The literature on the Russian revolution is enormous, although almost all the standard accounts focus on events in Petrograd. For an account of the impact of the revolution on Central Asia, see my "Tashkent 1917: Muslim Politics in Revolutionary Turkestan," *Slavic Review* 55 (1996): 270–96.

2. Sirojiddin Maxdum Sidqiy, *Toza hurriyat* (Tashkent, 1917), 2.

3. Muallim M. H., "Bukun qondoy kun?" *Kengash* (Kokand), April 15, 1917, 12.

4. For a more detailed discussion of the conflict in 1917, see Adeeb Khalid, *The Politics of Muslim Cultural Reform:Jadidism in Central Asia* (Berkeley, 1998), ch. 8.

5. These calculations were worked out through a careful analysis of contemporary statistical sources by Marco Buttino, "Study of the Economic Crisis and Depopulation in Turkestan, 1917–1920," *Central Asian Survey* 9:4 (1990): 61–64; see, more generally, his *La rivoluzione capovolta: l'Asia centrale tra il crollo dell'impero zarista e la formazione dell'URSS* (Naples, 2003).

6. The views of Olaf Caroe, *Soviet Empire: The Turks of Central Asia and Stalinism* (London, 1954), ch. 7, came to acquire almost a canonical status and are still repeated in print. The émigré position is best articulated by Baymirza Hayit, *Basmatschi: Nationaler Kampf Turkestans in den Jahren 1917 bis 1934* (Cologne, 1992).

7. For example, see Eden Naby, "The Concept of Jihad in Opposition to Communist Rule: Turkestan and Afghanistan," *Studies in Comparative Communism* 19 (1986): 287–300.

8. Vitaly V. Naumkin, *Radical Islam in Central Asia: Between Pen and Rifle* (Lanham, Md., 2005), 20.

9. Abdurauf Fitrat, "Hind ixtilolchilari" (1920) in *Tanlangan asarlar,* 3 vols. (Tashkent, 2003), 3:46.

10. Rysqulov's career has not received proper study. All existing biographies were written within Soviet ideological confines and therefore cannot address the complexities of his life. Many of his writings have been published since the collapse of the Soviet Union, however; the criticism of Lenin is in T. R. Ryskulov, *Sobranie sochinenii v trekh tomakh* (Almaty, 1997), 3:182–87.

11. The oft-expressed opinion that the Latinization of Central Asian languages was a deliberate policy of the Soviet regime to cut off Central Asians from their heritage or from Islam stands in need of correction. The standardization of language and the reform of its vocabulary and orthography were central to modernizing nationalist movements all over the world. This phenomenon was common in central and eastern Europe during the age of nation building (indeed, the

phonetic script for Czech provided the model for many orthographic reformers in the Soviet Union), and language standardization was an important part of the agenda of reform in Turkey in the same years. Latinization was largely carried out by radical intellectual elites of the nationalities involved, and the creation of a new uniform alphabet was high on the agenda. See Ingeborg Baldauf, *Schriftreform und Schriftwechsel bei den muslimischen Russland- und Sowjettürken (1850–1937): ein Symptom ideengeschichtlicher und kulturpolitischer Entwicklungen* (Budapest, 1993). A decade later, the Latin script was abandoned in favor of Cyrillic, and the new Cyrillic alphabets were often designed to maximize differences among the various Turkic languages.

12. Central State Archives of the Republic of Uzbekistan (TsGARUz), f. R-25, op. 1, d. 681, ll. 170–710b.

13. P. V. Gidulianov, *Otdelenie tserkvi ot gosudarstva v SSSR* (Moscow, 1926), 516–19, 375–76.

14. Steven Kotkin, *Magnetic Mountain: Stalinism as a Civilization* (Berkeley, 1995), 286–93.

15. Andrei Sinyavsky, *Soviet Civilization: A Cultural History*, trans. Joanne Turnbull (New York, 1988), 31–32.

16. J. Stalin, "Our Tasks in the East," in *Works*, vol. 4 (Moscow, 1953), 246.

17. V. I. Lenin, *Polnoe sobranie sochinenii*, 5th ed., vol. 53 (Moscow, 1965), 190; emphases as in the original.

18. Terry Martin, *The Affirmative Action Empire: Nations and Nationalism in the Soviet Union, 1923–1939* (Ithaca, 2001).

19. The account of the delimitation of Central Asian boundaries in this chapter differs substantially from the received wisdom on the topic, which holds that the delimitation was the work of "Moscow" or of Stalin himself, and motivated by a simple desire to divide and rule. Unburdened by archival research, this view reduces the complexities of actual history to a tale of political deceit practiced on hapless victims. The account here relies on archival resources (primarily the Russian State Archive of Socio-Political History, or RGASPI, f. 62, op. 2, dd. 100–12) and excellent recent scholarship that uses them. See Arne Haugen, *The Establishment of National Republics in Soviet Central Asia* (Basingstoke, 2003); Adrienne Edgar, *Tribal Nation: The Making of Soviet Turkmenistan* (Princeton, 2004), 51–69; Francine Hirsch, *Empire of Nations: Ethnographic Knowledge and the Making of the Soviet Union* (Ithaca, 2005), 160–86.

20. RGASPI, f. 62, op. 2, d. 734, ll. 47–55.

21. Karl Marx, *Critique of Hegel's "Philosophy of Right,"* trans. Joseph O'Malley (Cambridge, 1970), 131.

22. The Bolsheviks' assault on religion is often seen simply as yet another example of their malevolence. Yet, we cannot disassociate their actions from a long tradition of materialism in post-Enlightenment Western thought, which the Bolsheviks carried to its logical conclusion. The *philosophes*, we should remember, were highly critical of religion both for its role in obstructing a purely rational explanation of the world by providing supernatural and metaphysical explanations of natural phenomena and for its use as a tool in the hands of power to keep people ignorant and powerless. "The radical Enlightenment," writes José Casanova, "reveled in exposing sacred texts as forgery, sacred prac-

tices as contagious pathologies, religious founders as impostors, and priests as slothful hypocrites, imbeciles, or perverts" (*Public Religions in the Modern World*, Chicago, 1994, 32). Many currents of the Enlightenment, however, came to see religion as a useful glue for society and a source for public morality. Only the radical materialists, such as Marx, held to the harsh view of the *philosophes*. The Bolsheviks were here, as in many other instances, deeply rooted in the Enlightenment tradition.

23. Nazir To'raqulov, "Islom va ko'mmunizm: Nazir To'raqulov tezislari," *Qizil boyroq*, December 20, 1921.

24. Mannon Romiz, *Xoyoldon haqiqatga* (Tashkent, 1929), 19.

25. TsGARUz, f. R-94, op. 5, d. 62, l. 2

26. TsGARUz, f. R-94, op. 5, d. 1451, ll. 14–16.

27. RGASPI, f. 62, op. 2, d. 1145, l. 72.

28. Shoshana Keller, *To Moscow, Not Mecca: The Soviet Campaign against Islam in Central Asia, 1917–1941* (Westport, Conn., 2001), 175–87. Since the collapse of the Soviet Union, Central Asian historians have compiled several accounts of the terror and repression visited upon the region during the Stalin years, but few have had any interest in documenting the destruction of Islam and Muslim institutions in the region. There are two major reasons for this reluctance. First, for the reasons I explore in this and the next chapter, few Central Asia intellectuals are either interested in or sympathetic to religion per se. Second, the subject of religion remains sensitive in post-Soviet Central Asia, and none of the regimes in place has much interest in foregrounding the destruction of Islam as an aspect of national history.

29. Keller, *To Moscow, Not Mecca*, 188–93.

30. Gregory J. Massell, *The Surrogate Proletariat: Moslem Women and Revolutionary Strategies in Soviet Central Asia, 1919–1929* (Princeton, 1974).

31. The *hujum* has attracted considerable attention from Western scholars in recent years. Douglas T. Northrop, *Veiled Empire: Gender and Power in Stalinist Central Asia* (Ithaca, 2004), presents a relentlessly negative view of the hujum, which he sees as a case of imperial intervention into a pristine national community. He bases his account on much too clear a distinction between "Uzbek society" and "alien Bolsheviks." Northrop's account begins in 1927 and is thus oblivious to the conflicts that had beset Uzbekistani society in the decade before that date. There is no indication in his account that different actors within Uzbekistani society had different goals or that many Bolsheviks were also Uzbeks. Marianne R. Kamp, *The New Woman in Central Asia: Islam, the Soviet Project, and the Unveiling of Uzbek Women* (Seattle, forthcoming), offers a more nuanced account of the hujum that takes into account the longer-term development of Muslim attitudes on the question and the aspirations of women activists. For other excellent work, see Shoshana Keller, "Trapped between State and Society: Women's Liberation and Islam in Soviet Uzbekistan, 1926–1941," *Journal of Women's History* 10 (1998): 20–44; and Adrienne Lynn Edgar, "Emancipation of the Unveiled: Turkmen Women under Soviet Rule, 1924–29," *Russian Review* 62 (2003): 132–49.

32. Rustambek Shamsitdinov, *O'zbekistonda sovetlarning quloqlashtirish siyosati va uning fojeali oqibatlari* (Tashkent, 2001).

33. The most thoughtful estimates for casualties are in: Zh. B. Abylkhozhin, M. K. Kozybaev, and M. B. Tatimov, "Kazakhstanskaia tragediia," *Voprosy istorii*, 1989, no. 7: 53–71; S. Maksudov, "Migratsii v SSSR v 1926–1939 godakh," *Cahiers du monde russe* 40 (1999): 763–92; Niccolò Pianciola, "Famine in the Steppe: The Collectivization of Agriculture and the Kazak Herdsmen, 1928–1934," *Cahiers du monde russe* 45 (2004): 137–92.

34. Yaacov Ro'i, *Islam in the Soviet Union: From the Second World War to Gorbachev* (New York, 2000); Shamsuddinxon Boboxonov, *Shayx Ziyovuddinxon ibn Eshon Boboxon (ma'naviyat va ibrat maktabi)* (Tashkent, 2001), 36–41.

35. This quotation comes from the diaries of Enver Hoxha, *The Artful Albanian: The Memoirs of Enver Hoxha*, ed. Jon Halliday (London, 1986), 130.

36. For examples from Turkmenistan, see Adrienne Lynn Edgar, *Tribal Nation: The Making of Soviet Turkmenistan* (Princeton, 2004); for ones from Kazakhstan, see A. P. Kuchkin, *Sovetizatsiia kazakhskogo aula, 1926–1929 gg.* (Moscow, 1962), 190–206.

37. The number of well-placed individuals today who claim descent from prominent public figures of the 1920s or earlier is striking, as is the preponderance of surnames denoting august lineage (-xo'jayev, -bekov, and so on).

38. Donald S. Carlisle, "The Uzbek Power Elite: Politburo and Secretariat (1938–83)," *Central Asian Survey* 5, no. 3–4 (1986): 99.

39. Martin, *The Affirmative Action Empire*, 314–16.

4. ISLAM AS NATIONAL HERITAGE

1. Semën Gitlin, *Natsional'nye otnosheniia v Uzbekistane: illiuzii i real'nost'* (Tel Aviv, 1998), 224–25.

2. The proportion of Party members was lower in Central Asia, ranging from 4.6 percent in Kazakhstan to 2.35 percent in Tajikistan in the last years of the Soviet period; the numbers were lower still among the indigenous population of the region. Nevertheless, the point about the Party becoming a political machine stands.

3. Moshe Lewin, *The Gorbachev Phenomenon* (Berkeley, 1990).

4. Erika Weinthal, *State Making and Environmental Cooperation: Linking Domestic and International Politics in Central Asia* (Cambridge, Mass., 2002), 82–102.

5. The best account of how networks operate in daily life is by the young French anthropologist Boris-Mathieu Pétric: *Pouvoir, don et réseaux en Ouzbékistan post-soviétique* (Paris, 2002); see also Joma Nazpary, *Post-Soviet Chaos: Violence and Dispossession in Kazakhstan* (London, 2002), ch. 4. Elaborating the workings of these networks in the Soviet period is considerably more difficult, for little documentary evidence exists, and oral history is a difficult proposition. See, however, the excellent study by Victoria Koroteyeva and Ekaterina Makarova, "Money and Social Connections in the Soviet and Post-Soviet Uzbek City," *Central Asian Survey* 17 (1998): 579–96. Such networks of mutual obligation were not unique to Central Asia; the way they worked and still work in Russia is described in another fine ethnography: Alena Ledeneva, *Russia's Econ-*

omy of Favours: Blat, Networking and Informal Exchange (Cambridge, 1998). On "clans" in the political realm, see Edward Schatz, *Modern Clan Politics: The Power of "Blood" in Kazakhstan and Beyond* (Seattle, 2004); and Kathleen Collins, "The Logic of Clan Politics: Evidence from Central Asian Trajectories," *World Politics* 56 (2003–04): 224–61. See also E. Karin and G. Ileuova, eds., *Politicheskie elity Tsentral'noi Azii* (Tel Aviv, 2001).

6. Gitlin, *Natsional'nye otnosheniia v Uzbekistane*, 304–305.

7. James Critchlow, "Prelude to 'Independence': How the Uzbek Party Apparatus Broke Moscow's Grip on Elite Recruitment," in William Fierman, ed., *Soviet Central Asia: The Failed Transformation* (Boulder, Colo.,1991), 138–39.

8. For a contemporary description of these practices, see Nancy Lubin, *Labour and Nationality in Soviet Central Asia: An Uneasy Compromise* (London, 1984), 154–70.

9. Rashidov's career has not received the attention it deserves outside Uzbekistan. The best account of Uzbekistani politics in the mid- and late-Soviet periods is Donald S. Carlisle, "The Uzbek Power Elite: Politburo and Secretariat (1938–83)," *Central Asian Survey* 5, no. 3–4 (1986): 91–132. As chapter 5 discusses, Rashidov suffered posthumous disgrace, and his career remains controversial. All work on him in Uzbek or Russian is thus part of this debate; the most useful work is S. Rizaev, *Sharaf Rashidov: shtrikhi k portretu* (Tashkent, 1992).

10. Robert Conquest, *The Nation Killers: The Soviet Deportation of Nationalities* (London, 1970); Robert Conquest, *Stalin: Breaker of Nations* (London, 1991); Roman Smal-Stocki, *The Captive Nations: Nationalism of the Non-Russian Nations in the Soviet Union* (New York, 1960); Hélène Carrère d'Encausse, *Decline of an Empire: The Soviet Socialist Republics in Revolt*, trans. Martin Sokolinsky and Henry A. La Farge (New York, 1979).

11. Yuri Slezkine, "The USSR as a Communal Apartment, or How a Socialist State Promoted Ethnic Particularism," *Slavic Review* 53 (1994): 414.

12. As Lenin once put it, "If we say that we do not recognize the Finnish nation but only the toiling masses, it would be a ridiculous thing to say. Not to recognize something that is out there is impossible; it will force us to recognize it." Quoted by Slezkine, 420.

13. This discussion provides only a broad overview of a fascinating new literature that has reshaped our understanding of nation formation in the Soviet period. In addition to Yuri Slezkine's brilliant article cited above, see Ronald Grigor Suny, *The Revenge of the Past: Nationalism, Revolution, and the Collapse of the Soviet Union* (Stanford, 1994); Terry Martin, *The Affirmative Action Empire: Nations and Nationalism in the Soviet Union, 1923–1939* (Ithaca, 2001); Robert J. Kaiser, *The Geography of Nationalism in Russia and the USSR* (Princeton, 1994).

14. This phenomenon is scarcely limited to Central Asia but rather is the product of certain organic notions of national identity. Such debates have erupted with great ferocity since the end of Soviet-era checks on national expression, and they continue to rage throughout the former Soviet Union. See Victor A. Shnirelman, *Who Gets the Past? Competition for Ancestors among Non-Russian Intellectuals in Russia* (Washington, D.C., 1996).

15. This claim comes from Demian Vaisman, "Regionalism and Clan Loyalty

in the Political Life of Uzbekistan," in Yaacov Ro'i, ed., *Muslim Eurasia: Conflicting Legacies* (London, 1995), 107. The simplicity of the essentialist vision here is beguiling, and the argument is frequently trotted out in similar forms.

16. Koroteyeva and Makarova, "Money and Social Connections," 582.

17. Again, we lack ethnographic studies of *otins* during Soviet times; on the post-Soviet period, see Habiba Fathi, *Femmes d'autorité dans l'Asie centrale contemporaine: quête des ancêtres et recompositions identitaires dans l'islam post-soviétique* (Paris, 2004); Sigrid Kleinmichel, *Halpa in Choresm (H^warazm) und Ātin Āyi in Ferğanatal: Zur Geschichte des Lesens in Usbekistan im 20. Jahrhundert* (Berlin, 2000); Annette Krämer, *Geistliche Autorität und Islamische Gesellschaft im Wandel: Studien über Frauenälteste (otin und xalfa) im unabhängingen Usbekistan* (Berlin, 2002).

18. Yaacov Ro'i, *Islam in the Soviet Union: from the Second World War to Gorbachev* (New York, 2000), 371–72; on Sufi shrines and pilgrimages in Turkmenistan, see S. M. Demidov, *Sufizm v Turkmenii* (Ashkhabad, 1978).

19. Gillian Tett, "'Guardians of the Faith'?: Gender and Religion in an (ex) Soviet Tajik Village," in *Muslim Women's Choices: Religious Belief and Social Reality,* eds. Camillia Fawzi El-Solh and Judy Mabro (Oxford, 1994), 144.

20. Sergei Abashin, "Sotsial'nye korni sredneaziatskogo islamizma (na primere odnogo seleniia)," in Martha Brill Olcott, Valerii Tishkov, and Aleksei Malashenko, eds., *Identichnost' i konflikt v postsovetskikh gosudarstvakh* (Moscow, 1997), 447–67; Bruce G. Privratsky, "'Turkistan Belongs to the Qojas': Local Knowledge of a Muslim Tradition," in Stéphane A. Dudoignon, ed., *Devout Societies vs. Impious States? Transmitting Islamic Learning in Russia, Central Asia and China, through the Twentieth Century* (Berlin, 2004), 161–212.

21. Ro'i, *Islam in the Soviet Union,* 608.

22. Ibid., 560.

23. Gitlin, *Natsional'nye otnosheniia,* 219.

24. Quoted by Daniel Crecelius, "Al-Azhar in the Revolution," *Middle East Journal* 20 (1966): 42.

25. Gregory Starrett, *Putting Islam to Work: Education, Politics, and Religious Transformation in Egypt* (Berkeley, 1998).

26. Sam Kaplan, "*Din-u Devlet* All Over Again? The Politics of Military Secularism and Religious Militarism in Turkey Following the 1980 Coup," *International Journal of Middle East Studies* 34 (2002): 113–27.

27. Bakhtiiar Babadzhanov, "O fetvakh SADUM protiv 'neislamskikh obychaev,'" in Martha Brill Olcott and Aleksei Malashenko, eds., *Islam na postsovetskom prostranstve: vzgliad iznutri* (Moscow, 2001), 170–84; the texts of some of these fatwas appear in Shamsuddinxon Boboxonov, *Shayx Ziyovuddinxon ibn Eshon Boboxon (ma'naviyat va ibrat maktabi)* (Tashkent, 2001).

28. Ziyauddin Khan Ibn Ishan Babakhan, *Islam and the Muslims in the Land of Soviets,* trans. Richard Dixon (Moscow, 1980), 72–73.

29. The extent of this unsanctioned activity was of considerable interest to Western observers during the Soviet era, who saw it as politically subversive and a likely source of opposition to the regime. The only sources of information available on the subject were Soviet ethnographic or anti-Islamic publications,

and few Western observers had the training in Muslim traditions or Islamic dogma, or indeed in the academic study of religion or society, to make clear sense of what they found in their sources. Western observers therefore built up a large literature that was fundamentally flawed in its basic assumptions and its conceptual apparatus. For a critique of this literature, see Devin DeWeese, "Islam and the Legacy of Sovietology: A Review Essay on Yaacov Ro'i's *Islam in the Soviet Union*," *Journal of Islamic Studies* 13 (2002): 298–330.

30. Hindustoniy left behind a brief autobiography, which has now been published in the original Uzbek and a Tajik translation in *Yodnoma* (Dushanbe, 2003). The best scholarly account of this milieu is Bakhtiyar Babadjanov and Muzaffar Kamilov, "Muhammadjân Hindûstânî (1892–1989) and the Beginning of the Great Schism among the Muslims of Uzbekistan," in *Islam in Politics in Russia and Central Asia (Early Eighteenth to Late 20th Centuries)*, eds. Stéphane A. Dudoignon and Hisao Komatsu (London, 2001), 195–219. Hindustoniy's story has been recounted at length by Monica Whitlock, *Land Beyond the River: The Untold Story of Central Asia* (New York, 2003). Although Whitlock has a wonderful eye for telling detail, she cannot locate Hindustoniy in the context of religious debate.

5. THE REVIVAL OF ISLAM

1. Steve Coll, *Ghost Wars: The Secret History of the CIA, Afghanistan, and Bin Laden, from the Soviet Invasion to September 10, 2001* (New York, 2004), 104–105.

2. See, for instance, Alexandre Bennigsen and Marie Broxup, *The Islamic Threat to the Soviet Union* (New York, 1983).

3. Bakhtyar Bobojonov, "Le Renouveau des communautés soufies dans l'Ouzbékistan," *Cahiers d'Asie centrale*, no. 5–6 (1998): 285–311.

4. Cholpon Orozobekova, "Kyrgyzstan: Fury Over Lavish Funeral Ban," *Reporting Central Asia*, no. 105, February 22, 2002.

5. Bruce G. Privratsky, *Muslim Turkistan: Kazak Religion and Collective Memory* (London, 2001).

6. Ibid., 54–57, 90–92.

7. Barbara Metcalf, "'Traditionalist' Islamic Activism: Deoband, Tablighis, and Talibs," in Craig Calhoun, Paul Price, and Ashley Timmer, eds., *Understanding September 11* (New York, 2002), 58–59.

8. Bayram Balci, *Missionaires de l'Islam en Asie centrale: les écoles turques de Fethullah Gülen* (Paris, 2003).

9. See, for instance, Hélène Carrère d'Encausse, *The End of the Soviet Empire: The Triumph of the Nations*, trans. Franklin Philip (New York, 1992).

10. For an excellent survey of policies and legislation affecting the practice of Islam in Central Asia, see International Crisis Group, "Central Asia: Islam and the State," Asia Report no. 59 (Brussels, 2003); see also Sébastien Peyrouse, "La gestion du fait réligieux en Asie centrale: poursuite du cadre conceptual soviétique et renouveau factice," *Cahiers d'Asie centrale*, no. 13–14 (2004): 77–120.

11. Islam Karimov, *Uzbekistan on the Threshold of the Twenty-First Century: Challenges to Stability and Progress* (New York, 1998), 20.

12. Such rhetoric is routinely used in Uzbekistan; this particular statement comes from Rafik Saifullin, then an adviser to the president of Uzbekistan, at the conference Islam and Modern Society, Tashkent, February 1, 2001.

13. Nargiz Zakirova, "Tajik Women Want Polygamy Legalised," *Reporting Central Asia,* no. 151, October 4, 2002.

14. See, for example, Daina Stukuls Eglitis, *Imagining the Nation: History, Modernity, and Revolution in Latvia* (University Park, Penn., 2002).

15. Dale F. Eickelman and Jon W. Anderson, eds., *New Media in the Muslim World: The Emerging Public Sphere* (Bloomington, Ind., 1999).

16. Sébastien Peyrouse, *Des chrétiens entre athéisme et islam: regards sur la question religieuse en Asie centrale soviétique et post-soviétique* (Paris, 2003); Marlène Laruelle and Sébastien Peyrouse, *Les Russes du Kazakhstan: Identités nationales et nouveaux États dans l'espace post-soviétique* (Paris, 2004).

17. International Crisis Group, "Youth in Central Asia: Losing the New Generation," Asia Report no. 66 (Brussels, 2003), 24.

18. Olga Dosybieva, "Kazakstan: Muslim Villagers Lash Out At Sect," *Reporting Central Asia,* no. 139, August 20, 2002.

6. ISLAM IN OPPOSITION

1. Rafis Abazov, Aleksei Vasilivetskii, and Vitalii Ponomarev, *Islam i politicheskaia bor'ba v stranakh SNG* (Moscow, 1992), 11–12.

2. See, for example, Vitaly Naumkin, *Radical Islam in Central Asia: Between Pen and Rifle* (Lanham, Md., 2005).

3. Edward A. Gargan, "Afghan President Says U.S. Should See Him as Ally against Militant Islam," *New York Times,* March 10, 1992, A3.

4. Muhammadjân Hindûstânî, "Answers to Those Who Are Introducing Inadmissible Innovations into Religion," appendix to Bakhtiyar Babadjanov and Muzaffar Kamilov, "Muhammadjân Hindûstânî (1892–1989) and the Beginning of the Great Schism among the Muslims of Uzbekistan," in Stéphane A. Dudoignon and Hisao Komatsu, eds., *Islam in Politics in Russia and Central Asia (Early Eighteenth to Late Twentieth Centuries)* (London, 2001), 210–19.

5. Bakhtiyar Babadjanov, "Debates over Islam in Contemporary Uzbekistan: A View from Within," in Stéphane Dudoignon, ed., *Devout Societies vs. Impious States? Transmitting Islamic Learning in Russia, Central Asia and China, through the Twentieth Century* (Berlin, 2004), 51n. The text of the pamphlet is not extant, but Babadjanov has reconstructed its basic arguments from various sources.

6. *Kommunist Tadzhikistana* (Dushanbe), January 31, 1987, February 12, 1987, excerpted in *Current Digest of the Soviet Press,* 39:9 (April 1, 1987), 10–11.

7. The term *neo-Soviet* was coined by Muriel Atkin in "Thwarted Democratization in Tajikistan," in Karen Dawisha and Bruce Parrott, eds., *Conflict, Cleavage and Change in Central Asia and the Caucasus* (Cambridge, 1997), 277–311. This article provides one of the best analytical accounts of the Tajik civil war. Monica Whitlock, in *Land Beyond the River: The Untold Story of Central Asia* (New York, 2003), provides a longer account with greater attention to the human dimension of the events.

8. This quote is from Qadi Akbar Turajonzoda, "Religion: The Pillar of Society," in Roald Z. Sagdeev and Susan Eisenhower, eds., *Central Asia: Conflict, Resolution, and Change* (Chevy Chase, Md., 1995), 269, but numerous statements from the early 1990s corroborate this position.

9. Olivier Roy, *La nouvelle Asie centrale, ou la fabrication des nations* (Paris, 1997), 154–55.

10. Abazov, Vasilivetskii, and Ponomarev, *Islam i politicheskaia bor'ba*, 6.

11. Quoted in Human Rights Watch, " 'Straightening Out the Brains of One Hundred': Discriminatory Political Dismissals in Uzbekistan," *Helsinki Watch* 5:7 (April 1993), 1. The best account of Uzbekistani politics during these years is in William Fierman, "Political Development in Uzbekistan: Democratization?" in Dawisha and Parrott, eds., *Conflict, Cleavage, and Change in Central Asia and the Caucasus*, 360–408.

12. The most detailed information on the Islamic Movement of Uzbekistan (IMU) is in Ahmed Rashid, *Jihad: The Rise of Militant Islam in Central Asia* (New Haven, Conn., 2002), 145–82. Vitaly Naumkin's account in *Radical Islam in Central Asia* is seriously flawed.

13. "Uzbek Islamic Movement: Government Must Go or Be Removed by Force," Voice of the Islamic Republic of Iran, Mashhad, in Uzbek, March 19, 1999, BBC Worldwide Monitoring, via LexisNexis Academic; some spellings modified for consistency.

14. In May 2001, reports indicated that the IMU had changed its name to the Islamic Party of Turkestan, leading to speculation that it had broadened its goals to include all of Central Asia on a pan-Islamic basis. A spokesman denied that the group had this objective, adding, "We have only one enemy—the Tashkent regime. We have no problems with neighboring countries." See Bruce Pannier, "Central Asia: IMU Leader Says Group's Goal Is 'Return of Islam,' " Radio Free Europe/Radio Liberty, June 6, 2001, www.rferl.org/features/2001/06/06062001121150.asp.

15. "Uzbek Islamic Movement: Government Must Go or Be Removed by Force."

16. "O'zbekiston 'Birlik' xalq harakatining bayonoti," February 17, 1999, http://w1.920.telia.com/~u92003997/bayo1701.html. For a survey of theories about the causes of the bombings and the identities of their perpetrators, see Abdumannob Polat and Nickolai Butkevich, "Unraveling the Mystery of the Tashkent Bombings: Theories and Implications," *Demokratizatsiia* 8 (2000): 541–53. For the official Uzbekistani view of the events, see the book by the Uzbek-born Israeli author, Oleg Yakubov, *The Pack of Wolves: The Blood Trail of Terror; A Political Detective Story* (Moscow, 2000). This book was clearly commissioned by the government, and in typical Soviet fashion, published in several languages. The author quotes the indictments put together by Uzbekistani prosecutors as proof of the guilt of the accused and in general, follows official rhetoric to a T.

17. Reprinted in Rashid, *Jihad*, 247–49. The statement was released on the Internet and was, curiously, drafted in Arabic with an accompanying English translation that clearly derives from the Arabic version rather than the Uzbek one. This choice is a sign of the political orientation the IMU had acquired in

Afghanistan, as well as perhaps the audience to which the statement was directed. The original Arabic text is available at www.e-prism.org/images/balagho1.doc.

18. The discussion in the following paragraphs draws from the party's articulation of its mission on its website: www.hizb-ut-tahrir.org/english/english.html. See also International Crisis Group, "Radical Islam in Central Asia: Responding to Hizb-ut-Tahrir," Asia Report no. 58 (Brussels, June 2003).

19. The vision of the future is underpinned by a remarkably poor understanding of the past. HTI's founder, Taqiuddin an-Nabahani, saw the caliphate as the perpetual order of things in Muslim history, from the time of the death of the Prophet to the defeat of the Ottoman Empire in 1918, when it was finally extinguished by colonialism. Throughout this period, moreover, "Islam was implemented from the first year of the Hijrah until 1336 A.H. (1918 C.E.) and the Islamic *Ummah* did not apply any system other than Islam." See *The System of Islam* (London, 2002), 66; online at www.hizb-ut-tahrir.org/english/english.html.

20. International Crisis Group, "Radical Islam in Central Asia," 17.

21. Ibid., 19.

22. Ibid., 32.

23. See, for instance, "The Reality of the Sect, Hizb-ut-Tahrir," at www.htexposed.com, an anonymous Web site that carries Wahhabi-oriented materials.

24. Quoted in Muhiddin Kabiri, "PIVT i 'Hizb-ut-Tahrir': sovmestimost' i razlichiia," in A. K. Zaifert and A. Kraikemaier, eds., *O sovmestimosti politicheskogo islama i bezopasnosti v prostranstve OBSE* (Dushanbe, 2003), 215.

25. Qadi Akbar Turajonzoda, "Dukhovnoe nevezhestvo naselemiia sposobstvuet rostu ekstremizma v respublikakh Srednei Azii," *Nezavisimaia gazeta*, August 4, 2004, http://news.ferghana.ru/detail.php?id=15128390707.34,1337,3314123.

26. The best analysis of these events is by Alisher Ilkhamov, "Mystery Surrounds Tashkent Explosions," *Middle East Report Online*, April 15, 2004, www.merip.org/mero/mero041504.html.

27. The message is now available at "Srochno! Otvetsvennost' za vzryvy v Uzbekistane vziala na sebia gruppa 'Islomiy Zhikhod'," TsentrAziia, April 3, 2004, http://centrasia.org/newsA.php4?st=1080996900.

28. See the translation at www.globalterroralert.com/uzbekjihado704.pdf.

7. THE POLITICS OF ANTITERRORISM

1. "Macedonia Faked 'Militant' Raid," BBC Online, April 30, 2004, http://news.bbc.co.uk/2/hi/europe/3674533.stm. The quote is from the original story reported by BBC Online, March 2, 2002, http://news.bbc.co.uk/2/hi/europe/1850501.stm.

2. Bakhtyar Babadjanov, "Islam officiel contre Islam politique en Ouzbékistan aujourd'hui: la Direction des Musulmans et les groupes non-Hanafî," *Revue d'études comparatives Est-Ouest* 31 (2000): 151–64.

3. A businessman in Namangan told the International Crisis Group that "the authorities recommended that he not 'invest in the sphere of religion if he cares about his professional future.'" International Crisis Group, "Central Asia: Islam and the State," Asia Report no. 59 (Brussels, 2003), 10. The years from 1989 to

1992 had seen a great deal of Islamic publishing under the sponsorship of private individuals, but that practice has largely disappeared.

4. Igor Rotar, "Uzbekistan: State Control of Islamic Religious Education," *Forum 18 News,* May 11, 2004, www.forum18.org/Archive.php?article_id=318.

5. See the Web site of the university at www.tiu.uz.

6. *"Diniy ekstremizm va fundamentalizm: tarixi, mohiyati va bugungi xavfi" maxsus kursini o'rganish bo'yicha metodik tavsiyalar* (Tashkent, 1999).

7. Quoted by Muriel Atkin, "The Rhetoric of Islamophobia" (2000), www.ca-c.org/journal/eng-01–2000/16.atkin.shtml.

8. Quoted in Human Rights Watch, *Creating Enemies of the State: Religious Persecution in Uzbekistan* (New York, 2004), 197–98.

9. Ibid., 123.

10. Uzbek Radio, June 12, 1999, BBC Worldwide Monitoring, via Lexis-Nexis Academic; some spellings modified for consistency.

11. Human Rights Watch, *Creating Enemies of the State,* 43.

12. International human rights law defines a *disappearance* as any situation in which "persons are arrested, detained or abducted against their will or otherwise deprived of their liberty by officials of different branches or levels of Government, or by organized groups or private individuals acting on behalf of, or with the support, direct or indirect, consent or acquiescence of the Government, followed by a refusal to disclose the fate or whereabouts of the persons concerned or a refusal to acknowledge the deprivation of their liberty, which places such persons outside the protection of the law." United Nations Declaration on the Protection of All Persons from Enforced Disappearances (A/RES/47/133), December 18, 1992, available at www.unhchr.ch/ huridocda/huridoca.nsf/ (Symbol)/ A.RES.47.133.En?OpenDocument.

13. On Dodaxon and his message, see David Tyson, "The Role of Unofficial Audio Media in Contemporary Uzbekistan," *Central Asian Survey* 13 (1994): 283–93.

14. Human Rights Watch, *Creating Enemies of the State,* 23–24; Monica Whitlock, *Land Beyond the River: The Untold Story of Central Asia* (New York, 2003), 208.

15. This crackdown is meticulously documented in Human Rights Watch, "Crackdown in the Farghona Valley: Arbitrary Arrests and Religious Discrimination," *Human Rights Watch Report,* 10:4(D) (May 1998), www.hrw.org/ hrw/reports98/Uzbekistan.

16. Uzbek Radio, May 1, 1998, BBC Worldwide Monitoring, via LexisNexis Academic.

17. AAP Newsfeed, May 3, 1998, via LexisNexis Academic.

18. The text of the law appeared in *Narodnoe slovo* (Tashkent), May 15, 1998.

19. Rustam Eshmuradov and Muhsina Hamidova, "No Place for Uzbek Muslims," *Reporting Central Asia,* no. 213, July 1, 2003.

20. Human Rights Watch, *Creating Enemies of the State,* 94–95, 111–12.

21. Ibid., 88–89.

22. Ibid., 118–20.

23. Uzbek Television, April 1, 1999, BBC Worldwide Monitoring, via Lexis-

Nexis Academic. Karimov continued, "Why does he [the father] not ask his son where he has disappeared to and spent the last six or 12 months? Where have you been? What have you done? With whom you are fighting? He should cut off his son's head with his own hands, should he not? He should punish him, should he not? I am speaking for myself. If my son did such a thing would I tolerate him? What kind of man can tolerate such things?"

24. On contemporary mahallas in Uzbekistan, see Elise Massicard and Tommaso Trevisani, "Die uzbekische Mahalla zwischen Staat und Gesselschaft," *Anthropos* 95 (2000): 206–18; Marianne Kamp, "Between Women and the State: Mahalla Committees and Social Welfare in Uzbekistan," in *The Transformation of Central Asia: States and Societies from Soviet Rule to Independence*, ed. Pauline Jones Luong (Ithaca, 2004), 29–58; and Z. X. Orifxonova, ed., *Toshkent mahallalari: an'analar va zamonaviylik* (Tashkent, 2002).

25. "Uzbek President Speaks on Bomb Attacks," Uzbek Television, First Channel, Tashkent, February 16, 1999, BBC Worldwide Monitoring, via Lexis-Nexis Academic.

26. Human Rights Watch, "From House to House: Abuses by Mahalla Committees" (New York, 2003), available at www.hrw.org/reports/2003/uzbekistan0903/.

27. See Human Rights Watch, *Creating Enemies of the State*, 185–200, for several examples of such rallies.

28. All real opposition remains outlawed, and human rights activists are persecuted. In 2003, the regime turned on foreign nongovernmental organizations, passing a law that required all of them to reregister with the government and then using the process of reregistration to deny many groups the right to operate in the country.

29. Human Rights Watch, *Creating Enemies of the State*, 261.

30. "Status of International Religious Freedom: An Analysis of the State Department's 2003 Annual Report: Testimony by Tom Malinowski before the U.S. House of Representatives Committee on International Relations," February 10, 2004, available at http://hrw.org/english/docs/2004/02/17/uzbeki7481.htm.

31. Ibid.

32. Human Rights Watch, *Creating Enemies of the State*, 275, 285.

33. Ibid., 288–89; the medical report is quoted from the report of the U.N. rapporteur on torture who visited Uzbekistan in autumn 2002: United Nations Economic and Social Council, Commission on Human Rights, "Report of the Special Rapporteur on the Question of Torture, Theo van Boven: Mission to Uzbekistan," E/CN.4/2003/68/Add.2, February 3, 2003, 16; available online at www.unhchr.ch/Huridocda/Huridoca.nsf/TestFrame/29d0f1eaf87cf3eac1256ce9005a0170?Opendocument.

34. Steve Coll, *Ghost Wars: The Secret History of the CIA, Afghanistan, and Bin Laden, from the Soviet Invasion to September 10, 2001* (New York, 2004), 456–58, 525–27.

35. U.S. Department of State, "Background Note: Uzbekistan," www.state.gov/r/pa/ei/bgn/2924.htm#foreign. The last statement was removed from the text on the Web site after relations soured in the summer of 2005, but the first quote remained.

36. Vitalii Ponomarev and Saltanat Dzhukeeva, "Religioznyi faktor v politicheskoi zhizni Kazakhstana (1991–1996 gg.)," at http://eurasia.org.ru/archive/book/IEI/index.html.

37. Daur Dosybiev, "Kazakstan Tackles Hizb-ut-Tahrir," *Reporting Central Asia,* no. 276, April 14, 2004.

38. The foregoing comments are based on a visit to the university in July 2004.

39. Olga Dosybieva, "Kazakstan: Clerics Quizzed in Test to Root Out Radicalism," *Reporting Central Asia,* no. 333, December 11, 2004.

40. Stéphane A. Dudoignon, "From Ambivalence to Ambiguity? Some Paradigms of Policy Making in Tajikistan," in Luigi De Martino, ed., *Tajikistan at a Crossroad: The Politics of Decentralization* (Geneva, 2004), 125.

41. Author interview, Dushanbe, July 15, 2004.

42. Dudoignon, "From Ambivalence to Ambiguity?" 141.

43. International Crisis Group, "Central Asia: Islam and the State," 18.

44. For added measure, the refrain of the national anthem states, "The great creation of Türkmenbashy / Native land, sovereign state / Turkmenistan, light and song of soul / Long live and prosper forever and ever!"

45. The Niyazov regime has received sporadic international attention, mostly in the form of newspapers articles by bemused journalists. For a comprehensive survey, see International Crisis Group, "Repression and Regression in Turkmenistan: A New International Strategy," Asia Report no. 85 (Brussels, 2004).

46. From a speech on October 22, 2004, reported by Radio Free Europe/Radio Liberty, October 25, 2004, www.rferl.org/newsline/2004/10/251004.asp.

47. Saparmyrat Turkmenbashy, *Rukhnama: Reflections on the Spiritual Values of the Turkmen* (Ashgabat, 2003), 9. The English version used here was translated through the Russian; the title has therefore acquired an extra *k.* Portions of the texts are also available on the Web site of the government of Turkmenistan, www.turkmenistan.gov.tm/people/pep&ruh_eng.htm.

48. As if the Ruhnama phenomenon were not surreal enough, at the time of this writing, one could buy not just the English *Ruhnama* but also Ruhnama merchandise (including such typically Turkmen items as tote bags, coffee mugs, and T-shirts)—from a Web site based, of all places, in Peoria, Illinois!

49. Konstantin Arzybov, "Turkmen President's Prophet Motive," *Reporting Central Asia,* no. 55, June 8, 2001.

50. Felix Corley, "Turkmenistan: President's Personality Cult Imposed on Religious Communities," Forum 18 News Service, March 1, 2005, www.forum18.org/Archive.php?article_id=522.

51. Felix Corley, "Turkmenistan: 2004, The Year of Demolished Mosques," Forum 18 News Service, January 4, 2005, www.forum18.org/Archive.php?article_id=481.

52. Muhammadsharif Himmatzoda, "Politicheskie metody i protivorechiia pri regulirovanii otnoshenii mezhdu gosudarstvom i religiei," in A. K. Zaifert and A. Kraikemaier, eds., *O sovmestimosti politicheskogo islama i bezopasnosti v prostranstve OBSE: dokumenty svetsko-islamskogo dialoga v Tadzhikistane* (Dushanbe, 2003), 96.

CONCLUSION: ANDIJAN AND BEYOND

1. RIA Novosti, July 11, 2005, via LexisNexis Academic.

2. Islam Karimov sketched out this scenario on national television the day after the events; see the transcript in "Uzbek Leader Gives Press Conference on Andijon Events," Uzbek Television, May 14, 2005, BBC Monitoring, via Lexis-Nexis Academic.

3. Details of Yo'ldoshev's indictment are in S. Zainabitdinov, "'Akramiia': za chto boretsia religioznaia organizatsiia v Ferganskoi doline," http://centrasia.ru/newsA.php4?st=1093410660.

4. Bakhtiyar Babadzhanov, "The Ferghana Valley: Source or Victim of Islamic Fundamentalism?" (1999), www.ca-c.org/dataeng/10.babadzh.shtml.

5. Zuhriddin Husniddinov, *Islom: yo'nalishlar, mazhablar, oqimlar* (Tashkent, 2000), 107–10.

6. Akramjon Yo'ldoshev, "Iymonga yo'l," ed. Saidjahon Zaynabitdinov, at www.ozodovoz.org/uz/contents.php?cid=75. The structure of the document provides compelling evidence of its authenticity; Saidjahon Zaynabitdinov, the human rights activist who publicized the document, was disappeared in the aftermath of the Andijan uprising.

7. Igor Rotar, "Uzbekistan: Islamic Charitable Work 'Criminal' and 'Extremist'?" *Forum 18 News*, February 14, 2005, www.forum18.org/Archive.php?article_id=508.

8. *Islom: entsiklopediya* (Tashkent, 2004), 22–23.

9. Jenny Norton, "Uzbekistan's Most Orderly Protest," BBC Online, May 12, 2005, http://news.bbc.co.uk/1/hi/world/asia-pacific/4540041.stm.

10. Galima Bukharbaeva, "Blood Flows in Uzbek Crackdown," *Reporting Central Asia*, no. 377, May 14, 2005.

11. The following reports of the events are the most compelling: Peter Boehm and Andrew Osborn, "Uzbekistan: 'In the Narrow Lane, the Machine Guns Clattered Remorselessly for Two Hours,'" *The Independent on Sunday* (London), May 22, 2005; Human Rights Watch, "'Bullets Were Falling Like Rain': The Andijan Massacre, May 13, 2005" (New York, June 2005), http://hrw.org/reports/2005/uzbekistan0605; Organization for Security and Co-operation in Europe/Office for Democratic Institutions and Human Rights, "Preliminary Findings on the Events in Andijan, Uzbekistan, 13 May 2005" (Warsaw, June 20, 2005), www.osce.org/item/15234.html; and Ed Vulliamy, "Death in Bobur Square," *The Guardian* (London), September 13, 2005. Whereas the dominant note in the Western coverage of the events was one of shock and revulsion, the Uzbekistani regime found a few defenders, the most vociferous of whom was the British academic Shirin Akiner. Akiner traveled to Andijan on May 25 with the permission of the authorities and in the company of the governor of Andijan province. As a result, she claimed, she was able to travel freely and speak to whomever she wanted. Her account was skeptical of the media coverage and supported the official Uzbekistani view to the hilt. "The death toll," she concluded, "was *probably* closer to the government estimate (i.e. under 200 deaths) than to the high estimates (1,000 and above) given in media reports. . . . The action was initiated by armed, trained insurgents, some of whom came from out-

side Uzbekistan. . . . It seems likely that the motive was political, intended as the opening phase of a coup d'état, on the lines of the Kyrgyz model." See Shirin Akiner, "Violence in Andijan, 13 May 2005: An Independent Assessment," p. 12, at www.silkroadstudies.org/new/inside/publications/0507Akiner.pdf. Although skepticism of media reports was certainly in order (given the media blackout in Andijan, the exaggerated and contradictory nature of the early reports was not surprising), the fact that Akiner traveled in the company of officials and had full clearance from them scarcely helps her credibility. Her account is entirely devoid of the broader context of the uprising (the trial and the protests it had engendered or the regime's long-established persecution of Muslims), and she gives the regime the benefit of the doubt on every occasion. She was eager enough to lend her support to the regime that she agreed to appear on Uzbekistan's (tightly controlled) official television on May 27 to present her findings. See the transcript of her interview at www.centrasia.ru/newsA.php4?st=1117520280.

12. Boehm and Osborn, "Uzbekistan: 'In the Narrow Lane.'"

13. Norton, "Uzbekistan's Most Orderly Protest."

14. Human Rights Watch, "'Bullets Were Falling Like Rain,'"16

15. Ibid., 25

16. Human Rights Watch, "Uzbekistan: Dissident Forced Into Psychiatric Detention" (3 September 3, 2005), http://hrw.org/english/docs/2005/09/03/uzbeki11684.htm.

17. "Uzbek Uprising 'Chief' Confesses," BBC Online, September 21, 2005, http://news.bbc.co.uk/1/hi/world/asia-pacific/4266548.stm.

18. International Crisis Group, "Uzbekistan: The Andijon Uprising," Asia Briefing no. 38 (Brussels, May 25, 2005), 8–11.

19. "Targets Set for Uzbek 'Slaves,'" *Reporting Central Asia,* no. 249, November 28, 2003; "'Patriotic' Uzbek Child Labourers," *Reporting Central Asia,* no. 333, December 11, 2004; Craig Murray, "The Trouble with Uzbekistan," www.riia.org/pdf/meeting_transcripts/081104murray.pdf; see also the photographs of the 2004 cotton harvest by Thomas Grabka, "The Cost of Uzbek White Gold," at www.iwpr.net/index.pl?top_galleries_index.html.

20. International Crisis Group, "The Curse of Cotton: Central Asia's Destructive Monoculture," Asia Report no. 93 (Brussels, 2005), 12.

21. For a pessimistic assessment, see Eric Sievers, *The Post-Soviet Decline of Central Asia: Sustainable Development and Comprehensive Capital* (London, 2003).

Select Bibliography

I list below works cited in the notes that relate directly to the main themes of the book. I have left out incidental references but have included some important titles that do not appear in the notes. I have also included a short list of the most important electronic sources, indispensable for the contemporary period; all Web sites were last accessed on May 12, 2006.

BOOKS AND ARTICLES

Abashin, Sergei. "Sotsial'nye korni sredneaziatskogo islamizma (na primere odnogo seleniia)." In Martha Brill Olcott, Valerii Tishkov, and Aleksei Malashenko, eds., *Identichnost' i konflikt v postsovetskikh gosudarstvakh*. Moscow, 1997.

Abazov, Rafis, Aleksei Vasilivetskii, and Vitalii Ponomarev. *Islam i politicheskaia bor'ba v stranakh SNG*. Moscow, 1992.

Abylkhozhin, Zh. B., M. K. Kozybaev, and M. B. Tatimov. "Kazakhstanskaia tragediia." *Voprosy istorii*, 1989, no. 7: 53–71.

Ainî, Sadriddin. *Ta'rikhi amironi manghitiyai Bukhoro*. Dushanbe, 1987; orig. 1921.

Akiner, Shirin. "Violence in Andijan, 13 May 2005: An Independent Assessment." www.silkroadstudies.org/new/inside/publications/0507Akiner.pdf.

Algar, Hamid. "Shaykh Zaynullah Rasulev: The Last Great Naqshbandi Shaykh of the Volga-Urals Region." In Jo-Ann Gross, ed., *Muslims in Central Asia: Expressions of Identity and Change*. Durham, N.C., 1992.

———. *Wahhabism: A Critical Essay*. Oneonta, N.Y., 2002.

Atkin, Muriel. "The Rhetoric of Islamophobia." 2000. www.ca-c.org/journal/eng-01–2000/16.atkin.shtml.

———. *The Subtlest Battle: Islam in Soviet Tajikistan*. Philadelphia, 1989.

Babadjanov, Bakhtiyar, and Muzaffar Kamilov. "Muhammadjân Hindûstânî (1892–1989) and the Beginning of the Great Schism among the Muslims of Uzbekistan." In Stéphane A. Dudoignon and Hisao Komatsu, eds., *Islam in Politics in Russia and Central Asia (Early Eighteenth to Late 20th Centuries*. London, 2001.

Babadjanov, Bakhtyar. "Islam officiel contre Islam politique en Ouzbékistan aujourd'hui: la Direction des Musulmans et les groupes non-Hanafi." *Revue d'études comparatives Est-Ouest* 31 (2000): 151–64.

Babadzhanov, Bakhtiiar. "O fetvakh SADUM protiv 'neislamskikh obychaev.'" In Martha Brill Olcott and Aleksei Malashenko, eds., *Islam na postsovetskom prostranstve: vzgliad iznutri.* Moscow, 2001.

Babadzhanov, Bakhtyar. "The Ferghana Valley: Source or Victim of Islamic Fundamentalism?" www.ca-c.org/dataeng/10.babadzh.shtml.

Babakhan, Ziyauddin Khan Ibn Ishan. *Islam and the Muslims in the Land of Soviets.* Trans. Richard Dixon. Moscow, 1980.

Balci, Bayram. *Missionaires de l'Islam en Asie centrale: les écoles turques de Fethullah Gülen.* Paris, 2003.

Baldauf, Ingeborg. *Schriftreform und Schriftwechsel bei den muslimischen Russland- und Sowjettürken (1850–1937): ein Symptom ideengeschichtlicher und kulturpolitischer Entwicklungen.* Budapest, 1993.

Bobojonov, Bakhtyar. "Le Renouveau des communautés soufies dans l'Ouzbékistan." *Cahiers d'Asie centrale*, no. 5–6 (1998): 285–311.

Boboxonov, Shamsuddinxon. *Shayx Ziyovuddinxon ibn Eshon Boboxon (ma'naviyat va ibrat maktabi).* Tashkent, 2001.

Brower, Daniel R. "Kyrgyz Nomads and Russian Pioneers: Colonization and Ethnic Conflict in the Turkestan Revolt of 1916." *Jahrbücher für Geschichte Osteuropas* 44 (1996): 41–53.

Buttino, Marco. *La rivoluzione capovolta: l'Asia centrale tra il crollo dell'impero zarista e la formazione dell'URSS.* Naples, 2003.

———. "Study of the Economic Crisis and Depopulation in Turkestan, 1917–1920." *Central Asian Survey* 9:4 (1990): 61–64.

Calhoun, Craig, Paul Price, and Ashley Timmer, eds. *Understanding September 11.* New York, 2002.

Carlisle, Donald S. "The Uzbek Power Elite: Politburo and Secretariat (1938–83)." *Central Asian Survey* 5, no. 3–4 (1986): 91–132.

Carrère d'Encausse, Hélène. *Decline of an Empire: The Soviet Socialist Republics in Revolt.* Trans. Martin Sokolinsky and Henry A. La Farge. New York, 1979.

———. *The End of the Soviet Empire: The Triumph of the Nations.* Trans. Franklin Philip. New York, 1992.

Casanova, José. *Public Religions in the Modern World.* Chicago, 1994.

Coll, Steve. *Ghost Wars: The Secret History of the CIA, Afghanistan, and Bin Laden, from the Soviet Invasion to September 10, 2001.* New York, 2004.

Collins, Kathleen. "The Logic of Clan Politics: Evidence from Central Asian Trajectories." *World Politics* 56 (2003–04): 224–61.

Dawisha, Karen, and Bruce Parrott, eds. *Conflict, Cleavage, and Change in Central Asia and the Caucasus.* Cambridge, 1997.

DeWeese, Devin. "Islam and the Legacy of Sovietology: A Review Essay on Yaacov Ro'i's *Islam in the Soviet Union*." *Journal of Islamic Studies* 13 (2002): 298–330.

———. *Islamization and Native Religion in the Golden Horde: Baba Tükles and Conversion to Islam in Historical and Epic Tradition*. University Park, Penn., 1994.

———. "Sacred History for a Central Asian Town: Saints, Shrines, and Legends of Origin in Histories of Sayram, 18th–19th Centuries." *Revue du monde musulman et de la Méditerranée*, no. 89–90 (2000): 245–95.

"Diniy ekstremizm va fundamentalizm: tarixi, mohiyati va bugungi xavfi" maxsus kursini o'rganish bo'yicha metodik tavsiyalar. Tashkent, 1999.

Donish, Ahmad Makhdumi. *Risola, yo mukhtasare az ta'rikhi saltanati khonadoni manghitiya*. Dushanbe, 1992. Original ms. ca. 1895.

Dudoignon, Stéphane A. "From Ambivalence to Ambiguity? Some Paradigms of Policy Making in Tajikistan." In Luigi De Martino, ed., *Tajikistan at a Crossroad: The Politics of Decentralization*. Geneva, 2004.

Dudoignon, Stéphane A., ed. *Devout Societies vs. Impious States? Transmitting Islamic Learning in Russia, Central Asia and China, through the Twentieth Century*. Berlin, 2004.

Edgar, Adrienne. "Emancipation of the Unveiled: Turkmen Women under Soviet Rule, 1924–29." *Russian Review* 62 (2003): 132–49.

———. *Tribal Nation: The Making of Soviet Turkmenistan*. Princeton, 2004.

Eickelman, Dale F., and Jon W. Anderson, eds. *New Media in the Muslim World: The Emerging Public Sphere*. Bloomington, Ind., 1999.

Eickelman, Dale F., and James P. Piscatori. *Muslim Politics*. Princeton, 1996.

Ernst, Carl W. *Following Muhammad: Rethinking Islam in the Contemporary World*. Chapel Hill, N.C., 2003.

Fathi, Habiba. *Femmes d'autorité dans l'Asie centrale contemporaine: quête des ancêtres et recompositions identitaires dans l'islam postsoviétique*. Paris, 2004.

Fazl Allah b. Rûzbihân al-Isfahânî. *Kitâb-i Sulûk al-mulûk*. Ed. Muhammad Nizâmuddin and Muhammad Ghaus. Hyderabad, India, 1966 (orig. 1514).

Fierman, William, ed. *Soviet Central Asia: The Failed Transformation*. Boulder, Colo., 1991.

Fitrat, Abdurauf. *Bayânât-i sayyâh-i hindî*. Istanbul, 1911.

———. *Munâzara-yi mudarris-i bukhârâyî bâ yak nafar-i farangî dar Hindustân dar bâra-yi makâtib-i jadîda*. Istanbul, 1910.

———. *Tanlangan asarlar*. 3 vols. Tashkent, 2001–03.

Gidulianov, P. V. *Otdelenie tserkvi ot gosudarstva v SSSR*. Moscow, 1926.

Gitlin, Semën. *Natsional'nye otnosheniia v Uzbekistane: illiuzii i real'nost'*. Tel Aviv, 1998.

Haugen, Arne. *The Establishment of National Republics in Soviet Central Asia*. Basingstoke, England, 2003.

Hirsch, Francine. *Empire of Nations: Ethnographic Knowledge and the Making of the Soviet Union*. Ithaca, 2005.

Human Rights Watch. "'Bullets Were Falling Like Rain': The Andijan Massacre, May 13, 2005." New York, June 2005.

————. "Crackdown in the Farghona Valley: Arbitrary Arrests and Religious Discrimination." *Human Rights Watch Report,* 10:4(D) (May 1998).

————. *Creating Enemies of the State: Religious Persecution in Uzbekistan.* New York, 2004.

————. "From House to House: Abuses by Mahalla Committees." New York, 2003.

————. " 'Straightening Out the Brains of One Hundred': Discriminatory Political Dismissals in Uzbekistan." *Helsinki Watch* 5:7 (April 1993).

Husniddinov, Zuhriddin. *Islom: yo'nalishlar, mazhablar, oqimlar.* Tashkent, 2000.

Ilkhamov, Alisher. "Impoverishment of the Masses in the Transition Period: Signs of an Emerging 'New Poor' Identity in Uzbekistan." *Central Asian Survey* 20 (2001): 33–54.

————. "Mystery Surrounds Tashkent Explosions." Middle East Report Online. April 15, 2004. www.merip.org/mero/mero041504.html.

International Crisis Group. "Central Asia: Islam and the State." Asia Report no. 59. Brussels, 2003.

————. "Cracks in the Marble: Turkmenistan's Failing Dictatorship." Asia Report no. 44. Brussels, 2003.

————. "The Curse of Cotton: Central Asia's Destructive Monoculture." Asia Report no. 93. Brussels, 2005.

————. "Radical Islam in Central Asia: Responding to Hizb-ut-Tahrir." Asia Report no. 58. Brussels, 2003.

————. "Repression and Regression in Turkmenistan: A New International Strategy." Asia Report no. 85. Brussels, 2004.

————. "Uzbekistan: The Andijon Uprising." Asia Briefing no. 38. Brussels, May 25, 2005.

————. "Youth in Central Asia: Losing the New Generation." Asia Report no. 66. Brussels, 2003.

Islom: entsiklopediya. Tashkent, 2004.

Jones Luong, Pauline, ed. *The Transformation of Central Asia: States and Societies from Soviet Rule to Independence.* Ithaca, 2004.

Juvaini, 'Ala-ad-Din 'Ata Malik. *The History of the World Conqueror.* 2 vols. Trans. from the text of Mirza Muhammad Qazvini by J. A. Boyle. Cambridge, Mass., 1958.

Kaiser, Robert J. *The Geography of Nationalism in Russia and the USSR.* Princeton, 1994.

Kamp, Marianne R. *The New Woman in Central Asia: Islam, the Soviet Project, and the Unveiling of Uzbek Women.* Seattle, forthcoming.

Kandiyoti, Deniz, and Nadira Azimova. "The Communal and the Sacred: Women's Worlds of Ritual in Uzbekistan." *Journal of the Royal Anthropological Institute,* n.s. 10 (2004): 327–49.

Kappeler, Andreas. "Czarist Policy Toward the Muslims of the Russian Empire." In Andreas Kappeler et al., eds. *Muslim Communities Reemerge: Historical Perspectives on Nationality, Politics, and Opposition in the Former Soviet Union and Yugoslavia.* Durham, N.C., 1992.

Karamustafa, Ahmet T. *God's Unruly Friends: Dervish Groups in the Islamic Later Middle Period, 1200–1550.* Salt Lake City, 1994.

Karimov, Islam. *Uzbekistan on the Threshold of the Twenty-First Century: Challenges to Stability and Progress.* New York, 1998.

Karin, E., and G. Ileuova, eds. *Politicheskie elity Tsentral'noi Azii.* Tel Aviv, 2001.

Keller, Shoshana. *To Moscow, Not Mecca: The Soviet Campaign against Islam in Central Asia, 1917–1941.* Westport, Conn., 2001.

———. "Trapped between State and Society: Women's Liberation and Islam in Soviet Uzbekistan, 1926–1941." *Journal of Women's History* 10 (1998): 20–44.

Khalid, Adeeb. *The Politics of Muslim Cultural Reform: Jadidism in Central Asia.* Berkeley, 1998.

———. "A Secular Islam: Nation, State, and Religion in Uzbekistan." *International Journal of Middle East Studies* 35 (2003): 573–98.

———. "Society and Politics in Bukhara, 1868–1920." *Central Asian Survey* 19 (2000): 367–96.

———. "Tashkent 1917: Muslim Politics in Revolutionary Turkestan." *Slavic Review* 55 (1996): 270–96.

Khālidī, Qurbān-ʿAlī. *An Islamic Biographical Dictionary of the Eastern Kazakh Steppe, 1770–1912.* Ed. Allen J. Frank and Mirkasyim A. Usmanov. Leiden, 2005.

Kleinmichel, Sigrid. *Halpa in Choresm (Hʷarazm) und Ātin Āyi in Ferğanatal: Zur Geschichte des Lesens in Usbekistan im 20. Jahrhundert.* Berlin, 2000.

Koroteyeva, Victoria, and Ekaterina Makarova. "Money and Social Connections in the Soviet and Post-Soviet Uzbek City." *Central Asian Survey* 17 (1998): 579–96.

Kotkin, Steven. *Armageddon Averted: The Soviet Collapse, 1970–2000.* Oxford, 2001.

———. *Magnetic Mountain: Stalinism as a Civilization.* Berkeley, 1995.

Krämer, Annette. *Geistliche Autorität und Islamische Gesellschaft im Wandel: Studien über Frauenälteste (otin und xalfa) im unabhängingen Usbekistan.* Berlin, 2002.

Kuchkin, A. P. *Sovetizatsiia kazakhskogo aula, 1926–1929 gg.* Moscow, 1962.

Lapidus, Ira M. "State and Religion in Islamic Societies." *Past and Present*, no. 151 (1996): 3–27.

Laruelle, Marlène, and Sébastien Peyrouse. *Les Russes du Kazakhstan: Identités nationales et nouveaux États dans l'espace post-soviétique.* Paris, 2004.

———, eds. *Islam et politique en ex-URSS (Russie d'Europe et Asie centrale).* Paris, 2005.

Lawrence, Bruce B. *Defenders of God: The Fundamentalist Revolt Against the Modern Age.* San Francisco, 1989.

Ledeneva, Alena. *Russia's Economy of Favours: Blat, Networking and Informal Exchange.* Cambridge, 1998.

Levin, Theodore. *The Hundred Thousand Fools of God: Musical Travels in Central Asia (and Queens, New York).* Bloomington, 1996.

Levitin, Leonid. *Uzbekistan na istoricheskom povorote: kriticheskie zametki storonnika Prezidenta Islama Karimova.* Moscow, 2001.

Lewin, Moshe. *The Gorbachev Phenomenon.* Berkeley, 1990.

Lewis, Bernard. "The Roots of Muslim Rage." *Atlantic Monthly.* September 1990, 47–60.

Lubin, Nancy. *Labour and Nationality in Soviet Central Asia: An Uneasy Compromise.* London, 1984.

Mamdani, Mahmood. *Good Muslim, Bad Muslim: America, the Cold War, and the Roots of Terror.* New York, 2004.

Martin, Terry. *The Affirmative Action Empire: Nations and Nationalism in the Soviet Union, 1923–1939.* Ithaca, 2001.

Massell, Gregory J. *The Surrogate Proletariat: Moslem Women and Revolutionary Strategies in Soviet Central Asia, 1919–1929.* Princeton, 1974.

Massicard, Elise, and Tommaso Trevisani. "Die uzbekische Mahalla zwischen Staat und Gesselschaft." *Anthropos* 95 (2000): 206–18.

Mottehedeh, Roy P. *The Mantle of the Prophet: Religion and Politics in Iran.* New York, 1986.

Munis, Shīr Muhammad Mirāb, and Muhammad Rizā Mirāb Āgahī. *Firdaws al-Iqbāl.* Ed. Yuri Bregel. Leiden, 1988.

an-Nabahani, Taqiuddin. *The System of Islam.* London, 2002; online at www .hizb-ut-tahrir.org/english/english.html (under Books Published).

Naumkin, Vitaly V. *Radical Islam in Central Asia: Between Pen and Rifle.* Lanham, Md., 2005.

Nazpary, Joma. *Post-Soviet Chaos: Violence and Dispossession in Kazakhstan.* London, 2002.

Northrop, Douglas T. *Veiled Empire: Gender and Power in Stalinist Central Asia.* Ithaca, 2004.

Organization for Security and Co-operation in Europe/Office for Democratic Institutions and Human Rights. "Preliminary Findings on the Events in Andijan, Uzbekistan, 13 May 2005." Warsaw, June 20, 2005. www.osce.org/item/ 15234.html.

Orifxonova, Z. X., ed. *Toshkent mahallalari: an'analar va zamonaviylik.* Tashkent, 2002.

Pétric, Boris-Mathieu. *Pouvoir, don et réseaux en Ouzbékistan post-soviétique.* Paris, 2002.

Peyrouse, Sébastien. *Des chrétiens entre athéisme et islam: regards sur la question religieuse en Asie centrale soviétique et post-soviétique.* Paris, 2003.

———. "La gestion du fait réligieux en Asie centrale: poursuite du cadre conceptual soviétique et renouveau factice." *Cahiers d'Asie centrale,* no. 13–14 (2004): 77–120.

Pianciola, Niccolò. "Famine in the Steppe: The Collectivization of Agriculture and the Kazak Herdsmen, 1928–1934." *Cahiers du monde russe* 45 (2004): 137–92.

Polat, Abdumannob, and Nickolai Butkevich. "Unraveling the Mystery of the Tashkent Bombings: Theories and Implications." *Demokratizatsiia* 8 (2000): 541–53.

Ponomarev, Vitalii, and Saltanat Dzhukeeva. "Religioznyi faktor v politicheskoi zhizni Kazakhstana (1991–1996 gg.)." http://eurasia.org.ru/archive/book/IEI/index.html.

Privratsky, Bruce G. *Muslim Turkistan: Kazak Religion and Collective Memory.* London, 2001.

Rashid, Ahmed. *Jihad: The Rise of Militant Islam in Central Asia.* New Haven, Conn., 2002.

Reporting Central Asia. Electronic news bulletins. London: Institute for War and Peace Reporting, 2000–date. Archived at www.iwpr.net/index.pl?centasia_rca_archive.html.

Rizaev, S. *Sharaf Rashidov: shtrikhi k portretu.* Tashkent, 1992.

Ro'i, Yaacov. *Islam in the Soviet Union: From the Second World War to Gorbachev.* New York, 2000.

Romiz, Mannon. *Xoyoldon haqiqatga.* Tashkent, 1929.

Roy, Olivier. *La nouvelle Asie centrale, ou la fabrication des nations.* Paris, 1997.

Ryskulov, T. R. *Sobranie sochinenii v trekh tomakh.* Almaty, 1997.

Schatz, Edward. *Modern Clan Politics: The Power of "Blood" in Kazakhstan and Beyond.* Seattle, 2004.

Schoeberlein-Engel, John. "Identity in Central Asia: Construction and Contention in the Conceptions of 'Özbek,' 'Tâjik,' 'Muslim,' 'Samarqandi,' and Other Groups." PhD dissertation, Harvard University, 1994.

Shamsitdinov, Rustambek. *O'zbekistonda sovetlarning quloqlashtirish siyosati va uning fojeali oqibatlari.* Tashkent, 2001.

Shnirelman, Victor A. *Who Gets the Past? Competition for Ancestors among Non-Russian Intellectuals in Russia.* Washington, D.C., 1996.

Sidqiy, Sirojiddin Maxdum. *Toza hurriyat.* Tashkent, 1917.

Sievers, Eric. *The Post-Soviet Decline of Central Asia: Sustainable Development and Comprehensive Capital.* London, 2003.

Sinyavsky, Andrei. *Soviet Civilization: A Cultural History.* Trans. Joanne Turnbull. New York, 1988.

Slezkine, Yuri. "The USSR as a Communal Apartment, or How a Socialist State Promoted Ethnic Particularism." *Slavic Review* 53 (1994): 414–52.

Sokol, Edward. *The Revolt of 1916 in Russian Central Asia.* Baltimore, 1954.

Spuler, Bertold. *History of the Mongols, based on Eastern and Western Accounts of the Thirteenth and Fourteenth Centuries.* London, 1972.

Suny, Ronald Grigor. *The Revenge of the Past: Nationalism, Revolution, and the Collapse of the Soviet Union.* Stanford, 1994.

Tett, Gillian. "'Guardians of the Faith'?: Gender and Religion in an (ex) Soviet Tajik Village." In Camillia Fawzi El-Solh and Judy Mabro, eds., *Muslim Women's Choices: Religious Belief and Social Reality.* Oxford, 1994.

Tishkov, Valery. *Ethnicity, Nationalism and Conflict in and after the Soviet Union: The Mind Aflame.* London, 1997.

Tokhtakhodjaeva, Marfua. *Between the Slogans of Communism and the Laws of Islam.* Trans. Sufian Aslam. Lahore, 1995.

Turkmenbashy, Saparmyrat. *Rukhnama: Reflections on the Spiritual Values of the Turkmen.* Ashgabat, 2003.

Tyson, David. "The Role of Unofficial Audio Media in Contemporary Uzbekistan." *Central Asian Survey* 13 (1994): 283–93.

United Nations Economic and Social Council. Commission on Human Rights. "Report of the Special Rapporteur on the Question of Torture, Theo van Boven: Mission to Uzbekistan." E/CN.4/2003/68/Add.2. February 3, 2003. www .unhchr.ch/Huridocda/Huridoca.nsf/TestFrame/29d0f1eaf87cf3eac1256ce90-05a0170?Opendocument.

Vaisman, Demian. "Regionalism and Clan Loyalty in the Political Life of Uzbekistan." In Yaacov Ro'i, ed., *Muslim Eurasia: Conflicting Legacies*. London, 1995.

Weinthal, Erika. *State Making and Environmental Cooperation: Linking Domestic and International Politics in Central Asia*. Cambridge, Mass., 2002.

Whitlock, Monica. *Land Beyond the River: The Untold Story of Central Asia*. New York, 2003.

Yakubov, Oleg. *The Pack of Wolves: The Blood Trail of Terror; A Political Detective Story*. Moscow, 2000.

Yodnoma. Dushanbe, 2003.

Yo'ldoshev, Akramjon. "Iymonga yo'l." Ed. Saidjahon Zaynabitdinov. www .ozodovoz.org/uz/contents.php?cid=75.

Zaifert, A. K., and A. Kraikemaier, eds. *O sovmestimosti politicheskogo islama i bezopasnosti v prostranstve OBSE*. Dushanbe, 2003.

Zainabitdinov, S. "'Akramiia': za chto boretsia religioznaia organizatsiia v Ferganskoi doline." http://centrasia.ru/newsA.php4?st=1093410660.

IMPORTANT WEB SITES

EurasiaNet (information and analysis site operated by the Open Society Institute): www.eurasianet.org/index.shtml.

Fergana.Ru (news and commentary from Central Asia): http://news.ferghana.ru/ main.php.

Forum 18 (a Christian initiative in support of religious freedom worldwide, with a news service that provides reports from journalists in the field): www .forum18.org/.

Human Rights Watch (international human rights organization, with an office in Tashkent since 1994): www.hrw.org/. Most of its publications since 1997 are available on the site.

Institute for War and Peace Reporting (media development nongovernmental organization with major presence in Central Asia): http://www.iwpr.net/centasia _index1.html.

International Crisis Group (international think tank working on crisis prevention, with an office in Osh, Kyrgyzstan): http://www.crisisgroup.org/. All its publications are available on the site.

Muslim Uzbekistan (oppositional site): www.muslimuzbekistan.com/.

UzA (Uzbekistan's official news agency): www.uza.uz/.

Index

Text: 10/13 Sabon
Display: Sabon
Compositor: BookMatters, Berkeley
Cartographer: Bill Nelson